Organizational Knowledge

Organizational Knowledge
The Texture of
Workplace Learning

SILVIA GHERARDI

With the collaboration of Davide Nicolini

Blackwell
Publishing

© 2006 by Silvia Gherardi

BLACKWELL PUBLISHING
350 Main Street, Malden, MA 02148-5020, USA
9600 Garsington Road, Oxford OX4 2DQ, UK
550 Swanston Street, Carlton, Victoria 3053, Australia

The right of Silvia Gherardi to be identified as the Author of this Work has been
asserted in accordance with the UK Copyright, Designs, and Patents Act 1988.

First published 2006 by Blackwell Publishing Ltd

1   2006

Library of Congress Cataloging-in-Publication Data

Gherardi, Silvia.
Organizational knowledge : the texture of workplace learning / Silvia Gherardi.
p.   cm. — (Organization and strategy)
Includes bibliographical references and index.
ISBN-13: 978-1-4051-2559-8 (hard cover : alk. paper)
ISBN-10: 1-4051-2559-4 (hard cover : alk. paper)   1. Organizational learning.
2. Knowledge management.   I. Title.   II. Series.

HD58.82.G48 2005
658.4′038—dc22
2005014987

A catalogue record for this title is available from the British Library.

Set in 11/13 pt Bembo
by Graphicraft
Printed and bound in India
by Replika Press

The publisher's policy is to use permanent paper from mills that operate a sustainable
forestry policy, and which has been manufactured from pulp processed using acid-free
and elementary chlorine-free practices. Furthermore, the publisher ensures that the
text paper and cover board used have met acceptable environmental accreditation
standards.

For further information on
Blackwell Publishing, visit our website:
www.blackwellpublishing.com

Contents

Acknowledgements

I have contracted too many debts of gratitude during the years of work required by this book for individual acknowledgements to be possible. I shall therefore express my collective thanks to the many persons who have assisted me while writing this book and conducting the fieldwork in the previous five years. I begin with acknowledging my indebtedness to those who gave me their time and help during the field research, and to the organizations that afforded me access to their personnel and premises. I hope that my interpretations are respectful of their wishes.

I am grateful in particular to the Gottlieb Daimler and Karl Benz Foundation in Germany, which funded the 'Organizational Learning in Various Environmental Conditions' Kolleg coordinated by Meinolf Dierkes. From 1994 to 1998, this network of people from 16 countries (see http://duplox.wz-berlin.de/oldb) met twice a year to explore organizational learning by means of regular discussions and joint research. Members of the Kolleg produced the *Handbook of Organizational Learning and Knowledge* (Dierkes *et al.* 2001), a major collective effort which provided me with valuable occasions for the discussion and comparison of my ideas. I am indebted to all the members of the network. My empirical research was also supported financially by the Department of Sociology and Social Research, the University of Trento, and emotionally by my colleagues, especially those with whom I founded the Research Unit on Cognition, Organizational Learning and Aesthetics (RUCOLA, http://soc.unitn.it/dsrs/rucola). I am particularly grateful to those of my colleagues who conducted the fieldwork and with whom I wrote the many articles on which this book is based. My thanks accordingly go to Davide Nicolini and Francesca Odella, and to Antonio Strati for constantly reminding me of the importance of aesthetic understanding whenever we discussed the results of the fieldwork. I also wish to thank the doctoral students on the Information Systems and Organizations programme for our long and fruitful discussions.

Finally, my good wishes go to those colleagues who organized with me the symposium on 'Situated Learning, Local Knowledge, and Action: Social Approaches to the Study of Knowing in Organizations' at the 1998 American Academy of Management Annual Conference held in San Diego. Following the symposium, Dvora Yanow, Davide Nicolini, Frank Blackler, Etienne Wenger, Lucy Suchman and myself produced a special issue of *Organization* (7/2000) where our voices were joined by commentaries written by Yrjo Engeström, John Law, Alessia Contu and Hugh Willmott.

In recent years I have given numerous papers based on this research, and I have greatly benefited from discussions with colleagues at the meetings of the European Group for Organizational Studies (EGOS), at conferences of the Organizational Learning and Knowledge and Researching Work and Learning Networks, and the Center for Activity Theory and Developmental Work Research of Helsinki. Finally, I am especially thankful to the Centre de Recherche en Gestion de l'Ecole Polytechnique of Paris, where as visiting professor I found a welcoming environment in which to conclude my research work.

The assistance of Adrian Belton in translating the book into English is greatly appreciated. Notwithstanding the fact that a book is always a collective product, I alone assume responsibility for its shortcomings.

Finally, many of the concepts of this book stem from years of collaboration and discussion with Davide Nicolini. This applies in particular to Chapters 3, 4, 5 and 7, which derive from previously co-authored articles and unpublished research reports. References to the original articles are given in the footnotes at the end of each chapter. The caption 'with the collaboration of Davide Nicolini' is therefore an acknowledgement of this joint work, for which I am particularly indebted to him. Of course, while the individual concepts should be attributed as indicated in the footnotes, the way in which they are used and interpreted in this book should be attributed to myself alone.

Introduction

To play the violin – as Geertz (1973: 12) reminds us – 'it is necessary to possess certain habits, skills, knowledge, and talent, to be in the mood to play, and (as the old joke goes) to have a violin. But violin playing is neither the habits, skills, knowledge, and so on, nor the mood, nor (the notion believers in "material culture" apparently embrace) the violin'. Violin playing is an easily recognizable practice; it is more troublesome to recognize 'an organizational practice' or to detect how and when 'knowing in practice' occurs. This book aims to show how an organizational researcher can empirically describe practices like 'learning', 'knowing' and 'organizing'.

This book takes as its subject a body of practical knowledge – safety in the construction industry – and addresses the following question: how does safety become expertise conserved and transmitted within a texture of organizational practices and performed through being put-into-practice? Safety is thus treated as the *object* of knowledge, the result of the practical activity of knowing, and the *context* in which that activity is performed and institutionalized as 'organizational practice'. The theme of safety has been selected both because of its social importance and because there is growing awareness in the literature that safety failures often have an organizational aetiology. It is therefore important to acquire more thorough knowledge – using a microanalytical approach – of how practical knowledge about safety, risk and prevention is produced in the course of everyday work practices; how novices learn safe work practices and perform them, or abstain from doing so; how these practices are produced and institutionalized in everyday organizing; how organizations deal with safety failures; and how a safety culture is constructed within an interorganizational network which comprises safety-regulating institutions and organizations which abide by the rules that those institutions issue. Safety is therefore defined as a body of practical knowledge, as the emergent property of a set of social bodies whose interactions put a contextually developed body of knowledge into practice.

This book therefore aims to show how safety can be analysed as a situated 'feeling, saying and doing' (i.e. interpreted as a social practice) and how, within it, a researcher can empirically describe how 'learning', 'knowing' and 'organizing' are practised. In fact this book is situated within the growing debate on practice-based studies.

Since the 1980s, learning and knowledge in organizations have been subject to lively and sometimes heated debate in the field of organization studies. It is natural to enquire as to the reasons for this great interest, and the answers are as different as the voices that are ranged against each other. The aim of this book is to furnish an answer to the question and to support it with arguments founded on data and examples from empirical research.

The success of the theme of learning and knowing in organizations resides, I believe, within that complex and variegated intellectual movement which in the social sciences has exposed the limitations of rationalism (Elster, 2000), and which in organization studies has dismantled the functionalist paradigm from which the discipline sprang (Tsoukas and Knudsen, 2003). Consider, in fact, how organization theory used to be grounded on an image of the rational organization which privileged decision-making processes, first based on paradigmatic rationality and then on bounded rationality, and strategic planning predicated on a priori rationality. The shortcomings of the paradigm became evident as both scholars and practitioners in organizations came increasingly to realize that the theory was unable to account for ongoing changes in the everyday world.

The image of an organization guided by the optimization principle was gradually replaced by an image of the organization which proceeds by trial and error, which builds on its own experience and that of others, which extracts maximum value from the knowledge in its possession, which strives after constant improvement, and which networks with other organizations and institutions in order to develop collectively the knowledge that it is unable to produce only on its own. This is an image, therefore, which depicts a more modest rationality of incremental and distributed type. It interprets the spirit of an age which views knowledge as a production factor and the knowledge society as manifesting epochal changes.

I do not wish to argue that study of organizational learning and knowledge in organizations has proceeded homogeneously in an anti-rationalist endeavour; on the contrary, contradictions between a priori rationality and incremental rationality, between positivist research and interpretative post-modern research, have traversed the debate. More modestly, I intend to set the contribution of this book within a non-rationalist and non-cognitivist framework. Unquestioning faith in rationality has rendered it into one of the myths most deeply rooted in the Western collective consciousness, and the consequence has been that the mind has been given primacy over the body as the almost exclusive seat of the knowledge-building process. Associated with a mentalist image of knowledge, therefore, is a research methodology which views individual or collective cognitive processes as the appropriate domain in which to investigate the mental schemes and mechanisms by which knowledge is produced and stored.

The intention of this book is to investigate organizations from the viewpoint of cultural studies and from within a tradition critical of rationalism and cognitivism, doing so on the basis of a complex image of the relationship between organization and knowledge. It conceptualizes knowledge in the same manner as those analyses of social and institutional learning which assume the reciprocal constitution of the knower subject and the known object. We live in a world termed 'post-social' (Knorr-Cetina, 1997) in order to emphasize that it comprises the objects of our mode of conceiving sociality. Consequently, objects and their material world can be construed as materialized knowledge and matter which interrogate humans and interact with them. It is sufficient only to cite intelligent machines to demonstrate that the alleged superiority of humans over the material world is highly questionable. The Enlightenment faith in rationality was matched by an image of human beings who dominated nature and objects and were ontologically separate from the material world. In the post-social world, by contrast, human beings are constricted and made vulnerable by their humanity, and they use technology to create devices with which to extend their capacities to memorize, take action at a distance, see and feel. Knowledge is therefore distributed between humans and non-humans, and in terms of an ecology of knowledge the question consequently arises as to how knowledge is transferred, and of how it is transformed during this transference.

The book's intended contribution is encapsulated by the expression which represents its central conceptual pillar: 'knowing in practice'. This signifies that knowledge is studied as a social process, human and material, aesthetic as well as emotive and ethical, and that knowledge is embedded in practice, as the domain where doing and knowing are one and the same. The concept has a historical precedent of great importance which marks out an emergent strand of analysis centred on what are now known as 'practice-based studies' (Gherardi, 2000a).

The historical antecedent to which I refer, and which traverses all aspects of the critique against rationalism, is that strand of studies which the French have aptly termed the paradigm of 'l'action située' (situated action) (Conein and Jacopin, 1994; de Fornel and Quéré, 1999), although the expression is less current in the English-speaking countries. The core of the paradigm is contextualized as opposed to decontextualized rationality, and therefore the methodological principle that the logic of the situation is radically different from the logic of disembodied and disembedded rationality. The concept of 'logic of the situation' has sociological and philosophical origins in the works of Mead (1934), Dewey (1922) and Goffman (1971a, b). However, the contemporary point of reference is the book by Lucy Suchman (1987), *Plans and Situated Action*, in which, as one intuits from the title, 'situated' is set in opposition to 'plan'. The basic idea is that action is a process which moves gradually towards a final state through organizing work which unfolds over time and cannot be represented ex ante (in a plan, that is) because it is not possible to specify all the contingencies connected with the circumstances produced by the action, nor the consequences that ensue from it. Hence no distinction is drawn between knowledge (and learning) and action because both of them develop simultaneously within a course of action. This literature has directed attention to practical action and situated, contextual and pragmatic rationality in antithesis to axiomatic rationality. Situated action is studied not only in its 'becoming' but also in its 'co-becoming', together with the context in which it occurs, and constitutes an ecology of socio-material relations (Lave, 1988; Star, 1995). Also emphasized is the continuity between action and thought in the praxeological tradition that stems from Dewey (Elkjaer, 2000). Notwithstanding the numerous meanings that attach to the term 'situated', it is often synonymous with 'practical' or 'processual'. But practices are not yet first-level objects.

Practices focus attention when they are contextualized in the sociological debate and when 'the social is a field of embodied, materially interwoven practices centrally organized around shared practical understanding' (Schatzki, 2001a: 3). What matters is that the social is defined in its materiality, that humans and non-humans together form a nexus of activity, and that forms of individual activity depend on the practices in which people participate.

Practices therefore constitute the terrain on which subjects and objects take shape, language becomes discourse, and knowledge is mobilized and maintained. Giving priority to practices over individuals restores visibility to materiality and displaces mind and reason as the central phenomena of human life. From this I derive two methodological recommendations: (i) start from practices – as sets of seeing, doing and saying – not from the individual or the collective actor; (ii) consider materiality to be 'tangible knowledge'.

Central to practices is the relationship between practice/practising and institution/institutionalization, that is, the dynamic of reproduction, recursiveness and reflexivity. Giddens (1984) views recursive human practices as the key to definition of a social institution. Recursive human practices are repeated again and again, although not identically each time. Through recursive human practices, group members, in interaction with artefacts and in situated physical contexts, constitute and reconstitute social institutions. The same dynamic operates between knowledge as a system sustained by institutionalized values and knowing as the process by which knowledge situated in a context of action is produced.

In other words, the discourse on learning and knowing in organizations conceives the figure of practice as articulating knowledge in and about organizing as a practical accomplishment, rather than as a transcendental account of decontextualized reality. Learning and knowing become courses of action, materially mediated, situated within a field of practices. Practice is the figure of discourse that allows the processes of 'knowing' at work and learning in organizing to be articulated as historical processes, both material and indeterminate. Knowing in practice creates a 'third way' in the contemporary debate and, in so doing, avoids the dilemma of Scylla and Charybdis.

Charting a route between Scylla and Charybdis

The figure of Ulysses in the *Odyssey* has been interpreted as a metaphor for humanity in search of knowledge. When Ulysses took his leave of Circe – forgoing immortality out of his desire to know and/or to return home – the sorceress revealed the dangers that awaited him and how to overcome them. Among these dangers were two sea monsters dwelling on opposite sides of what has been identified as the Strait of Messina. One of them was Scylla, a dreadful creature that lurked in a cave and devoured sailors from the ships which came within reach of one of her six necks, each bearing a head with three rows of teeth. The other monster, Charybdis, took the form of a whirlpool which sucked in and belched forth the waters of the sea three times a day.

In everyday language, reference to Scylla and Charybdis denotes a dilemma in which both options are equally undesirable. In the relationship between knowledge and organizations, Scylla and Charybdis can be represented, respectively, by a mentalistic vision of knowledge in organizations and by a commodification of knowledge. The search for a route which avoids both Scylla and Charybdis has given rise to a third figure in the discourse on organizational learning and knowing, one centred on 'knowing in practice' (Gherardi, 2000b).

The first figure of the discourse[1] on knowledge in organizations states that knowledge resides in the heads of persons, and that it is appropriated, transmitted and stored by means of mentalistic processes. This figure works through the dichotomies of mind/body, thought/action, individual/organization. Its watchword is 'organizational learning', and also 'cognitive framework' or 'traditional cognitive learning theory'. The second figure of discourse has been constructed by conversations in the economics of knowledge and in knowledge management. The starting point has been identification of knowledge as a production factor distinct from the traditional ones of capital, labour and land. This distinction has led the resource-based theory of the firm to conceptualize knowledge as 'core competencies' or 'core capabilities', naturalizing the relationship by means of the metaphor of the tree of knowledge: the trunk and major limbs are core products and the root system is the core competence (Prahalad and Hamel, 1990). The reification of knowledge has grown more overt with the 'objectified transferable commodity' envisaged by the knowledge management approach, which treats knowledge as practically synonymous with information created, disseminated and embedded in products, services and systems.

The desire to avoid the two dangers (the two monsters) is shared – around the concept of practice – by intellectual inquiries which spring from different traditions, such as cultural and aesthetic approaches to learning, situated learning theory, activity theory and actor–network theory (Gherardi, 2000b). Both in Europe and the United States, and in both the debate on organizational learning and in the social sciences, the concept of 'practice' or 'practices' has been rediscovered (Schatzki, Knorr-Cetina and von Savigny, 2001). In particular, the concept of 'knowing in practice' (Nicolini, Gherardi and Yanow, 2003) seems to have opened up promising avenues for a strand of analysis that terms itself 'practice-based study'. Still lacking, however, is a theoretical framework which thoroughly establishes the premises and the empirical methodology so that the expression 'knowing in practice' becomes more than an evocative slogan. This book, which systematizes a broad research

programme begun in 1994, intends to remedy this shortcoming by
showing the empirical context in which the expression was born, and
by outlining a theoretical–methodological framework which I now
deem mature after its first adumbration some years ago (Gherardi and
Nicolini, 2000a).

How, then, can 'knowing in practice' be a third way for analysis of
organizational learning and knowledge management? And how can it
contribute to organizational studies in general? A suggestion is provided
by the conclusions drawn by Marjorie Lyles and Mark Easterby-
Smith (2003: 645) in *Handbook of Organizational Learning and Knowledge
Management* when they outline the agendas for future research and
write:

> Few studies address when knowledge is used and the timeliness of that
> usage. Examining real-time learning poses many difficulties beyond access
> to organization and data. (. . .). We want to understand organizational
> learning, but lack research on actual learning processes and actual
> knowledge.

The notion of 'knowing in practice' is a response to this methodological difficulty because it defines the field of practices as the context
in which the concrete activity of producing and using knowledge
becomes visible and observable, as well as describable, without one
having to assume the intentionality of people or having to delve into
what goes on inside their heads. It also responds to a second research
question raised by Lyles and Easterby-Smith and which concerns learning across boundaries and more generally the process by which knowledge is transferred. Social, work and organizational practices closely
interweave, and the interconnections between knowledge and individual, group and organizational learning constitute a field of practices
which the researcher can examine without having to assume differences
among levels of learning. These matters will become clearer in the course
of the book, but even at this introductory stage it is important to have
in mind the book's stance on current debate and the contribution that
it intends to make thereto. I consequently anticipate that this approach
to the study of knowledge-as-process assists analysis of organizing
by establishing an equivalence between the process of organizing
and the process of activating and utilizing practical knowledge. To organize is therefore to establish connections in action, and these connections are made possible and appropriate by the knowledge and power
deployed.

A field of practices

What is a practice? Let us look at an example. When I get up in the morning, I clean my teeth. I do so without thinking, without having to take a decision on what for me is everyday automatic routine. We may take teeth-cleaning as an example of practice, of individual practice which does not require communication with others and which is supported by simple objects like a toothbrush and a tube of toothpaste – objects laid out in plain view on the wash-basin to remind me to clean my teeth, so that I have prestructured a setting in the physical space of my home to help me regularly perform an activity.

Teeth-cleaning is a practice apparently very distant from the practices of organizing examined by this book. Yet if we trace the connections that lead from my daily action to the value of dental hygiene in Western society, we come upon a much more complex field of practices. We have learned, and in my case also taught, that teeth must be cleaned every morning: a practice that involves various people, both within the family and in wider society. Teeth-cleaning then pertains to a family of practices such as six-monthly check-ups by the dentist, oral hygiene, and use of the national health system. Moreover, when I compile my tax returns I deduct the relative expenses and thus involve yet another institution. Buying my toothbrush and toothpaste brings me into contact with the supermarket, and thence with the pharmaceuticals industry, with its advertisements for teeth whiter than white and other technologies to make my minor daily action more efficient. It may be that my city health authority adds fluoride to the water supply to improve public health. Behind my individual practice there lies the social organization that institutionalizes oral hygiene as a value, creates phalanxes of specialists to safeguard and develop the relative expert knowledge, and furnishes them with financial and symbolic resources to celebrate the value of healthy teeth and discipline citizens so that they reproduce that value constantly and irreflexively.

The purpose of this simple example is to direct attention to the fact that every individual practice is situated within a broader field of practices which ramify in every direction, from the individual to organizations to institutions to ever more complex systems. Consider a field of organizational practices present in all organizations: the hiring of personnel and their subsequent 'management'. A field of expert knowledge – human resources management – has developed around this set of practices; educational institutions have been created to transmit and certify them; various theories are ranged against each other in a scientific debate involving the international scientific community; techniques, technologies and increasingly sophisticated expert systems incorporate and give material form to this expertise. The core activities in this field of practices can be grouped into well-known patterns: selecting, hiring, training, etc. Obviously, the ways in which these practices are performed in specific organizational settings will vary greatly; but however much they do so, they will still be recognizable as 'selecting', 'hiring', and so on. Performance of the same activity pattern, as long as that pattern is still recognizable, disseminates it and constantly changes it recursively. Of course, the subjects of practices give rise to the greatest variability in diverse settings, but consider how appointing a human resources manager requires a company to specialize knowledge and to coordinate specialist bodies of expertise.

Further examples could be adduced to show the indefinite extension of the fields of practices which connect the individual with society. However, here I will stop, having shown that the distinctive feature of practices is the connectivity tying together activities as they are reproduced and disseminated. I would stress in particular that practices cover an entire course of action which does not halt at the invisible boundaries between individual and private action and the institution, nor at the boundaries of the organization or the industrial sector. Accordingly, the methodological principle of 'follow the practices' acquires concrete meaning when the researcher observes a situated practice and moves up from it to the institutional order or conversely moves down from it to the individual-in-situation. Or in other words, when she/he explores a connective web which branches in all directions.

We may therefore conclude that the concept of 'practice' is fruitful precisely because it enables analysis of the social connections among individuals, collectives, organizations, institutions, the situated contexts in which these connections take specific form, and all the intermediaries utilized by them – intermediaries that may be physical objects or artefacts, discourses or texts. And it enables such analysis to be conducted, not statically with a description of a structure of connections, but dynamically as the constant becoming of a form which self-reproduces but is never identical with itself in that practices are incomplete and indeterminate until they are situatedly performed.

My concern in studying a field of practices is to determine how connection-in-action comes about, how associations are established, maintained and changed among the elements of a partially given form. I have called this connection-in-action 'texture of practice', my purpose being to emphasize the qualitative aspect assumed by the connection once the relations have been activated and the weaving together of the relations-in-act has begun. Not all 'theoretically' possible connections are established 'in fact' and then endure. Hence power is the power to connect (or not to connect) and it results from the texture of the field of practice. Associated with power is knowledge, with the consequence that 'knowing in practice' acquires more definite meaning the more its embeddedness in a field of practices defines the spatiality, facticity and the weaving together of the connections that constitute the texture. A field of practices can be defined as composed of activities and practices interconnected in constantly changing patterns.

Outline of the book

When studying how the objects of knowledge, the knowing subjects and knowledge-building activities come about within a field of practices, I selected a context that seemed promising for several reasons. I chose a humble form of knowledge, which may stand as a model for both expertise and 'non-intellectual' knowledge. A craftsman can in fact be considered an ideal model of 'knowing how to do', just as a repairer can be considered a model of 'knowing how to understand', and a strategist a model of 'knowing how to combine'. Of interest to me in the case of artisanal know-how was tacit knowledge and the manner in which 'knowing how' is transmitted from master to pupil. Yet it was not the craftsman's know-how in itself that attracted my interest, but rather the social production of a non-material good like safety which, in the construction industry, rests heavily on traditional crafts and artisanal knowledge. The construction industry is well known for its high accident rate and for the importance which society attributes to safety as an object. I can confidently claim that safety is a social value, a body of institutionalized knowledge, and a field of situated practices which involves all levels of society and is supported by a set of legal precepts.

I therefore defined safety as a property emerging from a set of situated practices in an industry, and I drew up a research design which enabled me to conduct empirical analysis of how safety knowledge is formed and transmitted within a field of situated practices and within courses of action that integrate those on the construction site with an institutional context comprising all safety-engendering practices. The base hypothesis was that society as a whole can be studied within situated interaction construed as the fragment of a hologram.

In that this book is based on a particular type of case study (what I have termed 'spiral'), it will describe the contexts and processes of 'knowing in practice' and analyse how material-discursive practices mobilize the objects and subjects of knowledge. The third way between Scylla and Charybdis is defined thus: knowledge does not reside in cognitive activities, nor is it subject to particular production conditions; rather, it can be described processually through analysis of the material-discursive practices that deploy it within a given setting. The book is organized on a pattern inspired by grounded theory[2] in the sense that the various chapters deal in depth with individual elements, while the overall framework that binds them together is constructed gradually and discussed only in the conclusions. It is therefore a book based on inferential rather than deductive logic. This will require some patience on the part of the reader, for which reason each chapter finishes with a summary.

The book is organized to replicate the research process and it proceeds as follows.

The first chapter examines current debate in the literature on organizational learning and knowing. It rejects a strictly cognitive and instrumental account of organizational learning and also distances itself from knowledge management studies and their reifying view of knowledge. The purpose is therefore to introduce the cultural context which has fostered the development of a 'third way' in analysis of organizational learning and knowledge. Termed 'knowing in practice', this approach focuses directly on the process of creating and using knowledge while organizing. The chapter sets out the theoretical background of the book and illustrates how the concept of knowing in practice is founded on the sociology of organization and on a constructivist ontology. The overall argument of the chapter is that the literature on organizational learning and knowing at the moment comprises two competing narratives: a predominant one which depicts knowledge as problem-driven, so that the need to solve a problem or any other external stimulus occasions the search for knowledge; and an emergent 'mystery-driven' narrative which depicts knowledge as engaged and self-critical participation in making the world in which we live. My first task, therefore, is to describe how knowing in practice involves participation in a meaningful situation. To this end, I shall have to define the field of practices that I wish to describe and the research design I intend to use.

The second chapter introduces the concept of 'texture', which grasps the qualitative character of a set of interconnected activities with continuously changing patterns called 'a field of practices'. The key to describing the texture of a field of practices is the idea of 'connectedness-in-action', i.e. the endless series of relationships which continually move into each other. The metaphor of weaving, as the art of looping and knotting, provides an image of the work of knowing in practice. The act of knowing in practice is the art of establishing connections-in-action, performing relationships which hold, and repairing them when they do not hold any longer. The research design developed to capture the endless connections between practices and their movements in the construction and translation of knowledge from one context of use to another is the 'spiral case study'. By using the notion of the 'spiral' I intend to show that the reality that we social scientists use to slide down among 'levels' – the individual, collective, organizational, inter-organizational and institutional – is not only connected but also fused with action. The spiral can be followed in both directions, up and down, and it serves to construe the close interaction which obtains between whatever is divided between a macro- and micro-analytical level. The distinction between levels of analysis and between micro and macro is not necessary, even though it is a practical way to mark out a field of analysis; but to avoid using it the research strategy will have to be rethought. My proposal is to examine some of the practices involved in creating a field of safety practices in order to describe both how practices are disseminated and the social process that weaves individual and institutional practices together.

The third chapter starts by examining the practices by which safety knowledge is transmitted to a novice on a building site. The object of knowing in practice will be simultaneously knowing how to work, knowing how to co-produce a safe environment with workmates, and knowing how to 'perform' an occupational identity. By means of examples drawn from an ethnographic study of how to become an assistant manager on a building site, and how safety is learnt, the third chapter argues that it is not 'safety' that is learnt but safe work practices. By positioning knowing as the capacity to perform competently in a specific socio-cultural activity and learning as the process of changing participation, the focus shifts from the mental processes of the individual to the discursive relations generated by a common practice. Learning to become a competent member within a culture of practice is a process through which novices appropriate the language, morality and culture of the community that sustain this practice. The process is not a passive act of 'being absorbed' but an active, reciprocal endeavour put in place by both the novice and the community. Novices therefore learn to master safety as they become part of a situated culture of practice.

In the fourth chapter, the notion of 'situated curriculum' directs attention to the practices which institutionalize the transmission of knowl-

edge within a community and in the relations between communities –
the workplace and the school – the purpose being to describe how a
body of knowledge is differently shaped by different and interconnected
practices.

The theme of shaping objects of knowledge across interdependent
communities is taken further in chapter 5, where the discursive practices of engineers, site managers and contractors describe the existence
of diverse and concurrent cultures of safety which operate simultaneously within an organization and among communities of practitioners.
Each of these cultures has its own mode of understanding, making sense
of, speaking about and handling themes to do with workplace safety, and
it is on this basis that appropriate behaviours and admissible justifica-
tions are defined, as well as the attention rules to be applied and the
action that should be taken. The aim of the chapter is to show that the
different voices are dissonant and their disagreement is not an impedi-
ment to collective action. People engage in conversations in practice and
on practice not only to reach agreements but also to celebrate identity, the logic of the community and to participate in broader societal
discourses.

The aim of chapter 6 is to highlight the importance of discursive
practices for the enactment of knowing and for mending the texture of
organizing when a breakdown occurs. It is the moment of breakdown
that provides the knowing opportunities discussed in the chapter in light
of cases of organizational breakdown repair prompted by accidents. From
the sociological point of view, an accident is a cognitive, emotional and
social breakdown. It is a breach in the organizational texture through
which disorder enters and a change of practices may be prompted from
outside.

The previous chapter implicitly questioned the distinction between
organization and environment and illustrated how in cases of breakdown
knowing in practice is not confined within the walls of the organization, and how a collective knowledgeable actor is discursively constituted by a plurality of subjects which mobilize knowledge resources.
This introduces the notion of the network qua subject that acts and
learns. The methodological problem here is identifying how human and
non-human actors enact 'bodies of knowledge' which are shaped and
circulated within institutionalized knowledge/power relations.

In chapter 7 the actors already introduced are presented to the reader
in sequence: a community of practitioners; interdependent communities
within an organization; organizations belonging to the same organizational field; and institutions which are interdependent with the previ-

ous organizations in that safety is one of their institutional concerns. All together they create the texture of the field of practices by mobilizing the differences of perspectives inscribed in institutional discourses. The chapter will illustrate how a discourse on safety as surveillance and repression meets with the discourse of safety as safe technology and artefacts, and dialogues with the discourse of safety as training and consultation. The purpose of this chapter is to show in particular how knowing in practice is mediated by the differences of perspective among co-participants in a field of practices and how it is mediated by artefacts. The objects of the material world are actively involved in discursive practices, not just because they interrogate humans and prestructure the contexts in which practices take place, but also because they incorporate the materiality of knowledge. Technologies, texts, the physical environment perform the role of anchoring knowledge and interactional infrastructures between humans and non-humans. A field of practices can be regarded as a network of fragmented and distributed knowledge held together by the power to associate heterogeneous elements.

The concluding chapter discusses the relationship among the various forms of the production, circulation, appropriation or avoidance of knowledge that have emerged in the previous chapters, presenting them within a theoretical and methodological framework grounded in the research findings.

NOTES

1. When Roland Barthes (1977) introduced the concept of figure in *Fragments d'un Discours Amoureux*, he wrote that the word should not be understood in its rhetorical sense, but rather in a much more vivid way as the body's gesture caught in action. The figure is delineated in outline (as a sign) and is memorable (like an image or a tale). A figure is established if someone can say: 'That's so true! I recognize this scene of language' (Barthes, 1990: 4, English translation). The figure is a *topos* (a place) half coded and half projective: 'it is a modest supplement offered to the reader to be made free with, to be added to, subtracted from, and passed on to others' (ibidem: 5).

2. Grounded theory (Glaser and Strauss, 1967; Strauss and Corbin, 1990) is an analytic method oriented to theory building which seeks to provide a conceptual codification of a set of empirical indicators consisting of actions, behaviours or events grouped into categories and used to build the theory. Therefore when conducting inductive research, the researcher collects everything that might have a bearing on the topic of study and only later, after qualitative data analysis, presents the theory 'grounded' on field events.

CHAPTER ONE

From Organizational Learning to Knowing in Practice

*Knowledge is not something that people possess
in their heads, but rather, something that people
do together.*

(Gergen, 1991: 270)

1.1   Conventional wisdom

Our society is dominated by a view of learning, education and training as an endeavour of 'knowledge delivery' based on a notion of learning as a process of information delivery from a knowledgeable source (either a teacher or a text book) to a target lacking that information (Eckert, 1989). From this perspective, learning amounts essentially to the acquisition of the body of data, facts and practical wisdom accumulated by all the generations that have preceded us. This knowledge is 'out there', stored in some form of memory (usually books), and the main effort of the learner is to acquire it and to store it in the proper compartment of his/her mind for future use or reference as needed.

To a certain extent, when learning is viewed in this way it may be equated to eating (hooks, 1994) or to banking:[1] knowledge is food for the mind, and the learner seeks to find the right or necessary sort of food and to ingest or consume it. Teaching and learning consist in the transfer of the 'gold' to the pupils' heads. Learning therefore takes place mainly during our early development, as we move through schooling, instruction and training. People usually receive their training at the end of their educational careers, so that it is considered a specific and goal-oriented form of instruction which provides newcomers with the knowledge they require to perform their roles appropriately in some organization. Training may be acquired later, if for some reason (e.g., updating existing knowledge or preparing for a job change or a new assignment), new learning becomes necessary. Generally speaking, in such cases training takes the form of a supplementary dose of instruction and schooling.

Although this familiar conception of learning may seem quite reasonable, it is a highly reductive account of both how people learn in general and of how people learn in organizations, for at least two reasons.

In the first place, it suggests that learning is separate from – and to some extent opposed to – any other activity. According to the traditional view, not only do we learn solely in certain periods of our lives, but also our learning is restricted to specific occasions, such as when we take a class, or read a book, or watch an instructional video. However, this is an inaccurate description of how matters stand. Study and instruction 'per se' are indeed important, but learning is also deeply rooted in other everyday activities and experiences as well. Most of the relevant know-how that distinguishes an expert from a novice is acquired on a day-to-day basis by acting and reflecting, i.e., by thinking about what we are doing and why, and talking about it with others (Schön, 1983).

In the second place, the view of learning as a totally individual activity, like ingesting food, can be misleading. Learning is much more than, and very different from, finding and acquiring items of organizational knowledge. As much in everyday life as in work organizations, people and groups create knowledge by negotiating the meaning of words, actions, situations and material artefacts. They all participate in and contribute to a world which is socially and culturally structured and constantly reconstituted by the activities of all those who belong to it. Cognitive and practical activity can thus be pursued only within this world, and through this social and cultural networking. Knowledge is not what resides in a person's head or in books or in data banks. To know is to be capable of participating with the requisite competence in the complex web of relationships among people, material artefacts and activities (Gherardi, 2001b). On this definition it follows that learning is always a practical accomplishment. As Gergen (1991) aptly puts it 'knowledge is something people do together' and it is done in every mundane activity, in organizations when people work together and in academic fields like organization studies, even if we make distinctions between lay, practical and theoretical knowledge. But also the practices of science – like any other social process – are intrinsically reflexive, and they are practices situated in specific contexts of power/knowledge. Situated practices are both pre-reflexive (depending on unstated assumptions and shared knowledge for the mutual achievement of sense) and reflexively constitutive of the situated members' contexts from which they arise. The term 'organizational learning' not only acquires meaning from the context in which it appears but it also reflexively creates that context.

The discourse on knowledge in organization studies arose in the 1970s from a metaphorical operation which combined the terms 'learning' and 'organization' into the concept of 'organizational learning' (although the first mention of the concept can be traced back to March and Simon, 1958). This was a highly successful operation, judging from the welter of publications on the subject and the ability of the discourse to conceal its metaphorical origins to the point of asserting the subjectivity of the learning organization. Simultaneously, the limitations implicit in every metaphorical operation grew increasingly evident, although describing them all would be an arduous undertaking. Nevertheless let us summarize the main points.

As an area of inquiry, organizational learning and knowledge (OLK) has grown to such an extent that it can be described as the institutionalization of a body of knowledge, and it can therefore be analysed using the categories of the sociology of knowledge (Scheler, 1926). This line of analysis takes account, besides the theoretical foundations, of the actions and events that have influenced these foundations, even if they are extra-theoretical phenomena. The task of sociology of knowledge (Berger and Luckmann 1966) is to analyse the social construction of reality on the basis of a conception of knowledge as active action which reflects the conditions and problems of the particular contexts in which it arises. The reason for assuming this point of view resides in the Babel of languages that today confront each other in this field. But our intention is not to propose a universal language. This proposal has already been made, and the many reviews of the literature that have appeared (in chronological order: Argyris and Schön, 1978; Shrivastava, 1983; Fiol and Lyles, 1985; Huber, 1991; Dodgson, 1993; Nicolini and Meznar, 1995; Easterby-Smith, 1997) can be considered attempts to catalogue the languages of Babel. Some of them (Fiol and Lyles, 1985; Huber, 1991) have been an explicit invitation to find a common background against which to construct a paradigm for the scientific development of organizational learning.

The history of science (and more modestly the time that has elapsed since the proposal was made and reiterated) teaches that 'normal' science does not become institutionalized by means of a process of accumulation and reflection on the knowledge produced, but through the mobilization of power resources in support of claims for its legitimacy and validity. It is thus we may interpret the appeals for the construction of

4 FROM ORGANIZATIONAL LEARNING TO KNOWING IN PRACTICE

a universal language as a form of rhetoric of scientific writing which relies on the emotionality tied to the idea of universal and disinterested knowledge, to knowledge for the sake of knowledge itself. This is an idealist position.

In the same way, however, we may represent the production of knowledge about knowledge as a war game in which some forms of knowledge achieve hegemony (as refined, official or elite language) while others are marginalized (like the vernacular). This is a sort of militarist – or political – conception of knowledge institutionalization. As regards OLK we can for the moment say that the hypothesis of a common language has not been fulfilled, but nor has there been a diaspora whereby the community has split into numerous sub-communities each with its own journals, conferences and references (Easterby–Smith, Snell and Gherardi, 1998).

A third position, neither idealist nor militant, views the production of science as an open conversation (Clegg and Hardy, 1996) in which diverse discourses on knowledge meet and clash, each of them with its own system of representation (its own grammar and syntax). An open conversation is one in which the conversation itself creates the conditions for conversing – which is an image that expresses the institutional reflexivity that characterizes the production and reproduction of society in time. The term 'institutional reflexivity' (Giddens, 1976, 1990) refers to the fact that the institutional work of society reproduces the social order that has produced its institutions. And it does so via a twofold hermeneutics, that is, the constant reinterpretation of previous interpretations.

When sociology of knowledge is applied to OLK, it can be conceived as a cultural object created by artful practices of cultural work. At the same time it points to where one should look in order to understand how institutional reflexivity has created the conditions for subjecting conversation to further theory building. The rhetoric used in my arguments will be based on a *pars destruens* which will focus on the institutionalization of knowledge about organizational learning (OL) and the meta-theoretical assumptions on which it is based, and on a *pars construens* which will shed light on the spaces still available to theory building. The argument will frequently employ dichotomous categories, but not to represent the world in black and white, even less to divide the community of scholars between heroes and villains. The intention instead is to use these dichotomies as a rhetorical device which facilitates the process of differentiation. In fact dichotomous categories may be used in order to be discarded and reveal what is concealed in the interstices among them.

The first dichotomy that I shall explore is between OL and learning organization (LO). This will be the argument developed in the two sections that follow, where I contend that the institutionalization of the concept is based on a realist ontology which has prevailed over the metaphorical operation from which it was born, and then that the development of the concept as a set of managerial techniques has given rise to a technology of disciplining (Foucault, 1977). We shall then look for alternative discursive positions which lead towards a practiced-based theorizing on knowing and learning in organizations.

1.2 The institutionalization of the field: the birth of the learning organization

The field of OL has developed and been institutionalized as 'problem-driven', as the production of instrumental knowledge. But the knowledge thus produced sets the conditions for research to shift to 'mystery-driven' learning (Gherardi, 1999) which – in Derrida's (1967) terms – is supplementary to cognitive reflexivity. An episode (Gherardi, 1999) is paradigmatic of what happens in the community of scholars that studies organizational learning:

> I was at an international conference on Organizational Learning and had taken part in discussion of a paper presented by a colleague from a university in a developing country which empirically tested whether the most successful firms in her country were, or were not, learning organizations. Unfortunately, her data showed a low correlation between being an economically successful firm and being a learning organization, and she was puzzled by her findings.

This episode is paradigmatic of the social process of 'manufacturing knowledge': a heuristic concept – OL – acquires legitimacy in the scientific community, it spreads through the community of consultants and practitioners, it produces the 'characteristics' that distinguish the phenomenon (and thus proves its existence), and it coins the label 'learning organization'. This label travels though time and space (Czarniawska and Sèvon, 1996) and is appropriated by some organizations, which incorporate it into their identities. At this point a social phenomenon has been produced: a realist assumption replaces a heuristic device, and learning is defined a 'real' phenomenon which takes place 'out there' in organizations and can be measured, compared and validated. There 'really' exist learning organizations in the world – organizations which are presumably different from non-learning ones – and as corporate actors they learn by themselves,[2] either from each other or by being immersed in an ecology of learning. The touchstone with which to determine whether, how and in what circumstances learning has been produced is the concept of change.[3] Organizational change is the outcome of a more or less rational procedure of the production of knowledge and its practical application. If this does not come about, something 'has gone wrong' and dysfunctional learning has taken place.

This episode gives cause for much thought, but I shall examine only the aspect that concerns the social process internal to a community of scholars which – around 20 years ago – marked out an area of study by means of a metaphorical operation: that is, by juxtaposing the concept of learning with that of organization. A new area of study requires resources of legitimation (Astley, 1985; Whitley, 1984) not only internally to the restricted occupational community of academics or consultants but also to firms and to society in general. This process of mobilizing credibility creates cultural artefacts – books, conferences, university courses – as well as new identities: learning organizations (LO) are born. Companies with outstanding reputations – Shell, Mercedes Benz, Isvor Fiat – baptize themselves LOs and devote enormous resources to creating a 'corporate' identity that is recognizable, recognized and trustworthy in the eyes of its members and of society at large.

This social process of the creation of a new subjectivity for the firm and of the legitimation of new expert knowledge singles out a series of distinctive features of the LO[4] and of OL which, in their turn, find coherence within a normative model. It is often a short step from description to prescription in organizational studies, even more so if historical memory is lost.

The existence of the LO has become 'natural' because it has been institutionalized, and institutions give identity. Therefore the features of the LO have become attributes of the being of a category of firms. Mary Douglas (1986: 83–6) argues that institutions are founded on an analogy with nature. The naturalization of social classifications protects the institution when it is still at the stage of fragile convention: by being naturalized, it becomes part of the order of the universe and is therefore ready to function as a basis for argument. And this is when organization scholars – of the second generation, or forgetful, or subordinate to those who produce 'knowledge', or decentralized or marginal with respect to them – arm themselves with questionnaires, measuring scales and other scientific tools and set off to verify these distinctive features.

This account is simplistic and crude. It does not claim to be 'true'; it merely serves to highlight some of the turning points that have made the languages of Babel no longer mutually intelligible. A scientific community can therefore be identified as forming around the concept of LO, around a realist ontology, around a positivist epistemology, around a prescriptive intent, and around continued research into applied rationality. It should be borne in mind, in fact, that the term OL was first used in decision-making theory (Cyert and March, 1963), which subsequently developed the notion of learning as adaptation.

We may for the moment assume that the distinction between LO and OL is based on the dichotomy between prescriptive and descriptive research, as proposed by Tsang (1997: 73) for example. But, in my view, the issue is not the fact that some (academics) 'fail to generate useful implications for practitioners' and the others 'seldom follow rigorous research methodologies', *therefore* there is a need 'to integrate the two streams of research'. This too is a rhetoric of scientific writing which urges the search for a universal language. Consequently, in my opinion, it is not a matter of producing 'constructs [that] can be operationalized in empirical research' (ibid. p. 78) or of producing 'empirical evidence' (ibid. p. 77) when the contrast is between a realist ontology – which assumes learning as an empirical phenomenon – and a constructionist one. These are problems of knowledge that concern a realist ontology, but if organizational learning is a 'live metaphor' (Tzoukas, 1991), a metaphorical operation performed by the researcher (Gherardi, 1995b) – that is, a means to represent the organization *as if* it were a system that learns – then the problem of knowledge is not to establish what constitutes 'effective learning' but to determine the amount of further knowledge yielded by the metaphor proposed.

Therefore the interest of knowledge (Habermas, 1971) shifts from the question 'how does an organization learn or should learn?' to the question 'if we depict an organization as a system which learns, are we able to see something new and to see something that we already know differently?' The former question mainly concerns explanation of OL, while the latter more closely relates to understanding (*Verstehen*) of it (Weber, 1922). At this crossroads in the social sciences, the former community goes in quest of the founding myth of objectivity, while the latter pursues the myth of adequacy (Ricolfi, 1997: 38). Ricolfi writes 'explanation and understanding, positivism and hermeneutics, the primacy of method and the primacy of the subject-matter, are antitheses that were born together with the social sciences, and they have persisted because they represent different but functionally equivalent answers to the need for identity of the social sciences themselves'. From this latter perspective we may therefore enquire as to the 'goodness' of the models of knowledge produced when a scientific community is socially constructed around a topic.

1.3 Organizational learning as a disciplinary discourse

The literature on LO has been suspected of colluding with the 'ruling courts' which govern organizations (Coopey, 1995) and of employing ideologically a discourse of democracy and liberation (Snell and Chak, 1998). Easterby-Smith (1997: 1086) defines the literature on LO as having 'an action orientation', and being 'geared toward creating an ideal type, an organization in which learning is maximized'.

But it would be naive to create and represent a distinction between OL as a heuristic view and LO as a realistic one, when both converge on the same social practice which legitimizes the managerial techniques based on their claims of scientific knowledge. They share the same bias and both contribute to the institutionalization of the field as a disciplinary discourse and to its superseding through the process of constant reinterpretation of the previous interpretation known as 'institutional reflexivity'.

We may therefore view the manufacturing of a body of knowledge – a discipline – under the labels 'OL' and 'LO' as a situated practice in a community of organizations, in a community of practitioners, in a community of academics, in a society. We may explore that practice as a 'disciplinary discourse' which sustains forms of normative behaviour, supports knowledge claims and provides resources for normalization.

From a Foucauldian perspective, discourses are systems of thought which are contingent upon material practices and which inform those practices through particular power techniques. Much of nineteenth-century social science (social welfare, administration, statistics) was almost wholly shaped by the 'disciplinary gaze' (Foucault, 1977) of surveillance. In organization studies, for example, the personnel function, under the guidance of 'human relations', had a similar tutelary role (Hardy and Clegg, 1996), and 'organizational learning' is now following suit.

Foucault's concept of discipline has been usefully applied in postmodern analysis of power/knowledge relations (Alvesson, 1993, 1994; Deetz, 1996; Townley, 1993) in the area of knowledge firms or in the construction of the subjectivity of knowledge workers. Also the exploitative ethos of many organizational learning discourses has been underlined by postmodern scholars (Boje, 1994) and other critical scholars

(Huysman, 1999). I do not wish to pursue this line of analysis further; rather, I shall restrict my treatment to illustration of a set of premises implicit in OL and LO theorization in order to highlight how they sustain a disciplinary discourse which disciplines concrete behaviours:

1. *OL is always ameliorative and disinterested.*
   Learning is regarded as always positive, in the spirit of 'the more, the better'. OL as a discourse implicitly assumes an ameliorative vision in which learning is incremental and knowledge is a cumulative product which undergoes constant development (Miner and Mezias, 1996). The alleged universality, neutrality and transparency of knowledge presume that humankind is its beneficiary, thereby neglecting the role of power in structuring organizational knowledge. What is deemed worth learning has already been selected: only those in power learn the right things.

2. *OL is intentional.*
   If learning resembles a process of appropriation and capitalization of something external, or of a known product, then also the ways in which it is appropriated/produced can be specified and normatively sustained. OL may be embodied in SOPs (standard operating procedures), which are periodically overhauled and updated (Kieser, Beck and Taino, 2001). It may thus be envisaged as 'the one best way of learning'.

3. *OL is an extorted result.*
   The LO requires of work groups that they 'learn' and transfer the knowledge thus acquired to organizational structures, and that learning leads to an improvement in performance. The use of power in transferring knowledge is silenced and OL is conceived as grounded on free transfer, on transparency, on voluntariness and on the chain of authority, rather than residing in the murky depths of micro-conflictuality, micro-negotiation and the systematic and more or less deliberate distortion/extortion of knowledge.

4. *OL presumes change but not its understanding.*
   Learning proposes a change in the behaviour – actual or potential – of individuals or groups, or perhaps a cognitive change. It does not necessarily require individuals to understand the logic that has led to a change in SOPs (Child and Markoczy, 1993). This amounts to saying that if some change is manifest, then a learning process has taken place, but also that change does not require any learning. The problem thus arises of how the empirical evidence can be collected to demonstrate the relationship between change and learning.

Learning, writes Rorty (1989), is a term often part of a final vocabulary: it is a value in itself which cannot be further questioned. It is associated with improvement in performance, the rapid correction of errors and a fast reaction to environmental changes. The positive connotations associated with the word induces the a priori assumption of what needs to be empirically demonstrated. Learning, as the founding myth of the scientific community of OL scholars, obscures the myopia of learning from experience (Levinthal and March, 1993).

In short, we have described the theoretical construction of OL and LO as a discourse of disciplining when it is preselected as a managerial technique which contains a bias towards systematic and purposeful learning, a bias towards improvement, and a normative bias. These biases are composed of a specific structuring of power/knowledge which sustains them and perpetuates them as a discourse of power. This is even more evident when we consider the literature on knowledge management.

1.4   The reification of knowledge in the knowledge management literature

A quantitative bibliographical survey (Scarbrough, Swan and Preston, 1998) shows that since 1997 the term 'knowledge management' has supplanted 'organizational learning', and that the interest of the scientific community has switched from questions concerning the appropriation of knowledge by individuals and organizations to ones concerning the techniques and technologies of knowledge management. The academic disciplines now predominant in the organizational learning debate are not psychological but economic, and a new alliance has arisen between the economics of knowledge and information technology which now monopolizes the term 'knowledge management' (KM).

The concepts of 'knowledge work' and 'knowledge worker' were first introduced by Peter Drucker (1939), who set them in contrast to those of manual work and service work. Brief inspection of the relation between knowledge and wealth creation between the eighteenth and twentieth centuries reveals a series of epochal changes: first, knowledge was applied to artefacts, processes and products through technologies, patents and tacit knowledge; then it was applied to human labour through the scientific analysis of work; and finally knowledge was applied to knowledge itself, thus constituting knowledge work. Based on this new type of work is the endeavour to manage knowledge as if it were an organizational resource and as if its management were an organizational process to be safeguarded.

The idea behind KM is that if organizations can induce their employees to store the knowledge that they produce while they work, and if they can draw on the knowledge stored by others, then a network will be created which will enable firms to work more efficiently. This idea is therefore based on two assumptions: that knowledge is 'archivable' in some form by means of information systems; and that it is 'reusable' by others and can be capitalized. Given this view of knowledge managed as a stock of know-how, it is evident why an alliance has formed between KM and information technology, and why the economics of knowledge regard it as a resource and therefore as an 'object'.

The distinctive feature of current technological innovation – writes Manuel Castells (1996) – is not the central importance of knowledge and information in themselves but rather their application to produce knowledge and the technologies to develop it. The new technologies are not simply tools used in the production cycle; rather, they are processes that must be developed. Necessary, therefore, is analysis of how organizations create, use, institutionalize and maintain knowledge and knowledge processes. These developments have had direct consequences for management because male and female workers (whether blue-collar or white-collar) make increasing use of specialist knowledge, and their work grows increasingly technical. They acquire greater power and broader autonomy in the workplace, because expert knowledge is more difficult to control and may easily become a resource with its own market. Workers develop cultures in occupations which are not professional in the strict sense, and these cultures collide with the traditional managerial culture based on bureaucratic organizational control. Organizations must be able to rely on the commitment of knowledge workers to their goals, so that also organizational cultures become instruments of control.

This cultural and economic context has bred an economics of knowledge which is based essentially on the resource-based theory of the firm and envisages specialist knowledge as a new productive resource (besides the traditional factors of land, labour and capital) denoted by terms such as core competencies, skills, routines or special abilities.

Colourful metaphors abound. Knowledge is the root of production, while products and services are its fruits, so that competencies constitute the organization's genetic code (Prahalad and Hamel, 1990); distinctive skills are like passing the ball in soccer (Kay, 1993); organizational competence is like a chef's ability to transfer his experience to new recipes (Miyazaki, 1994). Davenport and Prusak (1998: 17) define knowledge as a tangible resource which can be mobilized to obtain a competitive advantage. Dixon (2000) defines it as a resource which the members of an organization must share, although she does not indicate or discuss why workers would have reason to do so.

In this cultural climate and within a discipline mainly concerned with the economic value of knowledge, it rapidly becomes not only objectified but also commodified: 'objectively definable commodities that can be used to create competitive advantage' as Empson puts it (Empson, 2001: 812). Knowledge and competencies become resources, commodities or goods which can be stored, transferred and reused, which produce wealth and are used as and when needed. Kalling and Styhre (2003: 25) argue that the term 'knowledge management' is an oxymoron, since knowledge is processual and fluid, while management is aimed at control and order. A similar case was previously made by Weick and Westley (1996: 440): 'to learn is to disorganize and increase variety. To organize is to forget and reduce variety'.

The theoretical assumptions of the KM literature have been criticized on several grounds. These are now summarized because the rest of this book will not deal with the said literature any further:

- it has a simplistic and objectifying view of both knowledge and how it can be managed.
- it shows scant interest in exploring the relation between knowledge and power.
- a large part of the KM literature adopts an IT-based approach which treats knowledge as information.
- it assumes that there is a linear relation between knowledge and action, without considering that knowledge extends beyond what is useful or strictly instrumental.

These criticisms can be tempered by pointing out that when a new research topic arises, especially in management studies, the normative and prescriptive approach often prevails over the analytical and critical one. The criticisms brought against KM in an attempt to extend its range of application has been well expressed by Knorr-Cetina (1997: 8):

> The traditional definition of a knowledge society puts the emphasis on the first term; on knowledge, seen as a specific product. The definition I advocate switches the emphasis to society, a society that, if the argument about the expanding role of expert systems etc. is right, is no more inside

knowledge processes than outside. In a postsocial knowledge society, mutually exclusive definitions of knowledge processes and social processes are theoretically no longer adequate; we need to trace the ways in which knowledge has become constitutive of social relations.

Alongside the position stressing that knowledge management entails a coherent knowledge culture we may put the positions of those who, while not rejecting a technological approach to knowledge treatment, stress the social component of technological management.

A well-balanced position on the matter has been taken up by McDermott (1999), who argues that information technologies may have inspired KM, but on their own they are unable to ensure the proper management of knowledge. As happened when the terms of 'organizational learning' and 'learning organization' were reversed, so today the expression 'knowledge management' is being replaced by 'management of knowledge'. But can knowledge be 'managed'? In what sense does the concept of management apply to knowledge?

I argue that both the OL and KM literatures are inadequate and that a third body of literature is emerging and forming an alliance around practice-based studies of knowing and learning and the study of knowing in practice (Nicolini, Gherardi and Yanow, 2003).

1.5   Knowing in practice: neither in the head nor as a commodity

One figure in the discourse on learning and organization states that knowledge resides in the heads of persons, and that it is appropriated, transmitted and stored by means of mentalistic processes. The figure works through the dichotomies of mind/body, thought/action, individual/organization. Its main catchphrase is 'organizational learning', but also 'cognitive framework' or 'traditional cognitive learning theory' (Nicolini and Meznar, 1995; Fox, 1997; Easterby-Smith, Snell and Gherardi, 1998). The second figure in this discourse has been constructed by conversations in the economics of knowledge and in knowledge management. The starting point has been the identification of knowledge as a production factor distinct from the traditional ones of capital, labour and land. This distinction has led to the definition of knowledge as 'strategic' and its location in the head of the organization (i.e., management), which through its work determines corporate performance. The catchphrase for this figure discourse on learning and organization, 'knowledge management', unites the image of knowledge as a commodity (or asset) with that of its intentional and deliberate control. The economics of knowledge is the political economy of knowledge as well.

Before considering a third figure in this discourse, *practice*, I will round off the discussion so far with a telling image garnered from a recent conversation with my colleague Pasquale Gagliardi. To explain why knowledge management cannot be based on a functionalist idea of knowledge, he used the following analogy: 'It's the difference between house architecture and garden architecture'. When a garden is laid out, the designer is aware that plants grow, that they grow and spread, and that they have lives of their own. Functionalist views of knowledge, like those of house architecture, are based on the fixity of structure and on the control of form. But if knowledge, like plants, is alive, then it can be talked about more like garden architecture as it becomes 'culturalized' in different discourses. That is, rather than focusing on knowledge as inert material, to be fixed and controlled, knowledge could be articulated both in its spatiality and in its fabrication, and in consideration of its transformative linkages between the human and the natural. The concept of knowing in practice enables us to focus on the fact that, in everyday practices, learning and knowing are not separate activities; they instead take place in the flow of experience, with or without our being aware of it. In everyday organizational life, work, learning, innovation, communication, negotiation, conflict over goals, their interpretation, and history, are co-present in work practices. They are part of human existence.

There is a need for a new vocabulary centred on the term 'practice', even if paradoxically the concept of practice has a long philosophical and sociological tradition. Several authors (Boisot, 1998; Contu, 2000; Barley and Kunda, 2001; Nicolini, Gherardi and Yanow, 2003; Kalling and Styhre, 2003) have complained that they are forced to work with concepts unsuited to building theories of post-bureaucratic organizing. An entire family of explanatory concepts such as 'tacit knowledge', 'shared understanding', 'communities of thought', 'communities of practice', 'epistemic objects', 'situated knowledge', 'forms of life', 'cultural practices', 'aesthetic understanding', 'negotiated order' denote the search for embodied and contextually located instances of discourse and action, of doing and knowing.

A unified field of practices or a social theory of practice does not exist. Nevertheless, I shall seek to explain why and how some traditions of research can be grouped under the heading of what I call 'practice-based theorizing on learning and knowing in organizations' (Gherardi,

2000b; Nicolini, Gherardi and Yanow, 2003). My intention is not to force diverse ontological and epistemological assumptions into a single framework; nor is it to resolve controversies among them with a view to constructing a single theory. More modestly, I shall attempt to show that among the manifold conversations now in progress on the theme of knowing and organizing, there is one that has an emergent identity which centres on the idea of practice. To do this, I shall contextualize the meaning of 'practice-based theorizing' within these ongoing conversations:

- *A cultural and aesthetic approach.* Culture can be seen as cultural practices (Swidler, 2001) which keep and transmit the context-specific, collectively held meanings embedded in practices. This approach highlights how mastery depends on social processes both for its existence and for its communication: the practice of flute making (Cook and Yanow, 1993) is at once the medium through which mastery is expressed and communicated, and the outcome of that mastery. The cultural perspective also shows how artefacts and interactions sustain both meaning and knowing in practice without having to focus on whether an actor thinks or believes or acts upon a specific idea or set of values or predispositions. A cultural and symbolic understanding of organization is also the bedrock of the aesthetic approach. Aesthetic knowledge is the form of knowledge that persons acquire by activating the specific capacities of their perceptive-sensorial faculties and aesthetic judgement in the day-to-day lives of organizations. The aesthetic dimension in organizations is not just aesthetic judgement; it is not solely what is beautiful, ugly, grotesque or kitsch. It is these things as well, but it is also what the five senses of sight, hearing, smell, taste and touch make known (Strati, 2003). It is a sensible judgement which does not yield judgements, but rather evaluations of perceived perfection or imperfection which have the nature of sentiment and taste or a judgement in harmony with feelings instead of concepts. This latter characteristic was considered by Polanyi (1962) when he drew the distinction between explicit, formalized knowledge and tacit knowledge, or knowing how to do something without being able to provide an adequate analytical description of it. If I were to choose a concept that represents the main contribution of this line of inquiry to practice-based studies I would select the idea of 'aesthetic understanding' (Strati, 1992, 1999), because this overcomes the mind/body dichotomy and introduces feelings as forms of non-cognitive knowing.

- *Situated learning theory*. Lave and Wenger (1991) and Wenger (1998) develop a now well-established way to talk about practice-based learning and knowing in organizations which uses the notion of 'community of practice'. The concept defines a collective subject, a special type of community defined by joint enterprise, mutual engagement, and a shared repertoire of actions, styles, artefacts, concepts, discourses, stories. Communities grow from the intersection between competence and personal experience within a context of mutual engagement in a common practice. Competence is historically and socially defined in communities, and knowing is a matter of displaying the socially defined competence sustained by the community. At the same time, however, because we experience knowing on the basis of our own personal stories, the enactment of such knowing is always a matter of negotiation. The interplay between knowing and competence gives all constituents opportunities for learning and innovation. The community of practice perspective thus emphasizes knowing in practice as joint enterprise and belonging. This, I believe, is its main contribution to practice-based studies.

- *Activity theory*. This originates from the work of Vygotsky and emphasizes the historical, mediated and transformational nature of collaborative endeavours. An 'activity system', to use Engeström's *et al.* (2003) as well as Blackler's (1995) term, is a disturbance-producing system constituted by incoherences, inconsistencies, paradoxes and tensions. Among other things, the concept of activity (cognate to practice) dissolves the distinction between order and disorder. Because activities are always enacted in communities and are oriented towards objects of work that are partly given and partly emergent and generated within the activity itself, the accomplishment of the object of an activity requires expansive learning. Such expansion requires the activity system to learn new ways of accommodating all different composing elements; an effort that inevitably affects the nature itself of the object of work and generates new inconsistencies and contradictions, thus triggering a new cycle of transformation. The idea of an object of work that is partly given and partly emergent, which reveals the tentative nature of knowing and acting, is the fundamental feature of this approach to practices.

- *Actor-network theory*. The framework of sociology of translation, also known as actor-network theory, began with the social studies of science and technology based on the notion that 'the social' is nothing other than a patterned network of heterogeneous materials – not only people but also machines, animals, texts, money, architectures – kept together by active processes of ordering (Law, 1992). According to the principle of symmetry, the knower and the known reciprocally define each other. Thinking of the world as a performative effect entails acknowledgement that if entities (human or non-human) achieve their form as a consequence of the relations in which they are located, and if relations do not hold fast by themselves, then they have to be performed in, by and through those relations. Organization, stability and persistence are consequently the result of an effort, not an intrinsic quality of things. The order and 'nature' of things is therefore always a reversible and uncertain outcome, an effect of operations, manoeuvres and processes that keep things in place. And knowledge and action are located in ecologies of social-material relations (Fujimura, 1995; Star, 1995) or action-nets (Czarniawska and Jorges, 1995). The approach contributes to the field of practice-based studies mainly by conceiving knowing in terms of performativity and its intermediaries, which not only mediate practices but also propagate them.

• *Workplace studies.* The term 'workplace studies' denotes a body of analyses that share an interest in the 'naturalistic' study of work settings. A workplace is conceived not in physical or static terms, but as socially constructed through interactions among participants, and through the use made by the latter of the artefacts and technologies present in the work setting. Workplace studies consider work as an activity in which the objects and subjects present in the setting constitute and give sense to the activities that arise from their interactions. By means of detailed analysis of the actions and interactions that take place in work settings, they seek to account for the 'taken-for-granted', and for the tacit routines which participants often do not experience as constitutive elements of work but which instead pertain to expert knowledge. Workplace studies are interested in technology as a constitutive element of workplaces, considering it as 'technology in use' or 'technology in action', and they are aware that it is produced by a specific culture: that of its designers. These studies pay particularly close attention to 'technology as a social practice' (Suchman *et al.*, 1999), firstly because they are engaged in the naturalistic study of work and its interaction with technologies, and secondly because they conceive objects and technologies as constitutive elements of the work setting (Borzeix, 1994; Luff, Hindmarch and Heath, 2000). Their main contribution to practice-based studies is the focus on conversation and interaction mediated by technology.

Conversation among these traditions of research has been made possible by their shared focus on situated practice, on practical rather than abstract and decontextualized forms of knowledge. In this regard it would be an unpardonable oversight (to say the least) if this section did not recognize the authority of the feminist voice in discussion of 'situated knowledge', and in revealing the androcentrism of both the structures and the practices of knowledge through which social experience has been understood. The feminist critique of science, and feminist works in the sociology of science and technology, have helped to show that even 'universal' knowledge is situated, while feminist objectivity simply means bodily-situated knowledge (Harding, 1986; Star, 1991; Mol, 1999). Feminist objectivity 'is about limited location and situated knowledge, not about transcendence and splitting of subject and object. In this way we might become answerable for what we learn how to see' (Haraway, 1991: 190).

There is a convergence with other thought positions on a critique of power/knowledge (Foucault, 1977), philosophy of science (Rouse, 2002) or social studies of science and technology (Pickering, 1992) emphasizing that knowledge is situated within forms of life and is the outcome of interests, ideologies and the contingencies of social negotiations, but it is important to stress that feminism is not just a theoretical position; it is mainly a practice intended to make knowledge more accountable by contextualizing questions of evidence, what counts as evidence, and how evidential relations are produced in practice.

Those post-structuralist feminist scholars working towards 'post-epistemological' conceptions of knowledge (Belenky et al., 1986; Barad, 2003; Haraway, 1991; Hawkesworth, 1989; Gherardi 2003) clearly depict the meaning of a 'politics of knowledge'. Their claims also concern the field of practice-based studies if the researcher wishes to engage with reflexive construction of the knowledge that s/he produces:

• *Knowledge is engaged and self-critical participation in making the world in which we live.* Accounts of the world, or of the world of science, do not depend on a logic of discovery of inner laws, but on the subjects' active construction and their power-based social relations in conversation with the world. Feminist studies are concerned with different ways in which knowers interact with the objects of knowledge, since knowing is embedded within specific ways of engaging the world, starting from the concrete particularity of bodies and social relations.

- *Knowledge is situated in historical practices.* Feminist studies take a participatory stance on knowing, reflecting and learning. That is to say, feminist scholars conceive 'knowing' as concretely situated in conversation among machines, people, other organisms and artefacts, more interactional than representational. They suggest that changes in knowledge are as much changes in practices as changes in beliefs and mental representations.
- *Knowledge is a multidimensional relationship between the knowers and the known.* Knowing is neither external to what is inside knowers' thoughts, culture and interests, nor merely instrumental to representations. Feminist scholars construe knowledge as a multidimensional relationship between knower and known, rather than as a simple relation of representation and correspondence. Moreover the relationship is intertwined with complex relations among knowers as well as with the object of knowledge. This is an attempt to hold knowers accountable for what they do, and to make explicit to whom and to what they need to be accountable.
- *Knowledge is transformative and futural.* Feminists seek to have an impact on important aspects of how the world is constituted, and to exert an effect upon the culture of practices that they study in order to legitimate the changes that they hope to engender. They therefore assert an alternative to the supposed neutrality and detachment of knowing as portrayed in science by propounding reflective and self-critical participation in the production of knowledge.

In summary, there are evidently numerous and diverse routes regarding 'knowledge' that can be followed under the umbrella concept of practice. These routes may meet and then once again diverge. Yet, as a figure of the discourse on knowing and learning, the term 'practice' is a *topos* that connects 'knowing' with 'doing'. It conveys the image of materiality, of fabrication, of handiwork, of the craftsman's skill. Knowledge consequently does not arise from scientific 'discoveries'; rather, it is fabricated by situated practices of knowledge production and reproduction, using the technologies of representation and mobilization. The connection between power and knowledge is thematized together with ethical questions and issues concerning social change.

However, my concern is not to go in search of a framework that comprises all these reflections in a single space, but rather to show how a practice-based theorizing arises from multiple perspectives and negotiations, and how in doing so it delegitimizes a univocal narrative of scientific authority. Altogether, *practice* articulates knowledge in and about organizing as practical accomplishment, rather than as a transcendental account of a de-contextualized reality, done by a genderless and disembodied researcher.

1.6   The philosophical roots of the concept of practice

The concept of 'practice' requires exploration because it is laden with diverse traditions of thought. I shall briefly recall the phenomenological account, the Marxist one, and that of the late Wittgenstein.

Heidegger (1969) and the phenomenological school used the term *Dasein* to denote the 'being-in-the-world' whereby subject and object are indistinguishable. They are both part of a situation and exist in a social and historical setting. The concept is taken further by Winograd and Flores (1986), who provide an illuminating example of the relationship among subject, object, environment and knowledge. Consider a carpenter hammering a nail into a piece of wood. In the carpenter's practical activity, the hammer does not exist as an object with given properties. It is as much part of his world as the arm with which he wields it. The hammer belongs to the environment and can be unthinkingly used by the carpenter. The carpenter does not need to 'think a hammer' to drive in a nail. His capacity to act depends on his familiarity with the act of hammering. His use of the practical item 'hammer' is its significance to him in the setting 'hammering' and 'carpentry'. The hammer exists as such when it no longer works or is missing. That is to say, when it becomes unusable. In the usable environment, the understanding of situations is pre-reflexive activity.

Reflexive, investigative, theoretical knowledge requires that something that was previously usable must now be unusable. The world of objects thus becomes 'simply present' (*Vorhanden*), no longer understood. This breakdown only occurs when the carpenter has already understood the hammer in practice. When the carpenter is hammering unimpededly, the hammer with its properties does not exist as an entity. Only when some breakdown or situation of non-usability occurs will the carpenter's activity of 'hammering' take problematic form.

Closely associated with the phenomenological tradition is the concept of tacit knowledge. This is what Polanyi (1962) meant when he said that we know much more than we know we know. He asks: does an analytical description of how to keep one's balance on a bicycle suffice as instruction to someone wanting to learn how to ride a bicycle? And he answers: 'rules of art can be useful, but they do not determine the practice of an art; they are maxims, which can serve as a guide to an art only if they can be integrated into the practical knowledge of the art. They cannot replace this knowledge' (Polanyi, 1962: 50).

In order to convey what he means by 'tacit knowledge' in the practice of skills, Polanyi draws a distinction between two types of awareness: focal awareness and subsidiary awareness:

> when we use a hammer to drive in a nail, we attend to both nail and hammer, *but in a different way.* We *watch* the effect of our strokes on the nail and try to wield the hammer so as to hit the nail most effectively. When we bring down the hammer we do not feel that its handle has struck our palm but that its head has struck the nail.
>
> **(Polanyi, 1962: 55)**

The focal awareness is driving in the nail, the subsidiary awareness is the feeling on the palm of the hand, and we pay close attention to these feelings not because they are the object of our attention, but because they are the instruments of our attention. The conclusion is that, in general, we do not have focal awareness of the instruments over which we have gained mastery.

The example of hammering is also paradigmatic of the knowledge that arises when breakdown occurs and reflexive activity intervenes. Accidents, for example, are cases of breakdown in everyday life which bring to the surface what was previously unproblematic. In organizational studies, the tradition of action research has made much use of the method of the critical incident as a stimulus for reflection on the conditions that govern normality. Ethnomethodology, too, has used the breaching of rules to show the operation of the rules that produce a 'normal' situation. Again, the method of reflection on quasi-incidents exploits the social, cognitive and emotional breakdown brought about by events. In the phenomenological tradition, therefore, the concept of practice shows how comprehension in situations where one is 'thrown headlong into use' is pre-reflexive and does not draw distinctions among subject, object, thing or environment, and it also shows how reflexive understanding arises at moments of breakdown. This signifies that organizations as systems of practices exist in the world of a tacit knowledge which is simply usable and becomes the object of reflection when a breakdown occurs.

However, the phenomenological concept of practice is less well known than the Marxist use of the term, which assigns it an emancipating force. Added to these is Wittgenstein's concept of practice (1953). Taken together, these three concepts have been influential on studies of computer hardware design (Ehn, 1988), since this technology breaks down the artificial distinction between workers and machines and is instead located within the interaction between human and non-human systems in a practice of situated activity.

Practice (praxis) is a notion central to Marxist epistemology, where it contrasts with the Cartesian notion of detached reflection, of the separation between mind and body, and stands in polemic with rationalism, positivism and scientism. Practice is an epistemological principle because if as knowing subjects we are to know that things are independent of us, we must first subject them to our own praxis, because in order to know how things are when they are not in contact with us, we must first enter into contact with them.

Practice is both our production of the world and the result of this process. It is always the product of specific historical conditions resulting from previous practice and transformed into present practice. The material process of production involves the production of society and its reproduction as emancipatory practice.

The Marxist tradition has recently been revived by so-called 'activity theory' (Engestrom, 1987), which draws on the work of Vygotsky and the Russian school of social psychology (Luria, Leontiev, Davydov). Engestrom (1987) utilizes the concept of 'activity system' to show how analysis of human activity must begin with study of material actions and of contexts of action. Unlike contexts of animal activity, human activity systems are distinguished by the presence of: (a) manufactured objects and concepts which mediate the interaction between individuals and concepts; (b) traditions, rituals and rules which mediate the interaction between individuals and the community; (c) the division of labour that mediates the interaction between the community and the actions of its members. It is in practical action, and not in thought, that social learning takes place, because the ambiguities, uncertainties and contradictions of praxis provide opportunities for individual and collective development (Blackler, Crump and McDonald, 2003).

The important contribution of this tradition is its methodological insight that practice is a system of activities in which knowing is not separate from doing, and learning is a social and not merely cognitive activity. Blackler writes (1993: 870): 'social learning is a creative achievement, therefore, which involves a degree of personal investment; it can only be achieved by active participation'. Participating in a practice is consequently a way to acquire knowledge-in-action, but also to change or perpetuate such knowledge and to produce and reproduce society.

Finally, language is a distinctive feature of human activity systems. Which brings us to Wittgenstein's (1953) notion of practice as a linguistic game. A language game may be defined as a whole consisting of language and the action into which it is woven (Wittgenstein, 1953: 7). Language is a social, not a private, fact: linguistic terms arise within a social practice of meaning construction. Participation in a practice entails taking part in a professional language game, mastering the rules and being able to use them. Having a concept means that having learnt to obey rules within a given practice. Speech acts are units of language and action; they are part of practice. They are not descriptions but types of action like any others in a given practice.

Language is not only the expression of social relations; it is also the medium for their creation (Czarniawska-Jorges, 1991). Those who participate in the practice of a linguistic game must share in the 'life form' that makes such practice possible, for sharing in a 'life form' is the prerequisite for understanding and transmitting so-called propositional knowledge. This is the type of knowledge acquired through the practical understanding of an operation. For example, carpenters participate in a professional language game, and they are able to 'tell' others the procedures that they follow to make a chair. But the (propositional) knowledge acquired in this way is different from practical understanding of the real operation of 'making a chair'. The propositional knowledge of how to make a chair, and how to describe the process, is qualitatively different from knowing how to use a hammer (practical knowledge) or from knowing when to change hammer and which type of hammer is best suited to a certain type of nail.

Those who participate in the practice of a linguistic game must share in the 'life form' internally to which that practice is possible: intersubjective consensus is more a matter of shared environment and language than of absent opinions (Wittgenstein, 1953).

1.7   The sociological roots of the concept of practice

I now briefly discuss, with the inevitable simplifications, the theories developed on the concept of 'practice' by three sociologists: Bourdieu, Garfinkel and Giddens. I shall do so without claiming to provide a summary of their thought.[5] My intention instead is to select the concepts that I found useful when setting up my research and developing the theoretical considerations that ensued from it.

I begin with the work of Bourdieu, from whom I have taken the ideas that practical knowledge is symbolic capital, that tacit knowledge can be viewed as a example of 'docta ignoratia', and that observation of practices enables simultaneous analysis of the reproduction and change of the social order. I shall not dwell on the points where I disagree with Bourdieu, although I may anticipate that I am contrary to his notion of 'habitus'.

Bourdieu's methodological point of view can be defined as simultaneously 'anti-functionalist, anti-empiricist and anti-subjectivist' (Sulkunen, 1982: 103). He is profoundly convinced that it is impossible to grasp the deepest-lying logic of the social world without immersing oneself in the particularity of an empirical reality, historically situated and dated, even if only to construct it as a 'particular case of the possible'. In this view, the science of society is a two-dimensional system of power relations and meaning relations among groups. It therefore requires a twofold reading. The first treats society as a 'social physics': that is, as an objective structure grasped from outside, whose articulations can be observed, measured and projected independently of the representations of those who live within it. This is the objectivist or structuralist point of view, which analyses society using statistical tools or formal models in order to bring out its regularities. Bourdieu believes that this is possible because people do not possess the totality of the meaning of their behaviour, as if it were a given of consciousness, and because their actions always comprise more meanings than they realize. However, a science of society must recognize that the awareness and interpretation of actors is also an essential component of analysis: individuals have practical knowledge about the world, which they invest in their ordinary activities. This second point of view is called subjectivist or constructivist. Characteristic of ethnomethodology and symbolic interactionism, this approach affirms that social reality is a contingent realization by competent social actors who constantly construct their social world through the practices of their everyday lives. On this interpretation – which Wacquant[6] calls 'social phenomenology' – society is the emergent product of the decisions, actions and cognitions of aware individuals to whom the world is given as immediately familiar and meaningful.

In other words, the objective/subjective and structural necessity/individual action antinomies are false to the extent that each term reinforces the other. It is by combining the two components of analysis that Bourdieu creates his 'social praxeology' (also called 'social constructivism'), in which, however, the two components, although both of them are necessary, are not of equal weight because epistemological priority is given to objectivist rather than subjectivist understanding. It is here that the gap with ethnomethodology emerges in so far as Bourdieu has the actor's point of view depend upon the place that s/he occupies in the objective social space. While this is an idea rooted in the structuralist tradition, Bourdieu introduces two new concepts to explain the importance of relations: (i) the concept of 'field' as constituted by a set of objective and historical relations among positions anchored in specific forms of power or capital; (ii) the 'habitus', defined as a set of historical relations deposited in the bodies of individuals in the form of mental and corporeal schemes of perception, evaluation and action.

Both these concepts – field and habitus – are relational in the sense that they function completely only in relation to each other, so that a field exists only if the actors in it 'play with or against the other'. This signifies for Bourdieu that there is action, history and the conservation or transformation of structures constituting a specific type of field only because there are agents 'in action'; and that these agents, in their turn, are efficacious only because they have not been reduced to the simple notion of 'individual' but are viewed as socialized organisms endowed with a set of dispositions which imply both the propensity and the ability to 'play the game' (Waquant, 1992: 19–21).

A field is also viewed as a social space in which agents confront each other with means and ends that differ according to their positions. The social space in which the social groups are distributed is charactertized by two factors of differentiation – economic capital and symbolic capital[7] – for monopoly over which the participants in the social space compete. Simultaneously with this conflict, however, the space itself and possession of these material and symbolic resources organize and determine practices and their properties. Differences in practices, but also in the goods possessed and the opinions expressed, become symbolic differences and constitute a sort of language – a set of distinctive signs for each position. The influence exerted by Bourdieu on organizational analysis is evident when it attributes the nature of symbolic capital to knowledge in general and to practical expertise in particular.

Bourdieu introduces the notion of 'habitus' in order to capture empirically the system of the structures of a particular field in the form of regularities associated with them. However, it is these same structures that produce the habitus, which is consequently constructed in practice and always geared to practical functions (Bourdieu, 1972: 206). In particular, habituses are produced by conditionings on a specific class of existence conditions. They can therefore be defined as sets of durable and transferable dispositions,[8] which as principles generating and organizing practices and representations can be objectively adapted to their

purposes without presupposing the conscious positing of ends or a profound and specific knowledge of the operations necessary to attain them.
Practices are collectively orchestrated without being the outcome of the
organizing action of an orchestra conductor (Bourdieu, 1972: 207).

This concept stands in a 'magical' relationship with the social game
that arises from a relationship of ontological complicity between mental
structures and the objective structures of the social space. It means that
we find interesting certain games because they have been imported into
and imposed upon our minds and bodies in the form of what
Bourdieu calls the 'sense of' or the 'feel for' the game. This type of
relationship arises in any social field which implicitly charges a sort of
entry fee: willingness to struggle for what is at stake in the field, even
against other individuals. Also to be noted is that there are as many kinds
of interest as there are fields. For Bourdieu, therefore, the practical world
is constructed in relation to habituses functioning as systems of cognitive and motivational structures. It is a world of already-achieved ends
– procedures to follow, moves to make – and of objects, instruments or
institutions endowed with 'permanent teleological character', to use
Husserl's expression.

In order to illustrate the logic of practice, Bourdieu repeatedly cites
the gift exchange described by Levi-Strauss as a striking example of how
individuals are able to construct a relatively simple generative model with
which to give value to the logic of practice. This generative model, which
reduces the exchange of gifts to a series of choices made on the basis
of a small set of principles with the assistance of a simple combinatory
formula, enables the attribution of economic value to an infinite number
of specific phenomena. It does so by reproducing the workings of a
habitus and the logic of practice that proceeds through a series of irre-
versible choices made under pressure, and often requiring close participation, in response to other choices complying with the same logic. The
logic of practice is thus constructed as a sort of practical participation
in a game about which its players possess tacit knowledge. To be stressed
is that Bourdieu uses the expression 'logic of practice' with the sense of
tacit knowledge in the form of 'docta ignorantia'.

Actors often employ ambiguous vocabulary to justify a social practice obeying rather different principles. They do so to disguise the true
nature of their practical knowledge as 'docta ignorantia', that is, a mode
of practical knowledge unaware of its own principles. It thus becomes
clear why rules are the chief obstacle against the construction of an adequate theory of practice. The practical sense – which is not weighed
down by rules or principles, even less by calculations and deductions –

is what makes it possible to grasp the meaning of a situation instanta-
neously, and to produce the appropriate responses at the same time. Only
this type of acquired knowledge, in that it functions with the automatic
reliability of an instinct, can furnish instantaneous responses to all the
uncertain and ambiguous situations of practice.

We may conclude by noting that Bourdieu has developed a theory of
practice on the basis of the relation between actors' practices and objective social structures by introducing the mediating concept of habitus
between the two dimensions. Hence practice in itself cannot be reduced
to either a habitus or, through this, to solely objective structures, or to
specific historical circumstances or forces; but rather to a constant process
of production and reproduction which comprises all these factors simultaneously. Bourdieu thus proposes a new model which includes both the
mechanism of reproduction and that of change because these are connected to the same factors, albeit to different extents.

It is not my intention to conduct a critique of Bourdieu's theory here.
I merely emphasize a point to which I shall shortly relate the ethnomethodological theory of practice. Bourdieu theorizes an ontological complicity ((his expression) between mental structures and the
objective structures of the social space. In fact, social actors possessing
the 'sense of' the game have incorporated a set of practical schemes for
the construction of reality mainly by dint of primary socialization agencies like the family and the school which reproduce social inequalities.
Bourdieu does not consider workplace practices; nor does he consider
the secondary socialization undertaken by the professions or by communities of practitioners – which are phenomena examined in subsequent chapters, but without assuming that mental structures and
objective structures are mirror images of each other.

I now turn to the ethnomethodological theory of practice, emphasizing in particular that this tradition of social analysis envisages knowledge as a practical accomplishment; that is, it views 'knowledge as a
situated doing'.

The term 'ethnomethodology' was introduced into sociology by
Harold Garfinkel in a study of jury deliberations. His intention was to
give definition to a body of studies which paid the same attention to
the most ordinary everyday activities as generally accorded to extraor-
dinary ones, on the assumption that practices of explanation, and explanations themselves, are incarnated in each other: 'the activities whereby
members produce and manage settings of organized everyday affairs are
identical with member's procedures for making those settings "accountable"' (Garfinkel, 1967: 1). Garfinkel has developed a new discipline

whose principal subjects of study are the properties of commonsense reasoning and knowledge, and how these are employed by social actors in their everyday lives. This means that the social world acquires meaningfulness at the level of the individuals who belong to it and who experience it as the routine reality of their lives. Ethnomethodology takes up Schutz's (1962) definition of working as *constituted by action in the external world based upon a project and characterized by the intention of bringing about a projected state of affairs by bodily movements.*

The study of practices by Bourdieu as well as by Garfinkel and Giddens is indebted to Schutz (1962), and to his definition of the social world as constituted by innumerable provinces of meaning viewed as particular sets of experiences, each of them manifesting a specific cognitive style and – with respect to this style – not only consistent in itself but also compatible with others. The world of everyday life is a province of meaning dominated and structured by what Schutz calls the 'natural attitude', so that the world is from the outset not the world of the private individual but an intersubjective world, shared by us all, and in which we have not a theoretical but eminently practical interest. However, individuals are usually aware that each of them has a different perception of reality. They are simultaneously aware that they have a sufficient degree of access to the perceptions of others to be able to perform their normal everyday activities. From this point of view, the meanings of our experiences of the outside world are considered for all practical purposes to be 'empirically identical' and thus give rise to the shared meanings indispensable for communication and for that particular 'accent' of reality conferred upon the world of everyday life. On this account, working represents the highest degree of interest in and attention to life, while simultaneously being the means with which individuals are able to alter the external world.

Put briefly, intersubjectivity gives rise not to a matching of meanings, but to the assumption that meanings are shared, or, as Garfinkel puts it, to an agreement on methods of understanding. Accordingly, the most significant innovation by ethnomethodology with respect to traditional sociology is its replacement of cognitive categories with the categories of action, and the consequent view of the creation and transmission of knowledge as a socially important practice. Which means that also sociology has taken up Austin's assertion that 'knowing is doing in everyday life, and it is doing society' (Giglioli, 1990: 85). In ethnomethodological studies, in fact, the transmission of knowledge as a social practice has been the focus of analysis by studies on work (Garfinkel, 1986). But because these studies have not overtly conceptualized working practice as 'learning', they have been largely ignored in the organizational field: only recently, in fact, has analysis of the social construction of technology and professional cultures by workplace studies resumed a number of ethnomethodological themes (Heath and Button, 2002).

Garfinkel (1967: 4) writes that one can discern the ethnomethodological method for analysis of social as well as working practices:

> wherever studies of practical action and practical reasoning are concerned, these consist of the following: (1) the unsatisfied programmatic distinction between and substitutability of objective (context free) for indexical expressions; (2) the 'uninteresting' essential reflexivity of accounts of practical actions; and (3) the analysability of actions-in-context as a practical accomplishment.

The discussion thus far has highlighted three essential features – indexicality, reflexivity and accountability – of the situated practices used by individuals to confer meaning on the social world.

The term 'indexical' was originally used in linguistics to denote expressions that are only completely comprehensible in the concrete context where they are produced and used. In ethnomethodological studies, however, the term has acquired specific connotations. The indexicality of social actions means that actors do not usually encounter problems in understanding each other, largely because comprehension is a constant and contingent achievement that depends on their interpretive work. Understanding situated practices therefore requires understanding of how individuals successfully use indexical behaviours and expressions whose meanings are constantly negotiated and renegotiated in the course of interaction. One meaning of 'situated' with reference to practices is that their performance depends on the manner in which indexicality is locally resolved. Also social norms are indexical, with the consequence that a rule of behaviour does not have a univocal meaning outside the concrete settings where it is applied. This thesis stresses in particular that the range of application of a rule is always constituted by an *a priori* indefinable number of different situations, so that a norm is always applied 'for another first time' (Garfinkel, 1967: 9)[9] and a routine work practice is always executed for 'another first time'.

Reflexivity, the second characteristic, is rooted in all order-producing social activities (Garfinkel, 1967: 67). It consists in the practices of accountability, observability and referability of social action, by which is meant making the world comprehensible to oneself and to the other members of a collectivity. 'Reflexivity refers to the dynamic self-organizational tendency of social interaction to provide for its own constitution through practices of accountability and scenic display' (Flynn, 1991: 28). It is therefore actions themselves that 'reflexively' display their nature as meaningful to social actors. It is this feature that enables the analysis of practices in that it renders their meanings accessible to 'outsiders' as well, or better, to 'external observers' (Fele, 2002). These observers consequently do not have to rely entirely on what people tell them – a method criticized by Zimmermann and Pollner (1970) because, they maintain, actions speak for themselves. However, this is not to imply that their meanings are abstract or decontextualized; rather, it depends on the fact that they inevitably participate in an organization of activity – they are, that is to say, embedded in a concrete situation.[10]

I finally deal with the notion of accountability. Generally used to denote a 'motive', a 'reason' or an 'explanation', the term is used by Garfinkel (1967: 1) as synonymous with 'observable-reportable, i.e. available to members as situated practices of looking-and-telling', that is, a constantly exhibited and public property of ordinary activities. In other words, accountability evinces the normal, ordinary, comprehensible and natural character of events. Consequently, social actions do not need to be 'baptized' by language for them to be intelligible and indexical to their participants. This signifies that accounts contribute to the setting of which they are part, and that they are interpreted and understood procedurally. 'Accounts, therefore, are not a terminus for social scientific investigation, they are, rather, a point of departure for it' (Heritage, 1987: 250). For that matter, Garfinkel himself maintains that a large part of our actions and interactions are not based on shared agreements but rather on a texture of tacit assumptions, neither explicated nor fully explicable, which are taken for granted. This, therefore, is yet another way to conceptualize tacit knowledge as 'taken for granted', which derives directly from Schulz (1962: 1964).

Finally, Garfinkel emphasizes the importance of social action as a moral phenomenon, where 'morality' is tied to patterns of action recognized by the entire community as those most correct, legitimate and adequate in a specific context[11] distinct from others. In this view, the members of society know the moral order when in the actions of others they recognize those models that represent the 'natural facts of life', not internalized social norms – as Parsons instead argued when he treated social norms as initially 'external' and then integrated into the personality by socialization to take the form of dispositions. This account of morality also views rules as assumed in constitutive function of the intelligibility of concrete actions. Indeed, it is precisely the self-structuring of behaviour in accordance with the prescriptions of a norm which enables the actor to recognize that behaviour as a given type of action.

Of principal interest for ethnomethodology, as it is for Foucault's theory,[12] is not the truth-value of knowledge systems but their architectonic-design aspect. The ethnomethodological version of the theory of practice brackets off the problem of truth, investigating instead the practical procedures of knowledge creation and their effects on the environment: 'knowledge is constituted by practices which construct truth and rationality in local settings' (Giglioli, 1990: 102).

I now move to consideration of the place occupied by the concept of practice in Giddens' theory, doing so by discussing one of his most significant but also controversial works: *The Constitution of Society* published in 1984. Like Bourdieu, Giddens argues against the dualisms of social theory: individual/society, action/structure, objectivism/subjectivism. He recasts the concepts of the human being and human actions, and of social reproduction and transformation. In doing so he emphasizes the importance of spatio-temporal relations, his conviction being that the structural properties of social systems exist only in so far as they are constantly reproduced as social behaviour over time and across space. Giddens maintains that the prime concern of the social sciences should be neither the experience of the individual actor nor the existence of some or other form of 'social totality', but rather a set of social practices ordered in space and time. Like certain self-reproducing phenomena in nature, human social activities are *recursive*. They are not brought into being by social actors but are constantly recreated by the same means whereby they express themselves as actors (Giddens, 1990: 4). The concept of recursiveness is central to Giddens' thought, and he seeks to remedy the weaknesses not only of classical sociological theory but also of, for example, symbolic interactionism, phenomenology and ethnomethodology in an endeavour to enable satisfactory analysis of crucial questions concerning in particular the recursive character of social practices. His theory of structuration views the production of social life as a 'skilled performance, sustained and 'made to happen' by human beings' (Cohen, 1987: 283), so that social practices are construed as procedures, methods or practical techniques appropriately performed by social agents – a definition, for that matter, which derives from ethomethodological theory.

In his attempt to reconcile and connect the concept of action with those of structure and institution, Giddens proposes the replacement of that dualism with the notion of 'duality of structure', where the latter is viewed both as a medium and as a result of recursively organized human action:'a medium because it is through its use that social conduct is produced, and an outcome because it is through the production of this conduct that rules and resources are reproduced in time and space' (Mouzelis, 1989: 615). The theory of structuration is therefore an attempt to analyse both structure and action within a single and coherent theoretical framework that yields an account of social life as a series of social activities and practices performed by individuals and by means of which, at the same time, those individuals reproduce social institutions and structures. Hence, structural properties exist in and through the use of resources employed by actors both to construct their action and simultaneously to reconstruct those same properties, so that institutions possess them by virtue of the continuity of the actions of their members. Giddens distinguishes between social systems and structure, defining the latter as an order of transformative relations, and consequently defining the former as reproduced social practices, concrete patterns of interaction, extended in time and space, which do not have structure but may have structural properties.[13]

These considerations suggest that one of the tasks of social theory should be to recover the theory of the subject, while at the same time discarding the functionalist conception of social systems as consisting of roles and their combinations and replacing it with that of social systems as constituted by 'reproduced practices'. It is consequently practices, not roles, which (via the duality of structure) should be viewed as the points of articulation between actors and structures.

By way of summary, therefore, analysing the structuration of social systems entails study of how those systems — founded as they are on the activities-with-knowledge of localized actors who exploit certain rules and resources in a variety of contexts of action — are produced and reproduced in the course of the interaction. The constitution of agents and that of structures, however, are not two distinct phenomena; instead they represent a duality: the structural properties of social systems are simultaneously the means and the outcomes of practices which organize recursively; and consequently, by reproducing their own structures, agents also reproduce the conditions that make those actions possible. The structure is therefore not something 'external': it does not exist, that is to say, independently of the awareness that agents, in their everyday activities, have of what they are doing.

Numerous criticisms have been brought against structuration theory (Bryant and Jary, 1991; Callinicos, 1985). Although this is not the place to review them, in order to forestall misunderstandings I must point out that in Giddens' theory the concept of reflexivity is fundamentally different from the ethnomethodological one that I embrace. Moreover, the conception of language in both Giddens and ethnomethodology differs from my understanding of discursive practices. Giddens often claims that reflexivity or 'being reflexive' is a methodological virtue, a source of priv- ileged knowledge and a cognitive activity of self-monitoring which, he maintains, pertain to particular conceptions of human nature and social reality. However, these various conceptions are called into question if one believes, as I do, that the true meaning of reflexivity is that con- ceived only by ethnomethodology, which defines it, in association with a particular research programme, as 'an unavoidable feature of the way actions are performed, made sense of and incorporated into social set- tings' (Lynch, 2000: 26). Finally, in Giddens, 'language exists only in so far as it is produced and reproduced in contingent contexts of social life in this fashion' (Giddens, 1986: 534). Hence, even if language is viewed in terms of its transformative properties, it is only one of the many activ- ities possible within the structure – as ethnomethodology also argues. It was not until the so-called 'language turn', or 'narrative turn', that lan- guage came to be attributed a more properly constructionist character and discursive practices were considered performative acts.[14]

I realize that giving a thorough account of three authors of such com- plexity, and often of difficult interpretation, would require a work of painstaking comparison. But I have briefly reviewed their theories in order to furnish the reader with three images with which to conceptu- alize the term 'practice' and thereby show how the methodology of empirical research may concern itself with very different phenomena. The best image with which to sum up Bourdieu's theory is that evoked by the expression '*sens pratique*', as the immediate and anticipatory per- ception of the sense of the social game. An expert's practical knowledge resides in the ability to understand immediately – for example, to rec- ognize a tune from its first two notes – to know, recognize and repro- duce a practice after seeing it done a number of times. In Garfinkel, the image of practices and of practising is 'mastery' of a method. Expert knowledge resides in being a competent member of a society, and of a specific community within it. Practical knowledge *par excellence* is knowing how to reproduce society in everyday interactions, whether these are meetings in the street or in the workplace. Finally, the image of practices in Giddens is that of the spatio-temporal 'recursiveness' which creates a reciprocal dependence between practice and practising. While structure relates to systems of rules and resources existing outside time and space, social systems indicate to individuals how to 'do' social life and how to reproduce activities in time and space.

The three images that I have selected to depict the sociological roots of the concept of practices highlight similarities more than differences, and I believe that they well illustrate themes that recur with a diversity of accents. In all three cases, the image of practice refers to tacit knowledge – whether 'docta ignorantia' or 'taken for granted' – embedded in the practice itself; it refers to the fact that knowing a practice is synonymous with knowing how to reproduce it with confidence (knowing-in-practice); and it refers to the institutionalized and institutionalizing character of reproduction and of simultaneous transformation, in that practices are indeterminate or, if one prefers, indexical.

1.8   What is a practice?

For the time being I shall propose a working definition of the concept of practice so that I can answer the question – what is a practice? – at the end of the book. Drawing on the phenomenological and eth-nomethodological traditions, I define a practice as a mode, relatively stable in time and socially recognized, of ordering heterogeneous items into a coherent set. This definition enables me to specify a number of elements:

- The qualitative and holistic aspect of a practice. This responds to the question of 'how' a set of activities acquires meaning and comes to be recognized as a unit. The attention is therefore directed not at the set of activities which make up the practice but at how these activities assume complete form within a context of situated action. By way of example, for many office workers 'claiming expenses' is a meaningful doing and a knowing-how that they have acquired as part of their professionalism independently of the organization for which they work. But what constitutes claiming expenses as a practice is knowing how it is done in the specific organization in which one works, and knowing that one's colleague will do it in an identical (or very similar) way, not the individual operations which produce the activity when summed together. The situated character of what we call 'practice' should be borne in mind, in fact, so that we may say that practices are constituted and reconstituted by embodied agents.
- Its relationship with temporality. In order to become such, practices must be repeated several times in order to be socially recognized as habitual modes of doing. They concern the reproduction of the social

world, but unlike mechanical reproduction by a photocopier, the reproduction of the social world does not preserve the identity of the original; rather, it is an open-ended process which in repeating the original maintains the constants and simultaneously introduces the change. It is more similar to human reproduction than to mechanical reproduction. The mode of claiming expenses may vary from one organization to another, from one department to another of the same organization, it may vary from year to year and according to the technologies used, but as long as it is recognized as 'claiming expenses', it is 'a' practice. Practices endure across time and space. They have a history and persist over time regardless of their continuous adaptation to changing circumstances.

- Its being socially recognized. Practices presuppose an institutional system which has inscribed the norms that enable those practices not only to be recognized as such but also to be sustained and therefore reproduced in accordance with rules of correctness. Those who bring a community of office workers into being also reproduce the meaning of what constitutes a 'well-executed expenses claim', as opposed to a badly executed one, and they do so from both a technical and aesthetic point of view. We can therefore say that practices are patterns of activities institutionalised by virtue of an ensemble of normative judgements which people negotiate among themselves, in the course of the actual practice, and express in terms of ethics, aesthetics and technical criteria of appropriateness. They constitute and reconstitute institutions through social activities which recur over time, and in so doing give form to collective and individual experiences.

- Its being a mode of ordering the world. As practices are performed, they introduce an ordering of human and non-human elements – an ordering which, though fragile, temporary and constantly threatened by disorder, becomes embedded in a network of practices anchored to each other. Making an expenses claim requires the production of correspondence between an entitled human and a set of papers attesting to a right and its quantification, and a set of technologies for inscription by computer (rather than by hand), a set of face-to-face rather than ICT-mediated communications, and so on. The trajectory of an expenses claim within an organization, and externally to it within the network of organizations activated by the claim (from those which have certified the expenses to those which are authorized to reimburse them) makes visible how a practice activates a socio-technical network of relations. Practices both constrain and facilitate actions by the people engaged in them. Practices constrain their practising by forbidding some alternatives and choices, while empowering others as possible, preferable or easier. In order to attain the goal, the physical environment of a set of practices is subjugated by means of intelligent artefacts.

In consequence of its long sociological tradition, 'a practice' has been given a wide variety of definitions. I have discussed the works of Bourdieu (1990), Garfinkel (1967) and Giddens (1984) in order to call attention to the subjectivity of the actors involved in a field of practices. But by proposing a simple definition of a practice, I risk failing to give due emphasis to the fact that practices have inscribed social positions and relations characterized by particular expectations, rules and procedures. People engaged in a working practice acknowledge a set of social positions which are interrelated, which make sense, and which are enacted. Practices impart identities and selves that are displayed on appropriate occasions. People's experiences in, with and within practices become incorporated into their identities, the social positions that they occupy, the status that they display while they enact the set of practices, and also when they do not perform it. Professional identities are linked to a set of institutional practices but they are also performed outside the profession. Classical sociology attributes logical primacy to actors, but this is a primacy which authors like Foucault, and subsequently actor-network theory,[15] have substantially tempered, in that they prefer to conceive actors as effects of the networks in which they are embedded, and to replace the term 'actor' with 'actant',[16] thereby including non-humans in the field of interactions that give rise to 'agency'. As we shall see in the chapters that follow, the notion that identity arises from a field of relations requires close attention to be paid to discursive practices as capacities to order heterogeneous elements and discursively to produce the positioning of things and persons within a practice. For the time being, however, we may adopt a methodological perspective which, once the nature of an 'institution of practices' has been established, views analysis of situated 'seeing, saying and doing' as an operational means to give concrete definition to a field of empirical analysis. This methodological approach has already been used with good results by studies of gender as a socially situated practice (Bruni, Gherardi and Poggio, 2004; Martin, 2003).

The concept of practice has recently acquired new vigour. Yet, despite the title of the book by Schatzki, Knorr-Cetina and Von Savigny (2001),

The Practice Turn in Contemporary Theory, which baptizes yet another 'turn' after the cultural, linguistic and narrative ones, a radical break with traditional programmes is not yet forthcoming, and a unified field of practice or a 'social theory of practice' does not exist. The philosopher of science Stephen Turner (1994: 116), who has worked for years on the theme, makes a pessimistic forecast: 'the idea of "practice" and its cognates has this odd kind of promissory utility. They promise that they can be turned into something more precise. But the value of the concept is destroyed when they are pushed in the direction of meeting their promise'.

I believe that the illusoriness that drains the term 'practice' of meaning is due to two tendencies which, although they differ considerably, produce a similar effect.

1. There is a romanticizing effect which exalts the indefiniteness and inarticulatability of practices. A practice is surrounded by an aura of the ineffable, of something that only adepts are able to describe and reproduce. This position has been efficaciously criticized by Michael Lynch (1995, 1997) in his interpretation of Turner's prophecy. He writes that behind concepts of shared understanding, forms of life or situated practices there is some sort of collective cognitivism[17] in so far as these forms of knowledge, lying above and beyond ordinary sensibilities, take the form of 'hidden abstract objects', characteristic of entire cultures.

2. There is then a reductionist tendency stemming mainly from Giddens (1984) which locates practices at an intermediate level between the actor and the structure. Explanations therefore oscillate between one level and the other, remaining trapped in the actor/system dichotomy first introduced by the researcher and from which s/he then seeks to escape.

With reference to scientific practices and to social studies of science – an area in which analysis of knowledge production practices has yielded significant results – Joseph Rouse (2001: 191) argues that there are at present two fundamentally different conceptions of practices:

1. practices identified with regularities or commonalities in the performances or presuppositions of some community of human agents;

2. practices characterized in terms of normative accountability of various performances.

Rouse criticizes the former conception and maintains that the accountability which binds a practice together need not involve any underlying regularity, nor even presuppose an uncontested formulation of norms. Of interest is the footnote where he argues in favour of the second conception by citing Davidson (1986: 445) to draw an analogy with understanding and using a natural language, which 'involves no learnable common core of consistent behavior, no shared grammar or rules, and no portable interpreting machine set to grind out the meaning of an arbitrary utterance'. This analogy with the use of a language and the concept of accountability highlights the crucial role played by language, which by means of discursive practices produces not only intelligibility but also moral order. The concept of accountability enables us to view reason not as an innate mental faculty but as a practical accomplishment.

We may therefore conclude that the concept of practice has two important implications: (i) social action and social knowledge must be regarded as activities inseparably woven together; (ii) knowledge cannot be viewed as a conscious activity involving meaningful acts, for it presupposes only presumed or indirect references to norms, meanings and values that it claims to apply or to follow. Study of the practical organization of knowledge, in the form of methods of reasoning and action and the association of human and non-human elements, is one of the most important directions taken by empirical studies which use the practice-based approach. Nevertheless, inspection of the literature shows that a unified field of practice studies does not exist; rather that there are three types of relations established between practices and knowledge:

- A relation of *containment*, in the sense that knowledge is a process that takes place within situated practices. In this view, practices are constituted as objective entities (in that they have been objectified) about which practitioners already have knowledge (i.e. they recognize them as practices) and which comprise bits and pieces of knowledge anchored in the material world and in the normative and aesthetic system that has elaborated them culturally.
- A relation of *mutual constitution*, in the sense that the activities of knowing and practising are not two distinct and separate phenomena; instead, they interact and produce each other.
- A relation of *equivalence*, in the sense that practising is knowing in practice, whether the subject is aware of it or not. Acting as a competent practitioner is synonymous with knowing how to connect

successfully with the field of practices thus activated. The equivalence between knowing and practising arises when priority is denied to the knowledge that exists before the moment of its application, so that when applying it something already existent is not performed but the action instead creates the knowledge formed in the action itself and by means of it.

However, although I prefer to base my work on the third type of relation — as shown by the rest of this book — I shall continue to use the expression 'practice-based approach' because the three relations do not exclude each other, and because emphasizing one of them does not prejudice the others.

In conclusion, we may say that the main reasons for adopting a practice-based approach are:

- To go beyond problematic dualisms like mind/body, actor/structure, human/non-human. In the practising of a practice all these elements are simply present (*Vorhanden*).
- To question the primacy of the actor and the individual action as the building blocks of social phenomena. It is within a situated practice that the knowing subject and the known object define each other.
- To see reason as a practice phenomenon and depict language as a discursive activity. Discursive practices, within a working practice, constitute a medium for the mode of ordering human and non-human elements in a coherent even if unstable and provisional alignment.
- To pay due attention to the materiality of the social world. Knowing and acting are located in ecologies of social-material relations and their intermediaries not only mediate activities, but also propagate practices.

1.9   To sum up: two narratives of learning and knowing

As a starting point for the exploration of the literature on learning and knowing in organizations. I took Weick's (1989) exhortation to consider theoretical construction in the study of organization as disciplined imagination, where the discipline arises from the coherent application of criteria, and the imagination is given by the diversity deliberately factored into the definition of problems. In the literature at least two narratives can be delineated according to their rhetorics.

Under the OL, LO and KM views, learning is principally 'problem-driven': the need to solve a problem (an external stimulus) occasions learning. These can be flanked by another view: learning as mystery-driven.

In Turner's (1991) words:[18]

> The distinction between problem and mystery was originally made by Gabriel Marcel, and transferred into organisational settings by Goodall (1991). To experience a problem, Marcel suggested, is to divide the narratives of 'us' from the narratives of 'them', and to see in this division a natural superiority of the observer, us, over the objects of observation, them. By contrast, mystery encourages us to see ourselves as integrally connected to others, as co-constructors of developing narratives of life which become entangled with our sense of being. To look at learning as a way of solving problems assumes the kind of dichotomy that Marcel refers to, assumes that good learning is that which produces a solution to a specified problem. Learning as a way of moving towards an understanding of mystery requires us to question both our own lives as members or managers of organizations, and the contribution that our organizations make to the development of shared activities, in a world in which we realize that we are increasingly interdependent with each other, and dependent, too, upon the way in which we negotiate our relationships with the material world and its ecosystems.

Whereas the organizational literature develops the rhetoric of learning as problem-driven, because this narrative has affirmed itself as disciplinary discourse, and is sustained by it, the second narrative is only at its beginnings. Taking the broader view which sees learning and knowing as practical accomplishments in organizations helps us explore a less intentional, less instrumental, more reflexive aspect of learning. Learning in the face of mystery also conveys the idea that not only is learning an activity, it is a passivity as well: its locus of control may be external to individuals. Activity, domination, rationality, instrumentality, masculinity are some of the symbolic meanings associated with problem-driven learning, while passivity, subjugation, emotionality, creativity, femininity can be associated with mystery-driven learning and its heuristics.

Polanyi (1962: 127–8) defines a heuristic process as a combination of active and passive stages: 'the admonition to look at the unknown really means that we should look at the known data, but not in themselves, rather as clues to the unknown, as pointers to it and parts of it'. Learning in a passive mode (and teaching how to learn) – according to Polanyi – is like teaching a person to surrender himself/herself to works of art:

'this is neither to observe nor to handle them, but to live in them. Thus the satisfaction of gaining intellectual control over the external world is linked to a satisfaction of gaining control over ourselves' (Polanyi, 1962: 196).

Experience is primarily an active-passive affair; it is not primarily cognitive. But the measure of value of an experience lies in the perception of relationships or continuities to which it leads. Learning as passivity reintroduces the body, the emotions, the affective mode of understanding, the intuition, receptiveness, empathy, introspection and aesthetic understanding.

When we give priority to practices over mind we contribute to a transformed conception of knowledge which is no longer possession of mind, which is mediated both by interactions between people and by the material arrangements in the world, which is discursively constructed, and which is diffused, fragmented and distributed as a property of groups working within a situated material environment. Gergen (1991: 270) writes 'knowledge is not something that people possess in their heads, but rather, something that people do together'. And Latour (1987) suggests that people interact not only with each other but also with the non-human that makes up the remainder of the natural world.

Practices, therefore, are modes of ordering which acquire temporal stability from provisional and unstable agreements in practice. We can say that people share a practice if their actions are regarded as answerable to norms of correct or incorrect practice, to criteria of aesthetics taste, and to standards of fairness. Consequently, we can ask the following question: how is practical knowledge produced, transmitted and circulated in a practice and among interdependent practices within a field of practices? The next chapter will propose a research methodology with which seek an answer to this question.

NOTES

1. Paulo Freire depicted the same situation when he suggested that modern education is often based on a 'banking model': the teacher possesses superior knowledge much like the owner of a bank possesses the gold stored in its vaults. Teaching and learning consist in the transfer of the 'gold' to the pupils' heads. Knowledge equals information that can be sold, bought and exchanged like any other good (Freire, quoted in Czarniawska-Jorges, 1996).

2. The risk of the anthropomorphization of the organization in the concept of OL has been dealt with in various ways. For example, Simon (1991:

125) argues: 'All learning takes place inside individual human heads; an organization learns in two ways: a) by the learning of its members, or b) by ingesting new members who have knowledge the organization didn't previously have'. One way, therefore, is to argue that the organization is a container within which individuals and groups learn. Another is to argue that the organization is both the subject and object of learning. And yet another is to maintain that learning is embedded in routine, everyday practices.

3. The best-known definitions of OL are based on actual or potential change in beliefs, behaviours, actions:

    'Organizational learning thus becomes that process in the organization by which members of the dominant coalition develop, over time, the ability to discover when organizational changes are required and what changes can be undertaken which they believe will succeed' (March and Olson, 1976: 78).

    'OL refers to experience-based improvement in organizational task performance' (Argyris and Schön, 1978: 323).

    'A continous process of information exchange (. . .) between a system and its environment, allowing the system to monitor changes and initiate appropriate responses' (Morgan, 1986: 87).

    'Organizations are seen as learning by encoding inferences from history into routines that guide behavior' (Levitt and March, 1988: 320).

    'A learning organization is an organization which facilitates the learning of all its members and continously transforms itself' (Garratt, 1990: 77).

    'an organization that is continually expanding its capacity to create its future' (Senge, 1990: 14).

    'An entity learns if, through its processing of information, the range of its potential behaviours is changed' (Huber, 1991: 89).

    For a critique of the traditional psychological definition of learning and a first proposal for an alternative search of non-traditional ones, see Weick (1991).

4. Pedler, Burgoyne and Boydell (1991) identify 11 'learning company' characteristics: the learning approach to strategy, participative policy-making, informating, formative accounting and control, internal exchange, reward flexibility, enabling structures, boundary workers as environmental scanners, inter-company learning, learning climate, self-development opportunities for all.

5. In what follows I have been greatly helped by discussions with Elena Cetto, who wrote her degree thesis on the three authors.

6. 'A total science of society must jettison both the mechanical structuralism which puts agents "on vacation" and the teleological individualism which recognizes people only in the truncated form of an "oversocialized cultural dope" or in the guise of more or less sophisticated reincarnations of homo aeconomicus' (Wacquant, 1992: 9).

7. Social capital is any property (physical strength, wealth, value) which –
    perceived by social agents endowed with the requisite perceptive and
    evaluative categories – becomes symbolically efficient because it exerts
    some sort of distance effect merely by fulfilling socially constituted
    collective expectations. Those who fulfil those expectations, or those,
    without having to calculate the matter, are immediately in line with the
    exigencies of a situation, enjoy all the profits of the symbolic goods
    market: 'symbolic capital is valid ever in the market' (Bourdieu, 1980/90:
    119).

8. The term 'disposition' is particularly appropriate to expressing the concept
    of habitus because, on the one hand it refers to the result of an organiz-
    ing action, while on the other it denotes a mode of being, a habitual state
    of the body, and specifically a predisposition, a tendency, a propensity or
    an inclination (Bourdieu, 1972: 206).

9. This has two fundamental consequences: the first is that the applicability
    of a norm necessarily depends on the content of that norm; the second
    is that norms in themselves are not sufficient to direct human action
    because they do not exhaustively define the components constituting the
    behaviour to which they apply, in the sense that it is always possible to
    find behaviours which are not regulated by any specific rule.

10. However, Garfinkel argues that in no case is the investigation of practical
    actions undertaken in order that the persons involved might be able to
    recognize and describe what they are doing in the first place and those
    conducting the analysis understand the manner in which they are talking
    about what they are doing. This entails that the actors assume 'the reflex-
    ivity of producing, accomplishing, recognizing and demonstrating the
    rational and wholly practical adequacy of their procedures; they rely upon
    it, require it, and make use of it' (Fele, 2002: 62).

11. Note that Garfinkel does not view the context as an entity which exists
    before the action and determines it by means of norms; rather, it self-
    organizes itself with respect to the intelligible character of its manifesta-
    tions. In other words, it is constantly reconstituted by actions so that it
    becomes at once the point of departure and arrival of the selfsame actions
    that constitute it (Nicotera, 1996: 53).

12. Although both theories are based on a distrust of universal concepts like
    social order, rule, norm or power, there is a fundamental difference
    between them. While Foucault's method investigates knowledge interac-
    tions together with power and the disciplining of society, ethnomethod-
    ology stops at its recognition of the institutionalization of social
    knowledge-creation procedures, although the analysis of social facts must
    nevertheless begin with the intellective, social, moral and commonsensi-
    cal procedures which make those facts recognizable.

13. The expression 'structural properties' denotes the most deeply embedded
    structural properties involved in the reproduction of social totalities. The

concept of institution thus refers to practices which have the greatest extension within such totalities (Giddens, 1990: 19).

14. I prefer to employ the concept of performativity, as formulated by Judith Butler (1990, 1993) and taken up by John Law (1994), because it is particularly able to grasp the dynamic between the pair of concepts, but maintaining their difference. In Butler's view, 'performativity is not a singular "act," for it is always a reiteration of a norm or set of norms, and to the extent that it acquires an act-like status in the present, it conceals or dissimulates the conventions of which it is a repetition' (or 'citation') (Butler, 1993: 12). 'Performativity is construed as that power of discourse to produce effects through reiteration' (1993: 20).

15. As defined by Latour (1999: 20), this is 'a theory that says that by following circulations we can get more than by defining entities, essence or provinces'.

16. An actant is defined (Latour, 1987) as any thing or person that acts. It is a semiotic concept more general than person or *dramatis persona*, whether individual (Peter) or collective (the crowd), animate or inanimate. Actants are all the elements which accomplish or are transformed by the actions through which the narration evolves. I prefer, however, to use the term 'actor' (human and non-human) in order not to excessively encumber the terminology.

17. Lynch states that this collective cognitivism is exemplified by Durkheim's notion of the collective conscience, which is still prominent in contemporary theories of practice, many of which, however, do little to acknowledge Durkheim's legacy.

18. 'Learning in the face of mystery' is an expression borrowed from Barry Turner with the intention of paying him homage. In a paper presented at Palermo (Italy) in 1991, Barry Turner drew a distinction between what he called 'old organizational learning' and 'new organizational learning', which can be considered two narratives on learning based on two different rhetorics. Turner viewed 'old organizational learning' as a functionalist narrative based mainly on a cybernetic model of organization and a feedback model of learning.

CHAPTER TWO

The Texture of Knowing in Practice

*Practice is where nature and society and the space
between them are continually made,
un-made, and remade.*
(Pickering, 1992: 21)

In the previous chapter I talked at length about practices and practising, but I did so in abstract because the 'practising' lacked a subject. Yet I do not believe that there is much point in discussing practices in abstract without asking the question of whether all practices are equal.

When practices are discussed in general, the danger arises of using the term 'practice' as synonymous with 'competence', 'skill' or 'tacit knowledge'. If we consult *The New Shorter Oxford Dictionary* (1993: 2317) we find, in fact, that the term 'in practice' has two meanings:

in reality, as a fact, when actually applied;
skilled at something through recent exercise in it or performance.

The former use of the term implies a contrast between something done 'in theory' and something done 'in practice'. Practice in this context is related to actual conduct as opposed to abstract theory, and it refers to the tension between interpretative theories and life-world understanding, between the world of work as it 'should be' and how it is in practice. One thus notes that there may be continuity between theory and practice, and not just an antithesis. Consider, for example, the relation between black-letter law and court procedures: both are constituents of legal practice. We may say that every professional or working practice has a body of abstract knowledge and another body of contextually situated knowledge, and that their practitioners develop their own personal knowledges while practising. I am interested here in the relations between abstract knowledge and situated and personal knowledge 'when actually applied' and when institutionalized in the form of a practice.

Implicit in the *Oxford Dictionary*'s second definition of 'in practice' is that practical knowledge comprises the form of wisdom that Polanyi (1962) terms 'personal knowledge'. This he considers to be an individual possession embodied in action but not expressed in rules of action and unconsciously transmitted from the master to the apprenticeship. The idea is that practice develops competence.

These two shades of meaning should be borne in mind, because when we delimit a field of practices which we intend to explore analytically, our concern is to study both knowledge 'when actually applied' and the performative aspect of knowledge which, when applied to itself, produces further knowledge.

How can a 'practice' or a 'field of practices' be defined? I shall consider the manner in which social and work practices are closely interwoven, and how their fields can be delimited, bearing in mind that practices merge into each other even though they have an internal structuration, for it is this that raises the question 'are all practices equal'?

To illustrate the difference I borrow an example provided by Ann Swidler (2001):

- Take a hypothetical architect's plan for a house. Long before the architect can draw up plans for the house, constraints on the possible design are built into taken-for-granted practices which involve standard kinds of materials (bricks, door frames, steel girders etc.). Like composers who cannot write music for which there are no instruments (Becker, 1982) architects assume the standard kind of materials that are available, and ignore the potentially infinite set of materials that are unavailable.
- The plans that architects draw up are inevitably incomplete. Even when the competence of a contractor or a builder is brought in, the plan for a house leaves most of what will be required to build it unspecified: the skill of the craftworkers, the ways in which different workers with different specialities coordinate their activities, what they consider to be the appropriate uses of standard objects and materials.
- Behind the plan lie other, almost invisible, practices. The architect's knowledge of what a house is, how people use one, whether sleep should take place in a room different from those reserved for eating or washing. Numerous cultural differences are inscribed in such a common, universal activity as living in a house.
- Also lying behind the plan is the set of professional practices against which the architect's aesthetic judgement is compared and which

furnishes the vocabulary of meanings with which s/he works in order to produce the aesthetic effect valued by his/her professional community.

• Another set of practices links the architect to the client: who decides what, how payments should be made, who, and how to own a house. A broad set of practices then link both the architect and the client to the capitalist market economy, mobilizing the work of other persons and institutions.

The example is a telling one for at least two reasons. First, it prompts reflection on the role of ideas versus material factors in causal explanations, and on the interpenetration of the material and ideational worlds (against idealism). Secondly, it raises the question as to whether in a field of practices the researcher should abandon his/herself to an endless deferral of nested practices, or if in concrete instances of practices there are some which anchor, control or organize others. In the case of the house, practices associated with capitalism, such as paying for a house or owning it, are more enduring and powerful than others.

We may therefore conclude from the above example that a field of practices arises in the interwoven texture that connects practices to each other, and that this texture is held together by a certain number of practices which provide anchorage for others. Moreover, from a methodological point of view, when we empirically mark out a field of practices we may first develop methodological knowledge on how we might *investigate* practices and only later consider how we can *theorize* them.

It was for this reason that I decided first to define a practice – safety as a social practice – and then to study it within a field of organizational practices – the construction industry – connoted by the objective importance of its high accident rate, and therefore by the subjective importance of that problem for those who work in the industry, for building firms and for the institutions that devise public policies on safety. I also had a personal and aesthetic reason for selecting the construction industry: I preferred a 'commonplace' field of inquiry into safety practices to 'heroic' ones like, for example, nuclear power stations, with greater impact on the imagination, because in my personal life I find everyday heroism more to my liking than sensational heroism.

I consider safety to be an emerging property of cultural systems – professional, organizational, industrial, social – which produce social conceptions of what is dangerous or safe, and of which attitudes and behaviours towards risk, danger and safety are appropriate. We may consider safety to be a collective ability to produce organizational and interorganizational work practices which protect both individual welfare and the environment. Safety is therefore a competence which is realized in practice, which is socially constructed, innovated and transmitted to new members of the community of practices, and which is embedded in values, norms and social institutions (Gherardi, Nicolini and Odella, 1998a, 1998b). It is the final outcome of a collective construction process, a 'doing' which involves people, technologies and textual and symbolic forms assembled within a system of social relations. In other words, a 'safe' workplace – a 'safe' organization – results from the constant engineering of diverse elements (for example, skills, materials, relations, communications) which are integral to the work practices of the members of an organization. Safety, then, is knowledge objectified and codified in an expertise and circulated within a web of practices. In order to exist it must be performed in, by and through safety practices, i.e. through discursive and material social accomplishments. Obviously, in talking of safety practices I am referring to a field of practices which range from the normative practices of the European Union and the member states to the individual one of the builder who does or does not put on a hard hat when entering a building site.

The next questions therefore are these: what connects one practice to another? How is that connection made or not made? How does a practice come to be regarded as an appropriate practice and is therefore sustained and transmitted?

Practices are nested (or un-nested) the one with the other. They form a 'texture' of practices, and this texture is locally dense to a greater or lesser extent. In the architect's plan for a house, his/her practice is simultaneously a doing, a saying and a knowing in practice which establish connections in action. I shall argue that knowing in practice is about accomplishing connectedness in action, and I shall provide a methodological framework for investigation of the texture of a field of practices. In order to do so, however, I must first outline the history of the concept of texture in organization studies.

2.1   Texture as connectedness in action

At the end of 1990 the *Journal of Management Studies* brought out a special issue, edited by Robert Cooper and Stephen Fox, on 'The texture of organizing'. The theme had been discussed a year previously at a seminar held in Bath, and the journal collected some of the papers discussed on that occasion. Together with Antonio Strati, I contributed an article which dealt with the texture of organizing a university mathematics department. Some years later I find that the concept of texture still serves to describe processes of organizing without having to assume the existence of 'an organization' as a distinctive system.

In opposition to the view of organization as structure and as the product and expression of rationality, there has always been a view, albeit a minority one, predicated on the formal/informal opposition and on the idea of endless movement or free-playing flow among elements (Morgan, 1986). It is in this terrain that the concept of texture is rooted, and we may trace its growth by following the account provided by Cooper and Fox (1990).

Emery and Trist (1965) introduced the idea of 'texture' into organizational studies in order to stress the connectedness between an organization and the environment. And they used the term 'causal texture' to highlight the dynamic interaction among environmental parts, as opposed to the conception of parts as relatively independent subsystems. They borrowed the idea from a much earlier psychological study by Tolman and Brunswick (1935) who, in their turn, adapted it from the philosopher Stephen Pepper (1942). The philosophical referent for the concept of texture is contextualism[1] as a root metaphor for seeing the world. For Pepper, texture is not only connectedness, it is also fused with action: 'It is doing and enduring, and enjoying: making a boat, running a race, laughing at a joke, solving a problem, communicating with a friend'(Pepper 1942: 232, quoted in Cooper and Fox, 1990: 575). These acts consist of interconnected activities with continuously changing patterns. In other words, we may call them practices.

Cooper and Fox (1990: 576) offer the following definition of the texture of organizing: 'The key to understanding texture is the idea of "connectedness in action"; this phrase brings out the definitive features of texture, its endless series of relationships which continually move into each other'. The woven text has a texture that stretches and shrinks, and 'to follow the pattern and interlacing of the composition requires the weaver's art of looping and knotting' (Brogan, 1989: 12, quoted in Cooper and Fox).

Texture is a strongly evocative concept which recalls the intricacies of networking but at the same time allows for an analytical, qualitative framework (Strati, 2000). The texture of organizing can be conceived as 'an imaginary territory, a circumscribed domain marked out by a plurality of organizational actors which comprises ideas, projects, emotions, that subjects assign to their organizational behaviour. (. . .) It is the symbolic territory of policies, conflicts, negotiations and exchanges, but also of reciprocal socialization by organizational actors to the diverse rationalities of their own activities' (Gherardi and Strati, 1990: 617). It represents 'the "decentring" of organizations as objects of study and gives priority to indeterminacies and contradictions intrinsic in organizational actions' (Cooper and Fox, 1990: 581).

The interest of organization scholars in the concept springs from their desire to move from the concept of 'organization' as an empirical reality to that of 'organizing', or as Weick (who in turn draws on Emery and Trist's concept of 'causal texture') has put it: 'Organizational theorists are concerned with developing more fine-grained analysis of the perceptual problems that organizational members face' (Weick, 1979: 59). Nevertheless, Weick's analysis is more concerned with the instrumentality of means–ends relationships (the causal) than with the rarefaction of the organizational field (the texture). The texture of organizing is not something that is explicitly linear, and the mental images best able to grasp it are a crossword puzzle (Cooper and Fox, 1990); the metaphor of flux and transformation (Morgan, 1996); the idea of tacit knowledge (Polanyi, 1966); or the 'et cetera' problem in Garfinkel and Sacks (1970), where any attempt at literal description simply multiplies the task in an infinite regress.

Cooper and Fox reprise Morgan's (1986) dual conception of order – implicate order (the raw material or flux) and explicate order (which derives from the implicate and expresses itself in rational, cause-effect terms) – and Polanyi's distinction between tacit and explicit knowledge, in order to talk of the tacit dimension of texture. They cite in particular Polanyi's assertion that 'while tacit knowledge can be possessed by itself, explicit knowledge must rely on being tacitly understood and applied. Hence all knowledge is either tacit or rooted in tacit knowledge. A wholly explicit knowledge is unthinkable' (Polanyi, 1966: 144). The distinctive feature of tacit knowledge is therefore that *we can know more than we can tell*.

Interestingly, Cooper and Fox juxtapose these ideas with the formulation offered by Garfinkel and Sacks (1970) in what they call the 'et cetera problem', i.e. the paradoxical process in which, as said, any attempt at literal description simply multiplies the task in an infinite regress. In this case, *there is always more than we can say*. For example, legal knowledge (and indeed any form of practical knowledge) is rooted in tacit knowledge, so that what laws actually mean is subject to subsequent persuasive interpretation in the courts. A lawyer's competence is simply one version of a glossing process general in social life, and it is a process that copes with the excess of 'open texture' in everyday life.

Garfinkel and Sacks introduced a reading of social life as 'text'. Cooper and Fox note that there are two basic ways to approach a text: glossing and weaving. Glossing is a socially controlled way to fix the mobile, and the gloss itself is meant for 'instant consumption': its fixed meaning implies that the reader is external to it, s/he is positioned in such a way that s/he believes the glossed text to be already constituted and beyond his/her influence. Weaving implies the tendency of an open text to transgress its socially contrived meaning: 'the woven text opens in a centrifugal way and can only be experienced as an activity of creative production, in which the agent/reader is caught up as an active element in the ongoing, unfinished movement of the text' (Cooper and Fox, 1990: 578). The reader is in the text, and in a very similar way knowing in the face of mystery presumes a subject who is inside the knowledge production process and abandons him/herself to the centrifugal connections of meanings/actions.

The framework that I propose for analysis of the texture of a field of practices is therefore indirect and metaphorical, since although texture can be shown or demonstrated it can never be defined. Explanation risks losing the very nature of what it seeks to elucidate. Weaving, i.e. following the multivalent process that constitutes texture, is the analytical metaphor most appropriate for its understanding (Brogan, 1989). Nevertheless, this is not to imply that texture is a hidden object that cannot be grasped; rather, we should develop a style of thinking and doing research that enables us to show the relevance of connectedness in action and its continuing deferral.

I maintain that the concept of texture paved the way for the study of organizing as a practical accomplishment and I consider it the antecedent of practice-based studies. In fact, regarding organizing activities as connectedness in action implies a sociology of verbs and not of nouns (Law, 1992), so that organizing is considered more than the organization, the mode of ordering more than the order; it entails, that is to say, a proximal view of work processes (Cooper and Law, 1995). Distal and proximal are two complementary but distinct ways of viewing human structures, just as a sociology à la Parsons is a sociology of being while a sociology à la Elias is a sociology of becoming. In the former case, social elements are conceived as self-sufficient; in the latter, as beginnings and transformations which constantly renew themselves.

Distal thought prioritizes results and consequences, the products and finished objects of thought and action, everything that is pre-packaged. Proximal thought instead addresses what is continuing and incomplete, towards which it constantly strives but never reaches. The proximal is always partial and precarious. The two authors – Cooper and Law – use the principle of symmetry (Law, 1992) to identify a methodological theory internal to contemporary sociology of science which eschews any principle of order and systematicity in phenomena. Distinctions in the sphere of human phenomena are not naturally given; rather, they are the products or effects of ordering and organizing activities. Thus, on a distal view, differentiation is presupposed; one sees functional problems and therefore the functional components of the organization; one sees part/whole polarities while the complex processes that operate between the parts and the whole are neglected. In proximal terms, instead, what stands 'between' is the privileged site of communication. Boundaries simultaneously divide and unite. This is the view of a process which – at least in the first instance – ignores distinctions among people, technologies and texts, and combines these elements in an engineering of the heterogeneous (Law, 1987), giving rise to an effect or a product. The idea is that the relations that constitute the social are continuous. They do not halt at the ontological barriers that separate nature and culture, actor and structure, organization and environment: the dynamics of interaction leaves aside these categories to form a seamless web.

This requires fresh consideration of the social order. Ethnomethodology, the sociology of science and technology, and practice-based approaches to learning and knowing in organizations share a common interest in the construction and maintenance of shared orders as emergent phenomena and interactional effects; but the challenge is how to translate these insights into a rigorous methodological framework without being lost either in a tendency to romance the texture or in a tendency to become ensnared in it.

2.2   A methodological framework: the spiral case study

The questions are therefore how the texture of a field of practices can be investigated empirically; how the achievement of connectedness in action can be analysed; together with how practical knowledge is enacted and circulates in a field of practices.

I shall proceed by differentiation, describing the solutions put forward in the literature and which I reject. The most common of them is to divide the learning and production of knowledge into qualitatively different levels: individual, collective, organizational and interorganizational. Corresponding to this categorization is a disciplinary division of labour whereby psychologists are principally concerned with individuals and groups, organizationists with the social and organizational dimension, cognitivists with cognitive activities, sociologists with social ones, and so on.

They then strive to explain the connections between one level and another: that is, they strive to remove the divisions produced by the categories that they themselves had introduced. From a methodological point of view, this is a problem common to analytical distinction by levels as well as by phases or cycles. A second problem concerns the conceptualization of temporality in social action (Gherardi and Strati, 1988) and in a field of practices that endures across time and space.

In this regard, attention should be paid to the metaphor used to describe the process of reproducing practices. There are two principal metaphors in the literature (Spinosa, 2001), and they reflect the difference between Heidegger's (1971) concept of articulation and Derrida's (1981) concept of dissemination.

Articulation assumes that practices tend towards their own elaboration. Heidegger speaks of this articulative nature of practices as gathering and as *Ereignis*: a *telos* guides the elaboration of practices around an event. Other authors (Spinosa, 2001; Schatzki, 2001b) use the notion of a practice's *telos* to explain what sustains stability and change in practices. Schatzki describes a 'teleoaffective structure' where teleology is orientation toward ends, while affectivity is how things matter. He argues that practical intelligibility is primarily determined not by understanding but by rules, teleology and affectivity. On his definition (Schatzki, 2001b: 53), practice is 'a set of doings and sayings organized by a pool of understandings, a set of rules, and a teleoaffective structure'. In my view, this form of explanation, too, presumes the existence of a 'hidden object' – the teleoaffective structure – in order to account for phenomena.

Those who take up the idea of articulation see the change in practices over time as an internal, regular tendency for self-elaboration which produces a better articulated core of practices, while those who opt for the metaphor of dissemination argue that elaboration involves discontinuity from the previous way of deploying a practice.

The idea of the elaboration of practices as a discontinuity-based process of dissemination should become clearer if I briefly outline its cultural context. To do so, I shall refer to the distinction drawn by Derrida (1981) between the metaphors of dissemination and polyphony. While the latter suggests the image of numerous meanings in one – and the possibility of collecting them and editing them – the former suggests the idea of the limitless generation of further meanings in an endless process.

Polyphony presupposes a community of speakers in which subjective and intersubjective processes enable the understanding and production of sense, the social construction of reality, and meaningful and intentionality-driven collective action. There may consequently be multiple meanings; but also presupposed is the possibility of a 'real' and final interpretation grounded on subjectivity and intersubjectivity. By contrast, dissemination evokes the idea of endless deferral and the recursiveness of language. For this reason it is the metaphor preferred by the deconstructionism which problematizes subjectivity and the existence of a subject separate from the language that the subject uses to signify itself and its world.

The idea of dissemination as elaboration of practices relates to that of citationality (Butler, 1990), a concept which Derrida uses to convey the idea of a text which cites another text, and by so doing inserts it in another context. Dissemination replicates identity by incorporating difference. For this reason I do not find that for Derrida the idea of dissemination is the same as that of dispersion, although they are very close. Dispersion principally concerns the progressive loss of identity, while the image of dissemination evokes the process itself of reproduction which simultaneously incorporates identity and difference. I consequently disagree with Spinosa (2001) and reach the opposite conclusion, preferring the concept of dissemination (not dispersion) to that of articulation.

My other reason for preferring the metaphor of dissemination is that it allows one to focus on the intermediaries of the dissemination process, so that practices are viewed not just as carriers of meanings, actions etc., but as propagators of practices as well, without assuming any 'hidden tendency' towards change or stability. The metaphor of translation, which I will introduce later, will take this point further.

We may now say that the texture of a specific field of practices is shaped by the processes of alignment of material and semiotic elements within the field and the modes of alignment are the effect of local connectedness in action. In order to conduct empirical investigation of the qualities of texture and the processes of its weaving, we must define and circumscribe some units of analysis within a seamless web. The units of analysis are not pre-given, nor do they rest on any natural distinction; they are arbitrary choices made by the researcher on the basis of a theoretical scheme.

I shall shortly describe how I selected my empirical units. First, however, I must introduce the concept of 'spiral case study' and then explain why I decided to conduct a case study.

There is an extremely large and diverse body of literature on case-study methodology: from Yin (1981, 1984) who described the design of case study research; to Jick (1979) on triangulation of data types; to

Silverman (2000) who discusses qualitative analysis more in general. But I do not believe that a detailed analysis of case-study methods is an appropriate way to introduce what I call 'spiral case study'.

I should specify what I consider to be of central importance when conducting case studies. I think that the case study is a research *strategy* which focuses on understanding the dynamics present within single settings (Eisenhardt, 1999: 135). It is a way of organizing social data so as to preserve the *unitary character* of the social object being studied (Goode and Hatt, 1952: 331, quoted in Mitchell, 1999: 184).

What is typical of case-study research is the combination of data-collection methods such as archives research, interviews, questionnaires and observations. The evidence thus provided may be qualitative (i.e. words), quantitative (i.e. numbers) or both. The aim of case-study research may vary and seek to provide a description, to test a theory or to generate a theory. And one should also bear in mind that case-study research may be conducted within a more traditional positivistic framework in which the research process is directed toward the development of testable hypotheses and theory generalizable across settings, or it may be conducted within a more interpretative framework in which the process is more concerned with a rich, complex description of the specific case under study and less concerned with development of generalizable theory. What is meant by 'generalization' is obviously a matter of dispute.

A feature shared by all kinds of case study is rich description. In my case I chose several qualitative methods of data collection – ethnography, interviews, group feedback analysis, discourse analysis – and qualitative and quantitative methods of data analysis.

The image of the spiral is intended to convey that, although my case study was 'unitary', it was made up of numerous case studies designed to bring out the connection among them woven by social action. In fact, safety as a social practice is the aggregate result of individual behaviours, the collective practices of various occupational groups, organizational practices and those of various organizations and institutions which cooperate and clash as they affirm safety standards, norms and cultures. Courses of action interweave in various ways, they concatenate, and they are changed over time by their reciprocal connections. The subject of the case study is the local texture of individual, group, organizational and institutional practices which, in a territorial setting circumscribed by reciprocal interactions, interweave, dissolve and become institutionalized.

The units of analysis were selected so that attention could focus on the process by which practical knowledge is institutionalized – that is, the moments when knowing in practice becomes 'knowledge' – and simultaneously on the manner in which the 'known' is enacted in actual 'knowing'. The image is that of a spotlight trained on the scene of an action (becoming a practitioner) which then moves to the next one. Hence, the scenes presented in the following chapters are these:

- A young assistant building site manager begins his new job by flanking the site foreman. How does he learn safety, and how does the community of practices that he is now joining teach him safety? An ethnography of the work entry process recounts the development of a knowledge base and an occupational identity, as well as the practical acquisition of a situated curriculum.
- Several communities of practice perform interdependent tasks in the same construction company and are therefore co-responsible for the production of safety. How do the engineers, the site foremen and the project managers explain the causes of accidents and ways to prevent them? A causal analysis of their accounts sheds light on practical reasoning processes, and examination of their discursive practices shows that as diverse communities 'talking in practice' they sustain their respective identities and socialize each other into their respective logics of action.
- Accidents represent breakdowns in practices; they are moments when quotidian 'normality' disintegrates and must be reconstructed. Can these moments occasion organizational learning? How is the texture of a field of practices repaired? Comparative analysis of the organizational processes enacted after a serious accident is the methodology of these case studies in my spiral case study.
- Within a circumscribed territory, construction companies and institutions with competence for safety encounter each other and come into conflict. The interactions in which they negotiate their power relations give rise to a local safety culture. How are interorganizational relations woven together, and how is the learning network constructed? Qualitative network analysis will answer the two questions.

These four units of analysis (Figure 2.1) are therefore four points of observation: individual, collective, organizational, societal. But they focus on the fact that the field of safety practices is a single seamless texture, and that all the levels of reality and all the different *loci* of social identity are interwoven and co-present in becoming an assistant site manager.

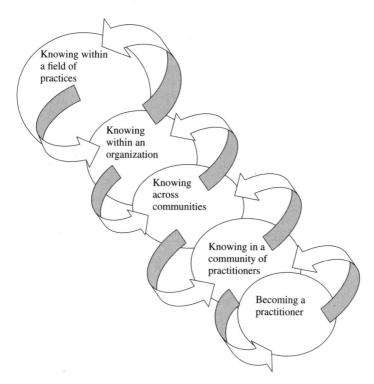

Figure 2.1 A graphic representation of the case study

If we consider a novice learning a trade, we may imagine that during his learning trajectory he also learns to develop a 'performed self' (Goffman, 1959), so that individual and social learning are somehow interconnected. Learning a trade means also developing one or more social identities. Occupational and organizational social identities are built upon individual identity but they have highly significant social referents, for the definitions which individuals give to their selves are also based on group or other social categories to which they feel that they belong and on the situations in which they find themselves. The relationship of social identity to organizational learning is still largely unexplored, although we know that the social identity of organizational groups 'is vested in the systems and bodies of knowledge that they perceive they own. Their members attribute symbolic value to that knowledge and regard themselves as having a right to arbitrate over this value' (Child and Rodrigues, 2003: 540); but 'since the ways social identities and organizational learning interact are complex they have to be exam-

ined at different levels: individual, group, organization and network'
(Child and Rodrigues, 2003: 553).

Simultaneously, in order to enable analysis of the situation, I have indi-
viduated each unit so that it represents situation types in which knowing
in practice can be more easily accessed. Definable as situation types are
the following:

- The entry of a novice in a community of practitioners. This is a
  typical situation of knowledge transmission, and it affords important
  information on knowledge-acquisition practices. Many of the indexical contents of practices are explained to the novice, and s/he
  has not yet taken them for granted precisely because s/he is still
  learning them. From a methodological point of view, moreover, the
  novice's trajectory of participation allows reconstruction of his/her
  situated curriculum as a set of work coding practices.
- Accounting practices among interdependent communities. These are
  situation types which represent the handling of boundary relations
  between one community and another. They are therefore situations
  in which members place particular emphasis on rendering each other
  accountable and consequently verbalize their grounds for claiming
  expert knowledge.
- Repair practices. These re-establish order after breakdowns. They are
  situation types where the modalities that normally sustain a set of
  practices become more salient because the connection holding them
  together has failed. The repair work reveals and questions the connection's resilience.
- The cultural practices within an interorganizational network which
  link the various institutional and organizational actors together and
  collectively institutionalize a body of knowledge. These are situation
  types evincing the production of socially sustained knowledge
  deployed by means of discourses and intermediaries.

I could probably have chosen other situation types; nevertheless, I
believe that those listed above very likely pertain to other research
designs as well, given that they well represent the nodes among social
interactions which range from the individual to the institutional level.
The spiral thus becomes a heuristic device for analysis and interpretation which unpacks the elements co-present. If we conceive the spiral
as a spring, we can say that its extension is followed by its compression,
and that when it is extended its interstices can be examined, given that
stretching a spring amplifies its spaces of connection in action.

2.3   The power of associations

When one sets out to analyse connections in action, a number of questions arise. What is it that holds the connections together? How are they established? Conversely, how are associations dissolved and connections severed? The answer that I intend to give and to illustrate with the empirical study is a simple one. It is power that holds connections together, and power is the resource that enables establishment of the associations that interweave and materialize the texture of a field of practices. Of course, clarification is required of what conception of power gives plausibility to this interpretation, and explanation is required of how it is then translated into the empirical research methodology of my spiral case study.

Researchers have long noted the confusion that exists over the definition of power (Hardy and Clegg, 1996) and I do not wish to enter into a detailed analysis of the debate. I only recall the main traditions of research. The older tradition originated in Marx and Weber who acknowledged that power derives from owning and controlling the means of production and (especially Weber) pointed to the fact that power derives from knowledge of operations as much as from ownership. While the founding fathers were interested in the processes through which power is legitimated in forms of domination (and resistance to it), management theorists saw power in the form of legitimated organizational structures and functional authority. As Clegg (1979) noted, management theorists defined power as those actions that fell outside the legitimated structures and which threatened organizational goals. In the functionalist approach, power is a political 'disorganizing' tool used by the opponents of managers; and in the critical approach it is a means of domination and resistance to it is an emancipatory tool. But now – as Hardy and Clegg write (1996: 636) – 'it is time for both functionalists and critical theorists to pause'. I strongly agree and propose that power should be looked at from a different point of view.

I begin by citing the title of an article by Latour (1986), 'The power of association'. The article first puts forward a relational conception of power which affirms that 'power is not something one can possess and hoard' but rather something that is exercised. The distinction rests on the fact that the difference between power 'in potentia' and power 'in actu' springs from the actions of others. Power must therefore be explained by the actions of others who obey an order, or follow a leader, not by a sort of 'hidden virtue' possessed by the leader. The amount of power exercised by a leader varies, not according to the power that s/he possesses but according to the number of other people who enter into the business. Latour's point is that the exercise of power is an effect rather than a cause, and he makes it by contrasting a diffusion model of power with a translation one.

In the *diffusion model*, in order to explain the spread in time and space of an order, a claim, or an artefact (Latour calls these items 'tokens') one has to presuppose an inner force – similar to inertia in physics – which imbues the token so that it moves in the same direction as long as there is no obstacle against it. In society, fashions, ideas, gadgets, goods and lifestyles spread smoothly as long as they do not encounter resistance. The diffusion model comprises only three important elements: the initial force which triggers the movement, the inertia which conserves the energy, and the medium through which the token circulates.

In the *translation model*, the diffusion in time and space of a token is brought about by people, each of whom may act in a different way: they may let it drop, modify it, deflect it, betray it, add to it, or appropriate it. In the diffusion model the token has no impetus in itself but receives it from the player who gave it its first kick, as in a rugby game. And if it has to move it must constantly find new sources of energy. The actors in the chain not only resist a force, but also transmit it and shape it according to their own ends. The token changes as it moves from hand to hand.

Comparison of the transmission of a managerial order in the diffusion and translation models reveals that, in the former, obedience to the order is explained by the power exercised by the manager, while in the latter it is explained by the alignments of all the people concerned; and the likelihood that it will be modified in the process depends on those who seek to achieve their own goals in the meantime. The question of power, then, is the question of what holds people and things together.

The concept of 'translation' has been taken from Michel Serres (1974). According to Callon (1980: 211) 'translation involves creating convergences and homologies by relating things that were previously different'. The concept of translation is used to direct attention to what classical social theories neglect: the set of transformation, transfer, translation and spatio-temporal processes. It is a concept akin to that of Deleuze and Guattari's (1983) 'rhizome' or 'rhizomatic knowledge', by which they mean the horizontal propagation of knowledge which, like the roots of certain plants, extends itself rapidly through the surrounding terrain in all directions.

This therefore is a semiotic operation – 'socio-logical' as Callon terms it – with the purpose of bringing knowledge and social actors together. The concept was intended to convey the idea that entities acquire form and attributes through their relations with other entities, thus counter-ing the essentialist assumptions which define entities in and of them-selves. The conception derived from the thought of Michel Foucault, but it departed from post-structuralism by not referring solely to lan-guage but also including the objects and materiality of the social world in the field of semiotics. In doing so, it removed the distinction between persons and things, between humans and non-humans: both being effects of a network of relations, the actants of a semiotics of materiality – or of a relational materialism, as Law (1999: 4) prefers.

The metaphor of translation[2] oscillates between two ambits of interpretation:

- *That of language,* where it denotes the process by which a concept is converted from one language to another, and the difficulty of rendering the meaning of a word in one language with a word in another. Shades of meaning, the musicality of words, 'untranslatable' terms, the concepts that express the culture of a people, these are the joy and torment of every good translator aware that something is always lost in translation, and perhaps something unwanted is added. The commonsense dictum runs: to translate is always to traduce. For example, the bureaucrat as translator interprets legislative texts (as well as others), fills their gaps and provides an exegesis but in doing so traduces and transforms them. His function as the 'middleman', like that of the 'intermediary', is that of acting in the spaces where rules are incomplete.
- *That of geometry,* where it denotes the process by which a perspec-tive or an object is shifted in space. The ideas of movement and ma-teriality focus attention on the fact that meanings arise and travel in a spatio-temporal continuum. Too often has the materiality of the social been virtually removed by locating thoughts, ideas, politics, the law and culture in an ethereal domain or in one which only exists in the world of ideas and in the heads of people. Social and work practices have material consistency. They are inscribed in written texts, symbolic objects, artefacts and ceremonies which travel from place to place carrying with them the persistence of their origin, the signs of their use and the change of destination made to them by the communities that receive them and propagate them. A circular, a book, a PowerPoint presentation, is an artefact which travels from one place to another and transports (translates, incorporates) the knowledge of its author. Culture is material (as archaeologists, for example, remind us), and the materiality of the social offers as many resistances against as opportunities for creative uses of an artefact.

The metaphor of translation is a way to describe movements between different forms of knowledge and cultural practices, but also of technology and artefacts. It has both a geometric and a semiotic meaning: translation is both the movement of an entity in space and time and its translation from one context to another – as in translating from one language to another, with the necessary transformation of meaning that this always implies. Any translation is the result of the active work of an array of heterogeneous entities that, as the process proceeds, either find a place or are locked into place. The set of entities that enter into the translation are called both 'actor-network' (whence the name of the approach) and 'action-net' (Czarniawska-Jorges, 1996). The former term is used to describe the fragmented composition of the 'agent' of the translation in response to the question 'who is responsible for the ordering process and its outcome'. The latter refers more or less to the same thing when the attention concentrates on the texture of the relations among the entities that constitute the arena and on the force field for the manoeuvres and processes of translation. To be emphasized, however, is that action-nets/actor-networks, unlike telephone networks or the world wide web, do not exist prior to the process of translation: action-nets/actor-networks should be understood as verbs, not nouns, as relational effects that recursively generate and reproduce themselves thanks to the manoeuvres and strategies of translation.

The metaphor of translation evokes power and distributed knowledge, the dissemination of meanings and of learning processes. It highlights that power is the effect of processes that associate humans and non-humans: the power of a manager is the effect of association obtained by means of long telephone calls, record keeping, clothes, machines, secretaries, other managers and so on. That which we call 'organization' is the relatively stable pattern in which these and many other elements are held together; it is the material manifestation of networks of knowledge and power.

Organizational studies have treated power in many ways. Hardy and Clegg (1996), in charting the key developments in functionalism, critical tradition and post-modernist scholars, argue that corresponding to the loss of faith in rational analysis is recognition of the close relationship between power and knowledge. They suggest that power should be studied as the *medium of responsible collective action*, and citing Callon and Latour (1981), they suggest that researchers should explore how, in particular situations, voices are heard or are silenced in order to illustrate how actors participate in a web of relations that they help create. They state that all forms of power play, including its theorizing, are 'moves in games that enroll, translate and treat others in various ways, in various situated moralities, according to various code of honor or dishonor which constitute, maintain, reproduce and resist various form of practices of power under their rubric' (Hardy and Clegg, 1996: 636).

To this definition of power Blackler and McDonald (2000: 835) add the refinement whereby power is *both the ongoing product and the medium of collective activity*. Moreover their discussion of power, mastery and organizational learning gainsays the widespread belief that scholars working in this field have neglected the issue of power. When the literature is examined in terms of how work groups achieve collective agency and mastery, one finds a large body of work (Chaiklin and Lave, 1993; Engestrom, 1987; Hutchins, 1991; Star, 1996; Suchman, 1987) dealing with the relationship between pragmatic activity and social processes, and highlighting how mastery is achieved through people's ability to co-operate and co-construct their workplaces in situations of high interactive complexity. Nevertheless, the focus on collective self-regulation emphasizes one aspect of power while usually failing to address its broader societal aspect.

Blackler and McDonald quote Raeithel (1996) who in a review of this literature stresses that ethnographic reports may present a romanticized view of organizing processes which tends not to address:

* the hierarchical aspects of group regulation in complex organizations;
* the politics of relationships between different experts or functional groups;
* the nature of the broader institutional context within which the teams and their organization are located;
* the way in which participants have become socialized to participate within these structures.

I have taken up the suggestion implicit in the critical analysis of the above authors. By proposing an empirical interpretation of safety practices put forward in my spiral case study, I intend to show that the texture of knowing in practice is woven together by power and through power.

The dynamic between mastery as relationships enabling collective agency, on the one hand, and power as the effect of associations among heterogeneous elements on the other, is reflected in the way that I have circumscribed the portion of texture of practices which I intend to analyse. I shall describe collective agency in light of how an apprentice is socialized into the practices of a building site. I shall also examine the

practical reasoning of three occupational groups working on that building site, doing so in terms of power effects and the performance of discursive practices. These latter I shall frame within the organizational and
interorganizational dynamics of a territorial area delimited by the courses
of action described. This way of marking out a field of practices is
entirely arbitrary. I could have done it differently, but because it corre-
sponded to my knowledge interests I decided upon this construction of
the empirical object. However, the field of practices is a constant interweaving and other delimitations would have been equally legitimate,
both in extension and profundity.

2.4   To sum up: weaving the texture of situated practices

The purpose of this chapter has been to describe a methodological
framework which enables empirical analysis to be conducted of a field
of practices in which a body of knowledge is stored, transmitted and
transformed.

Against this background, I have decided to focus on safety as an
example of a social practice and to study it within a field of working
and organizational practices pertaining to the construction industry, this
being a sector where safety is a major problem that technology has so
far failed to solve. I consider safety to be an emerging property of a cultural system which produces social conceptions of what is dangerous or
safe, and of what attitudes and behaviours towards risk, danger and safety
are appropriate. We may consider safety to be a collective ability to
produce organizational and interorganizational work practices which
protect both individual welfare and the environment. Safety, then, is
knowledge objectified and codified in an expertise and circulating (in
form of knowing) within a web of practices. The texture of the web
may assume different qualities, and it is precisely this that I aim to
describe as the result of a complex system of weaving.

Weaving will be the metaphor for knowing in practice, for the key
idea behind 'the texture of practices' is connectedness in action, i.e. the
endless series of relationship which continuously move into each other.
The woven texture opens in a centrifugal way and the weavers and
the reader/writer are caught up in the ongoing movement of the text/
texture as active elements. Consequently, the conceptual framework for
studying the texture of a field of practices is indirect and metaphorical.
Texture can be shown and demonstrated but not defined, because as
practices are reproduced over and over again, they disseminate and

generate new practices. The process of dissemination of practices displays active weaving work by the intermediaries of practices, these being the elements – people, things, technologies, tools, ideas – that enable the connections to stay in place and hold. They are the enabling elements for the translation of knowledge into actual 'knowing'. But what keeps the elements in place is power, the power to associate elements into a more or less stable and durable modes of ordering.

How can empirical research be conducted on a set of connections in action when the researcher/researchers are the active constructors of the relations that they intend to study?

I have defined four observation points on the texture of safety practices described in the chapters that follow:

- the learning of safety as a practice which socializes newcomers and simultaneously transmits practical knowledge in the course of every-day routine on a building site;
- the production of accountability and discursive practices among diverse communities of practices;
- the reconstruction of order when a breakdown occurs in the texture;
- the cooperative production of a safety culture in a particular territorial area.

NOTES

1. Pepper's characterization of contextualism is the absence of distinctions between up and down, inside and outside, big and small, etc.: they simply merge into each other, they are implicated in each other (without assuming for example that the big contains the small).
2. The term 'sociology of translation' made its official appearance in the vocabulary of the social sciences in 1986 (although it had previously been used in Callon, 1980 and 1981) when Michel Callon published his 1986 article 'Some elements of a sociology of translation: domestication of the scallops and the fishermen of St. Brieuc Bay'. This was an odd title, but it illustrated the translation of a scientific project – to stop the decline of a marine species – into an economic policy. The article was part of a broader intellectual movement which began in those years within the sociology of science and technology and which still today comprises one of the most animated and innovative debates ongoing in sociology.

CHAPTER THREE

On Becoming a Practitioner

The central issue in learning is becoming a
practitioner, not learning about a practice.
(Brown and Duguid, 1991: 48)

Imagine that you are engaged in the renovation of a mediaeval convent.
The work involves a certain amount of demolition but it concerns only
one storey of the building. The design engineer has estimated the costs
and has worked on the reliefs and drawings. These show that no but-
tressing or reinforcement work has ever been carried out on the masonry
to be demolished. What should be done? Demolish the upper storey?
Risk a collapse? Start the complex installation of temporary support
braces? Alter the original design?

Whereas building work has to cope mostly with 'external' constraints
(weather, delivery times, the availability of labour), restoration work must
also, and especially, cope with internal ones arising from the fact that the
building has a history 'wrought in stone' and cannot be treated as a *tabula
rasa*. Constructing a totally new building is a relatively linear activity
(though one not without its obstacles and unexpected difficulties). It is
easy to follow the architect's drawings in an 'ordered' sequence of actions
determined by a set of pre-established canons. The persons involved can
therefore act in a more 'organized' manner according to bureaucratic
principles, because the work has been organized so that it is compatible
with them. Conversely, it is often impossible to plan restoration work
beforehand and thereby have time to deal with the unforeseen. The
various layers of the building generate constraints which can almost
never be predicted when the work begins, but which arise as it proceeds. These constraints raise both operational and economic problems,
they rule out some forms of action, they require complicated 'dodges',
and they sometimes conflict with plans and designs, which must be recast
in an often non-linear and non-sequential process that instead resembles conversation and continuous negotiation.

In this chapter I shall present an ethnographic study of how safety is learnt on a building site, and how it is transmitted and circulates. The purpose of the ethnography is not to describe an entire cultural system, i.e. the safety culture of the firm; rather, it takes a situational focus (Alvesson, 1996), describing the practical accomplishment of becoming a member of a community of practices within that firm. A situational focus means that a particular situation, delimited in time and space, is considered a core phenomenon and 'in a situational focus actors as well as the institutional context are present' (Alvesson, 1996: 476).

I shall reconstruct how 'our hero' – Gianni, the person who was shadowed, and the researcher[1] who shadowed him – entered a community of practices (Lave and Wenger, 1991), namely the building site, as novices. Lave and Wenger (1991: 98) define a community of practice as:

> a set of relations among persons, activity, and world, over time and in relation with other tangential and overlapping communities of practice. A community of practice is an intrinsic condition for the existence of knowledge, not least because it provides the interpretative support necessary for making sense of its heritage.

The chief feature of learning in communities of practices is that it is conceived as participation in situated activities and as involving acquisition of a new identity, rather than merely the acquisition of cognitive contents. I shall show, in fact, how the subject of knowledge and the object of knowing emerge as an outcome of situated working practices. Learning 'safety' will therefore be framed in terms of learning to become a competent member of a community of practices in interaction with other communities of practices within a working place. In fact, safety is not a property 'added' to action; rather, it is a characteristic of action, or one of the characteristics that denote competent action in the workplace. The work required to mobilize heterogeneous elements in order to obtain a 'safe' organization includes the effort to integrate modes of action proper to several work practices present in the organization and employed by members who, because they bring different occupational cultures with them, may have different ways of understanding and dealing with safety.

'Safety knowledge' therefore takes the form of 'cultural' competence able to influence the style and manner in which meaning and value are attributed to events and to determine the use to which the resources, technologies, artefacts and knowledge of a group or organization are put. As such it offers a vantage point for reflection on the fundamental social and cultural features of learning and knowing in organizations.

3.1   Being 'on site'

A building school[2] was concluding the 'classroom' phase of a training course for assistants on restoration building sites, and all the participants were about to spend three-month traineeships at small and medium-sized firms in the district. This was an opportunity to observe at first hand the trainees' entries into a community of practices, their early socialization and apprenticeships.

Having obtained permission from both the firm and the trainees, the ethnographic observation involved the 'shadowing'[3] of one of the trainees – whom we shall call 'Gianni' – on the site. Shadowing Gianni required the researcher to become an active member of the organization by participating fully, for three months, in its life and activities. The shadowing took place on the building site, where the 'immersion' was made possible by the fact that few people were aware of the researcher's real activity and identity. Only the assistant site manager (that is, the trainee's supervisor) and later the site foreman were told that the researcher was a student gathering data for his degree thesis.

Access to the field was facilitated by the fact that both Gianni and the researcher were novices. The aim of each of them was to learn as much as possible from every opportunity; and of this all the site workers were aware, albeit in different versions. While for the insiders the roles were soon confused, a constant concern for the researcher was the fact that for Gianni this represented a real opportunity to find a job (although this did not in fact prove to be the case). The researcher therefore constantly tried to play a secondary and rather passive role, and to avoid interfering with Gianni's traineeship.[4] He justified his reduced working hours on the site by saying that he had another job, and his obvious lack of experience by the fact that he had joined the course late, whereas Gianni had attended it from the beginning.

In small and medium-sized Italian building firms engaged in restoration work, two figures coordinate on-site operations: the (traditional) site foreman and the (emerging) assistant site manager.

The site foreman is responsible for the workmen and is accountable for the standard of their work: he corresponds largely to the foreman in the manufacturing industry. His role (which is rapidly evolving) and functions depend closely on the organization of the firm (which in turn relates to its size: the larger the firm, the more marked its division and specialization of tasks). He is usually a skilled mason, well trusted by the owners, who has learnt the logistics of site management (stock-piling, ordering materials) and safety measures (scaffolding, first aid, personal protection devices) on the job. He also, indeed principally, monitors on-site events and reports directly to the surveyor or the site manager. It is he that is consulted by the workers for instructions on what to do when doubts arise; it is he who allocates the workmen on the basis of the work schedule negotiated with the site surveyor; it is he who is the target of on-site micro-conflict concerning working hours, breaks, leaves of absence, productivity; and it is he who serves the site manager as a repository of memories about the work and actions performed on the building (and usually keeps a daily log, which is the basis of his accountability).

The assistant site manager is progressively replacing the traditional site foreman. His work is substantially relational as he coordinates and mediates among technical and economic matters. He therefore constantly uses both categorial systems of reference. He is able to liaise with all the figures in his professional circle (architects, engineers, suppliers, surveyors, bricklayers, carpenters, excavators, lorry drivers, etc.) using different languages and applying different types of knowledge. Of the managerial staff (engineer, architect, surveyor) he is the only one who wears heavy boots and has mud on his trousers. This accounts for his ability to enter areas of situated knowledge in which the ideal constructions of the designer enter into 'conversation' with the building – that is, are moulded to the concrete reality of the work situation. At the same time he must apply economic criteria and negotiate competently among the various needs voiced by the actors on the building site (the firm with its concern for profit, the employees with their shortcomings, the customer and his representatives with their desire for everything immediately and at the lowest price possible), given that he is in charge of the building site *qua* economic unit and his every act has repercussions in both the short and long term.

How, therefore, does a novice learn the trade? How does safety knowledge circulate in a community of practices? Lave and Wenger (1991) put forward the concept of 'legitimate peripheral participation' to signal the particular mode of engagement of a learner who participates in the actual practice of an expert, but only to a limited extent and with limited responsibility for the ultimate product as a whole. Through this process the learner acquires community membership i.e. belonging, engagement, inclusiveness, developing identities:

> Absorbing and been absorbed in the 'culture of practice'(. . . .) might include (knowing) who is involved, what they do, what everyday life is like, how masters talk, walk, work, and generally conduct their lives, how

people who are not part of the community of practice interact with it, what other learners are doing, and what learners need to learn to became full practitioners. It includes an increasing understanding of how, when, and about what old-timers collaborate, collude, and collide, and what they enjoy, dislike, respect, and admire. In particular it offers exemplars (which are grounds and motivation for learning activity), including masters, finished products, and more advanced apprentices in the process of becoming full practitioners.

(Lave and Wenger, 1991: 95)

We expected Gianni to receive instructions, advices, tips and whatever had to do with the discourse of safety. Instead, our first and most striking finding was the silence of the organization.

3.2 Safety and silence of the organization: the culture of practice

The culture of practice that arose from the ethnography was characterized by the silence of the host organization on danger and safety. For the entire time spent on the building site, in fact, the two issues were never addressed explicitly and systematically, nor was particular attention paid to them. This experience was repeated, with different nuances, in the case of Gianni's co-trainees as well. It is not that the issue was non-existent; but the way in which it was treated, or ignored, assumes a specific significance. What does this silence indicate?

The story that follows helps shed light on the question. It was recounted by one of the workmen:

One of my mates told me this story. He'd gone to work for one of those firms that build the piers for motorway viaducts. They were working on an enormous overpass on the *** ring road, you know, one of those really high flyovers. They work like this in that firm: they have scaffolding all round the pillar, mounted on rails, which extend bit by bit. Every day they'd bolt together, say, 30 metres, and then they'd pour the concrete. You know, they use special prefabricated panels. The next day they come back, unclad the piece, extend the rails, climb the stretch that they'd done and then start again. You begin at the ground, but after a week you're 150, 200 metres high. Anyway, my mate was up there on the scaffolding and he saw that down in the yard, slightly apart from the others, was a hut which no one ever entered. He was curious, and a few days later before he clocked off work, he went to the hut, without anyone seeing him . . . who knows what was inside. So, he went to the hut, and he saw that it wasn't even locked. He opened the door and went inside. In the middle of the room he saw two coffins. Yeah, two brand-new coffins with their lids propped against the sides. Ready and waiting. He went straight into the office and quit . . .

The silence of the organization was matched by the stories that circulated in the community of practice. The story of the coffins has all the features of a 'paradigmatic story' (Martin *et al.*, 1983). That is to say, it is of less importance whether the episode actually happened or not, whether it happened to the man who told it or whether he had imagined himself in a story heard from someone else, than the social function performed by telling the story in a community, and the fact that the knowledge which circulated in the form of that story became the basis for individual action, and also of a social process. The silence of the organization therefore assumes meaning when it is indirectly addressed within a community of interpreters and is offered to Gianni both as a way of settling him in and furnishing him with a norm of conduct for his occupational life.

The story suggests certain features of the building industry and its power structure. In the working culture of Gianni's organization, as in the overwhelming majority of small and medium-sized building firms, safety is an issue deemed relevant not to the organization but to the individual. In other words, the silence of the organization often indicates that the dominant culture regards safety, and therefore accidents, as attributable solely to the individual and to his/her errors. The purpose of the story, recounted in that particular community, was to admonish the novice as to what 'safety' meant in that organizational culture and to provide him with a normative example, which if translated into advice would run as follows: 'when you come across safety cultures like that it's better to leave the firm and look for a safer one'.

Story-telling was thus the means to circulate practical knowledge on the extent to which the organization cared about safety, to transmit a rule of personal choice to the novice, and to start a social process of reciprocal choice among individuals able to set in train an exodus from less safe firms to safer ones which attracted 'safety-minded' workers, also according to their power on the labour market. Immigrant workers, with few skills and less protection, move into firms working on subcontracting orders, with higher turnover, and which invest less in safety.

The episode highlights two main features: the cultural practice of the owners and management whereby they suppress the discourse on safety by removing it from the 'organizational' sphere and relegating it to the 'private' one; and the cultural practice of the occupational community, which used story-telling to teach novices how to interpret silence, how to gauge the reliability of the organization for which they work and how to defend themselves by learning to manoeuvre in a hierarchized labour market. Story-telling is therefore an indirect discourse method used to transmit the 'wisdom' specific to an organization, which requires knowledge of the standards used to assess one's own person (can I change the organization?) in relation to assessment of the organization itself (how good is this job?). But the moral of the tale is hidden: not only must it be found, but also it must be found in a context that legitimates silence and attributes responsibility to the individual. The second episode now described shows, by drawing directly on the researcher's experience, how this principle is so widespread that it has been internalized acritically and unconsciously.

The idea that the individual alone is responsible for what happens rests on the deep-lying notion that those who hurt themselves have committed a wrong, not that they have suffered one. This is a value that is rapidly absorbed, to the point that the researcher himself had internalized it after only a few weeks:

> I was climbing down a very dangerous ladder which was used instead of scaffolding to speed up the work. I banged my shin against the edge of a small cement wall that had just been poured. The edge was still rough, and it gave me a cut, not serious but painful, which started to bleed. An elderly bricklayer saw what had happened and muttered reprovingly 'You should pay attention – you should be careful!' I answered defensively 'Right . . . yes . . . but I haven't hurt myself, no . . . it's nothing, just a scratch'. I limped for days afterwards.

An accident thus becomes an individual shortcoming, something of which to be ashamed (Douglas, 1985). It is an index of weakness, and weakness is morally condemnable in a working culture like that of the construction industry. While prevention is subtly codified as cowardice, risk-taking is rewarded with social recognition and the celebration of bodily skills. Mastery of the trade and bodily ability are interconnected and enacted in a context of affirmative working-class culture (Collinson, 1992).

Becoming a competent member of a community of manual workers entails performing the body and language in relationships appropriate to class and gender. Risk-taking figures as something gratifying, something to be proud about: 'a caress to the ego', as suggested by the following situation.

In order to get up to the roof, you had to climb a ladder about six metres high which, as was almost invariably the case, was makeshift and rickety. The engineer, egged on by the 'lads', had to overcome his fear of heights and climb the ladder. He concealed his nervousness with a series of jokes (first. 'You don't really want me to go up there, do you!?' The assistant site manager's reply: 'Look at him, he goes around in helicopters and boats and he's afraid of climbing a ladder.' Then came self-reassurance – he also had to climb down – 'Look what I have to do to earn a living . . . it's certainly high . . . look, I've still got palpitations' (seeking support). Answer: 'Get on with it. Be a man' (look at us real men . . . we've got other things to worry about).

In a traditionally male culture like that of the builders, risk-taking – that is, knowingly breaching the rules in non-ordinary situations – is considered to be appropriate behaviour which demonstrates strength, courage and virility. Gender codes are transmitted by gendered practices and organizational cultures sustain hegemonic masculinity. Since gender may be conceived as a cultural enactment learnt and displayed in appropriate situations (Gherardi, 1995a), we may say that in learning a practice one also learns the gender (and class) codes implicit in it.

Working-class masculinity has developed in accordance with the notion of the breadwinner, but in contrast to another type of masculinity which arises from class relationships: bourgeois masculinity. The latter, although it reflects the assumption of separate productive (male)/ reproductive (female) spheres, from the point of view of working class masculinity is 'unmanly' because it does not involve physical strength and is excessively polite (Morgan, 1992). This has been well documented by Linstead (1985) and Collinson (1988) when they illustrate the importance of humour in organizational cultures – and in particular when Collinson describes what happens when joking and vulgarity are taken to symbolize independence and freedom, as opposed to the more 'reserved' nature of office work. Risk, danger, rough humour and dirty work are the ingredients of a male working-class identity, and in order to socialize newcomers to it, their bodies must be disciplined and their ability to associate all these elements while working must be performed in practice. Foucault (1984), and feminist scholars after him (De Lauretis, 1987; Hassard, Holliday, and Willmott, 2000), have used the concept of technologies of self to describe how societal values become inscribed in the body and in the individual/collective identity. To their findings I would add the observation that the disciplined body and the learned social identity must be performed on appropriate occasions: that is, they form a class/gender practice which anchors working practices.

This set of cultural practices was sustained by the employer as well. On the one hand he complied with working-class masculinity and partly shared its convictions; on the other he found it a useful ally when he contended that prevention was too costly and of little use ('bad luck is always lying in wait', was the expression he used). When the informants were asked if any serious accidents had occurred in the firm ('luckily, no . . . in all these years there's been only one fall, he broke his leg; just bad luck') a further interesting feature emerged. In cases where the behaviour of the injured worker did not show signs of transgression, for which reason he had been punished, or in cases where the punishment was deemed excessive (death or serious disablement), the incident was blamed on bad luck, a residual category used as a device to prevent perilous breakdowns in the collectively sustained culture. Bad luck or chance were conjugated as 'there was nothing you could do about it' or 'it's a dangerous job'. This closed the circle and forestalled other explanations of what had happened.

Consequently, the employer both sustained and was sustained by the workers' culture. His actions were aimed on the one hand at evading normative annoyances: 'complying with the rules', at least nominally, was an action which reflected the conception of safety as an organizational commitment. On the other, his actions were intended to promote and perpetuate the workers' culture. As several informants told us, when the workmen started working for the firm, they were issued with the equipment stipulated by the regulations, but they then signed a 'release' form which shifted all responsibility back to the individual. The employer's actions thus confirmed the idea of the work as risky, of the inevitability of accidents and of the consequent implicit pointlessness of investing resources in accident prevention, given that it was bound to be useless. At the same time a counter-narrative based on the script 'the smart worker leaves' competed with the first. But both narratives could be told by the same person; they were just juxtaposed and interconnected, and not as clear-cut as rationality would like them to be.

The silence of the organization revealed another silence, on the emotionality of workplaces, and on how emotionality is socially constructed. The story that circulated within the group of workers was not only emotively charged, it was also an intermediary that enabled learning of the expressive forms of emotions. In the case just seen, it shifted emotions to the private sphere, where they were recounted indirectly, concealed behind words, but shared in already elaborated cultural forms. The affective domain of learning is always at work when we consider learning in its social context. Emotionality is a social process; it 'is given meaning and substance through interactions, expressed through culturally available symbols, particularly language and stories' (Fineman, 2003: 567).

In Gianni's trajectory of becoming an insider it was not 'safety' as a specific topic − a cognitive object of knowledge − that he learnt, but safe work practices. Although apparently banal, this observation says a great deal about the implicit assumptions of those who engage in research and how they circumscribe the domains of knowledge. The researcher, like the teachers at the building school, abstracted a body of knowledge from its context of production and use and elaborated it into texts describing or prescribing behaviours correlated with the production of knowledge. Accident prevention regulations provide an example. When the students had studied 'safety' at the school, they had acquired familiarity with a discourse representing a form of decontextualized knowledge. When they began to work, it was expected, by both us and them, that this knowledge would be re-contextualized in relation to specific cases − in the same way as a general rule is first learned at school and then applied to a certain number of concrete instances. This did not happen. The abstract knowledge remained abstract and pertinent to another field of practices (teaching, project design, analysis). The novice (and the researcher with him) accessed the knowledge embedded in working practices in a different way. We have just seen that this knowledge was contained in, and reproduced through, discursive practices like story-telling, jokes and humour, as well as practices which shaped physical abilities, and practices which institutionalized differences of gender and class. The same cultural practices that shape the 'right' worker for the 'right' company comprise a process of social matching between managerial accident prevention and safety measures, individual choices in the labour market, and the positioning of companies/workers on a hierarchical scale within the industrial sector. The next section investigates what type of knowledge is embedded in working practices and how it is transmitted principally through the activity of issuing/obeying instructions.

3.3   The knowledge pointers

A building site is a context in which the members of several occupations shape events subject to their professional scrutiny. The shaping process creates objects of knowledge (epistemic objects[5]) that form bodies of expertise and become the insignia of the craft and the stuff of their lifeworld. In the same way that a medical student learns how to read an X-ray picture through his/her exposure to the relevant material and to the specialized language that s/he is presumed to apply to that material (Polanyi, 1962; Schon, 1983; Lakoff, 1987), our novice Gianni learned what elements were important within the domain of building construction. Knowing how to act within a domain of action is learning to make competent use of the categories and the distinctions constituting that domain.

Charles Goodwin (1994) has investigated three practices that shape a domain of occupational knowledge:

- coding, which transform phenomena observed in a specific setting into the objects of knowledge that animate the discourse of an occupation;
- highlighting, which gives salience to specific phenomena in a complex perceptual field by marking them in some manner;
- producing and articulating material representations, which embed and structure the knowledge produced and transfer it through space and time.

I shall not describe similar practices in the apprenticeship of an assistant site manager. I prefer to focus only on the practice of highlighting, my purpose being to stress the role of what I have called 'knowledge pointers', that is, linguistic devices used mainly when giving instructions and shaping how a novice learns to see when following those instructions.

The notion of 'instructed action' was first formulated by Harold Garfinkel and Harvey Sacks (1970). Their observation was that the production of social order through everyday activity has, as both a primary resource and an ongoing practical problem, the task of bringing various forms of occasioned instruction into productive relation with specific circumstances of action. Common examples are maps and written directions on how to get from place to place, recipes, procedures and the like; and, more generally, learning to become a competent societal member in a plethora of ways. The key insight provided by ethnomethodology is that, far from determining courses of action in any strong sense, instructions of whatever form presuppose competences for their enactment which the instructions themselves do not fully specify.

A mechanism of instruction/imitation/emulation operated on the building site: 'you learn the job by watching. All right, you do it, but first you watch how it's done'. Moreover, imitation involved complex micro-social interactions in which language, observation and workmanship mixed and merged.

Looking and seeing are two forms of action essential for the learning of practice and for teaching it. Seeing and looking are components of watching, but the difference between them is difficult to determine. We may say that looking involves a metacognitive intentionality, a 'change of gear' whereby attention is focused on the fact that I am seeing (as the focus of attention) as well as on what I am seeing (which becomes a focus of attention temporarily placed in the background). Looking is therefore a transitory state in which, at least initially, two levels can be perceived: it may be spontaneously initiated by somebody who 'wishes to see', but it is more often the result of an associated linguistic (performative) behaviour: 'look here', 'go and look carefully', etc. The difference between seeing and looking lies in the linguistic expression used to describe the action. 'I've seen that . . .' describes both seeing and looking. 'I've looked carefully at . . .' instead corresponds to fulfillment of a prescription to pay attention in the act of seeing.

The use of the performative utterance 'Look!' can be considered a knowledge pointer because it signals the importance of what is happening. More specifically, 'look' implies 'look carefully because what is happening is important and should be understood and remembered for the same occasion or similar ones in the future'. Looking carefully – 'stealing the job with the eyes', as an expression collected in the field aptly put it – means understanding the prescription by making the effort to watch and memorize.

However, knowledge and competence are also acquired through simple perceptive exposure, that is, through automatic non-reflexive 'seeing'. The habits of a community do not need to be explicated or explicitly talked about; they are probably 'picked up' through 'constant seeing'. Looking, with its 'intentional' dimension, is utilized only in situations of microdifficulty when it is necessary to redirect the action ('look, this is how you do it', or simply 'this is how you do it' – the 'look' and what to look at being implicit in the latter utterance).

Language is used in other learning situations as well, often in concomitance with ostensive reference to examples and with suggestions ('you do it like this . . . no, not like that'), in judgements ('well done', 'good work', 'that's the way to do it'). It this case parsimonious use is made of language for the sake of practical economy. Ostensive reference allows use to be made of the entire information capital acquired in the community (and which in its turn is based on information acquired in social life). The combination of language, observation and ostensive reference thus reduces the need for extensive linguistic explanation without losing comprehension and coordination.

The skill of seeing (and looking) is structured through constant and situated use of directions and micro-explanations: the novice is *taught how to see* (Goodwin and Goodwin, 1996). The ability to see a meaningful event is not an individual and psychological process; rather, it is a social situated activity accomplished through discursive practices which employ specific knowledge pointers.

Goodwin (1994: 606) states that: 'all vision is perspectival and lodged within endogenous communities of practice'. An archaeologist, a farmer or a builder will see different things in the same patch of dirt, because they look at it from different professional 'visions'.[6]

The grammar of the expression 'be careful' is another interesting example of how language, vision and practice interact in the learning of situated skills.

'Be careful' is a performative utterance: saying the words 'be careful' produces a change in the emotional state of those present, who look for the source of the danger and turn to the others involved in the situation to understand how to react. The state of alert continues until:

1. the tension has been dispelled by the passage of time, and attention moves elsewhere;
2. someone gives a signal that the danger has passed; this signal is usually a statement, a phrase or (more rarely) an act which 'releases tension' and restores calm.

To illustrate the situated meaning of the utterance 'be careful', or similar ones which involve the act of *listening and understanding* as social processes, we give the example of the moving roof beam.

> New roof beams were being installed. Repairing the roof is a critical phase in restoration work because it is a key element in the stability of the whole building (restoration should begin with the roof, but this never happens), and also because the work should be performed rapidly so that rain water does not damage the rest of the building. In special cases (for example the restoration of buildings of great cultural value like the basilica of S. Lorenzo in Florence, on which one of our informants had worked) a provisional second roof is constructed over the original one. However, this is an extremely expensive method which requires a large amount of manpower and overtime. Usually the work is carried out rapidly with one eye on the weather forecast. Consequently, the restoration of roofs – especially in the case of buildings of great value – is carried out quickly and by as many workmen as possible. On our construction site, the 'filler' (diagonal) beams supporting the roof had to be laid with

a specific slope. They consisted of several timbers joined lengthways which rested on the internal load-bearing walls. Workers were therefore needed to lay the beams as they were hoisted up to them by crane, pushing them into the correct position and fixing them with temporary clamps. Other workers altered the masonry to provide support points for the beams. Yet others installed the reinforced concrete armatures of the 'yoke' which held the four outer walls of the building together. Finally, other builders installed the rafters to which the covering materials were to be fixed (the stringers beneath the roof, the intermediate layer of lightened cement, and the tiles); to do this they had to remove the tarpaulins used as temporary covering overnight.

All this work was going on at around 20 metres from the ground and 6–8 metres above the upper storey of the building. The building was surrounded by solid scaffolding which enabled the workers to move around without difficulty. However, all the operations on the roof were carried out with the sole support of the older beams or the new ones, which together with the walls also served as precarious walkways. If a workman wanted to move, he had climb onto a beam or a wall top and use the thickness of the masonry as a pathway with a sheer drop on either side. In this mid-air network of walkways, the workers contrived to make sure that they did not block each other's path. If this was impossible, they had to get past each other, which often meant squeezing past on a platform measuring only a few square centimetres.

The hoist operator, sitting at the highest point of the roof with his legs dangling, was manoeuvring one of the large filler beams. He was hoisting it up from the ground and had to swing it around to the other side of the building, where around 10 builders were working. The arrival of the beam was preceded by warnings. The 'beware' signal was echoed by everyone present and repeated to the new arrivals on the roof (even if they were some distance away): 'Watch out for the beam!' While everyone got on with their work they paid 'attention' to what was happening, to the position of the beam, and how the others were reacting. They watched each other, and especially the hoist operator, seeking to interpret their intentions. If there was any doubt, verbal negotiation began: 'Move over there a bit'. 'Yes, but give me a moment'. The operation was commented on by the others 'more slowly . . . now lower it', which among other things heightened the tension. Finally, the beam was laid in place. A shout 'Bloody hell, you took a week' signalled that the danger was past. The tension, and mutual observation to coordinate the operation, returned to their usual levels.

'Watch out!' is also a sort of reproof which serves the purpose of learning. If something unexpected or dangerous happens, a near-accident or a minor one, the statement is used as criticism which indicates what should have been done – for example, 'You should have been careful, and you weren't, and this is what might have happened' – and as a generalization, as shown by the following fragment in which after a near-collision one of the two workmen involved generalized the need to give proper warnings:

> Beware of moving loads . . . always call out (emphatically). . . you should
> . . . be careful lads . . . when you're walking around the site, be careful.

In Gianni's learning trajectory, the access to the knowledge diffused in the community of practice was mediated by the form of the linguistic and relational modalities that we have called 'knowledge pointers' because they called the novice's attention to the knowledge items that the community deemed important to ensure safe working practices. Ordinary language was used to transmit the specific content of how the work was or was not to be done. That content was reinforced by the transmission of a practical ability which consisted in the capacity to *look and see, listen and understand.*

In becoming a practitioner, Gianni developed the ability to grasp the knowledge pointers contained in the instructions he received and which gave him access to socially organized ways of seeing and understanding. It was through the social relations that tied Gianni to his workmates that the opportunity arose for him to learn and tacitly to coordinate himself with them, both to understand the implied meanings of the language they used and to develop the capacity to view the work with the eyes of an expert. Becoming an insider requires the ability to participate with competence in the discourses of a community and to look at a shared reality with a gaze situated within that community's culture of practice.

As we have seen, objects of knowledge emerge from the interplay between a domain of scrutiny and a set of discursive practices deployed within a specific activity (Goodwin, 1994). But indexicality is not usually a problem for practical action, as we shall see.

On a building site, it is not necessary to transmit *all* the aspects of danger, because in many cases the situation is already familiar and those concerned are already competent. While it is necessary to learn '*ex novo*' how to build a wall or to write an estimate, because these activities require entirely new competences of the novice, we know that we should not step on a nail or drop a brick which might hit a colleague (these are already 'taken for granted'). It is therefore sufficient, rather than necessary, to transmit the bodily capacity to sense where nails may be, and where colleagues are. Knowledge pointers, made up of simple and succinct linguistic and indexical expressions, help direct attention to specific objects of knowledge (and in so doing construct them) and shape what should be 'known' through the capacities to look and see and to listen and understand. The ability to see and to listen in occupational contexts is a social competence and a kind of unarticulated expertise involving the mind and the body. It is aesthetic knowledge, and as knowledge pointers perform their highlighting role they indicate a knowledge that should be acquired in sensorial terms.

3.4 Knowing as aesthetic understanding

Observations on our construction site as well as others (Strati, 1999) provided some interesting examples of how experts acquire, or better develop, a 'sense of what is safe'.

During the ethnography we observed the following:

> A heavy load of bricks had to be lifted off a lorry and stacked in an area of the site some distance away. Although a special crane sling was available for this kind of operation, it was complicated and too time-consuming to fit. The senior operator decided to use the sling already mounted on the crane, although it might have been undersized for the job. After positioning and securing the load, he told the crane operator to hoist it a few centimetres off the ground. He then glanced at it, looked at the crane, felt the tension of the sling and gave clearance for the operation to begin.

To the question: 'How could you be sure it wouldn't fall?', his unequivocal answer was: 'you know it in your fingers and in your tools'.

Strati reports another significant example. He observed three men dismantling a roof:

> I was struck by the fact that as the three workmen dismantled the roof, they were in a literal sense removing the ground from beneath their feet. I was also struck by the speed at which they worked . . .What I still couldn't understand, though, was why they never slipped nor even put a foot wrong. [Later] I spoke to the stout man who seemed to be the leader and asked him: 'But how do you do it?' He laughed, the others joked and nudged each other. He stamped his feet and, as if he was speaking for all of them, told me that the secret lay in *feeling the roof* through your feet as if they were fastened to it.

(Strati, 1999: 89)

The two excerpts testify to a form of aesthetic understanding in which feeling, understanding and knowing are intermeshed.

Michael Polanyi described this form of expert knowing as 'personal' knowledge. His main target was the erroneous neopositivist idea that scientific knowledge results from the application of impersonal methods, and he made a case for expert knowing as a form of action which is not rule based, which does not exclude the body by eulogizing the mind, and which remains mostly unsayable; knowing, in other words, which is tacit (Polanyi, 1966). Strati (2003: 54) defines aesthetic knowledge as 'the form of knowledge that persons acquire by activating the specific capacities of their perceptive-sensorial faculties and aesthetic judgement in the day-to-day lives of organizations. The aesthetic dimension in organizations, that is to say, is not just aesthetic judgement; it does not solely concern what is beautiful, ugly, grotesque or kitsch. It is this as well, but it is also what the five senses of sight, hearing, smell, taste and touch make known. As the act of perceiving and judging sensorially, *aesthetics is that form of organizational knowledge which is personal.* Which once again brings to the fore the connection between aesthetic understanding and tacit knowledge'.

The aesthetics debated in organizational theories (Dean, Ottensmeyer and Ramirez, 1997; Gagliardi, 1996; Strati, 2003) concerns 'feeling the *pathos*' of an organization's material and non-material artefacts, perceiving an organization's beauty, appreciating the grandiosity of certain organizational practices, feeling disgust at certain courses of organizational action. People participate in organizational life on the basis of their individual capacities to see, hear, smell, taste, feel and judge aesthetically. It is this that differentiates among them, given that not everyone sees the same things, reacts to the same odours, or has the same taste: there are those who 'have an eye' for things while others do not; those who have an 'ear' or a 'nose', those who are 'good with their hands', 'have taste'. This is personal knowledge that is ineradicable and irreducible. Aesthetic understanding therefore constitutes a form of knowledge acquired through the senses and which is collectively negotiated and perpetuated, a knowledge which individuals are able to put into practice but are unable to describe in formalized terms. In commenting on his observations, Strati (1999) states that the sort of competences described by the workers (how to 'feel the roof', for example), must be learned by novices through the creative appropriation of the community's skills: how to climb a ladder; how to look up and never down and use one hand to grip while climbing; how to counteract the slope of a roof without bending; how to hold one's body as if leaning on the air between oneself and the roof. Practice is acquired as aesthetic knowledge from clues and 'sensory maps' arising out of sensory experiences, and it relies on ineffable and incommunicable subtleties (Gagliardi, 1990: 20). Gagliardi stresses the coexistence of *logos* and *pathos* in the understanding of organizational life. Nevertheless the meaning of 'ineffable and incommunicable subtleties' should not be taken as mystic knowledge only because is difficult to articulate in words. When Strati describes the workmen on the roof, he reports his observation as follows:

> What I observed was not slow and deliberate movements but:
> a) confidence in footwork and posture, and manual dexterity,
> b) speed, as if the roof had to be stripped as quickly as possible,
> c) the rhythm of the work set by the regular cadence of the pieces of roof crashing into the yard below,
> d) the focusing of attention on the task at hand,
> e) organizational communication made up of gesticulations and few words,
> f) the performance of several tasks, which required changing place on the roof as the work progressed, changing posture according to the operation to perform, moving across the roof to help a workmate.
>
> **(Strati, 2003: 59)**

What is difficult to articulate in words, both for the researcher who tries to describe it, and for the workman who tries to teach it to a novice, is the feeling of the game: what Bourdieu called 'le sens pratique'. I have argued that it is communicated with help of the knowledge pointers which give the clues for appropriating and keeping that knowledge in bodily schemata.

This special sense is described by Bourdieu (1980/90: 81–2) thus:

> A player who is involved and caught up in the game adjusts not to what he sees but to what he fore-sees, sees in advance in the directly perceived present; he passes the ball not to the spot where his team-mate is but to the spot he will reach a moment later, anticipating the anticipations of the others. He decides in terms of objective probabilities, that is, in response to an overall, instantaneous assessment of the whole set of his opponents and the whole set of his team-mates, seen not as they are but in their impending positions. And he does so 'on the spot,' 'in the twinkling of an eye,' 'in the heat of the moment,' that is, in conditions which exclude distance, perspective, detachment, and reflexion.

As noted, insofar as these skills can be practised but not fully described, they depend on social processes of interaction and participation in joint activities to be 'transferred' to the body and kept alive.

When learning is construed as participation in a practice, the body and the mind, the knower and the known, feelings and emotions, understanding and knowing are intermeshed. Nevertheless, a distinction can be drawn between aesthetics and emotionality, even if both yield knowledge on organizational life and involve the body. In fact aesthetic feelings relate not so much to the heart and the sentiments as to the senses and to physical perceptions. Seeing, hearing, feeling, tasting and smelling 'are actions which provoke emotions in both organizational actors and the researcher' (Strati, 2000a: 18). On the other hand, anger and bitterness, boredom, disappointment, fear, anxiety, joy, enthusiasm and passion are all emotions tied to ethical codes, rights and obligations, and values specific to collectivities which operate in organizational contexts (Sims, Fineman and Gabriel, 1993; Antonacopoulou and Gabriel, 2001).

Without entering into overly long discussion[7] of the meaning of 'tacit knowledge' I should note that the term 'tacit' has been used in three main ways:

- to convey the meaning of 'docta ignorantia', a form of knowledge which does not comprise knowledge of its principles;
- to denote what is tacit because it has become 'tacit-ed' and is just as taken for granted as, for example, knowing that it is dangerous to step on a nail;
- to denote what cannot be fully articulated in words but is grasped through bodily experience and the intelligence of feelings.

Aesthetic understanding refers to the second meaning of 'tacit', although the elaboration of an aesthetic professional code within a community concerns the elaboration of criteria for a normative appreciation of practices generally articulated in open debate on what makes one particular way of doing things better then another; and usually, when it is not contested, it becomes taken for granted.

The aesthetic approach emphasizes the corporeality of personal knowledge in organizational life. It shows that knowing cannot be confined to the sphere of cognition and the translation of all forms of knowledge into cognitive knowledge. On this rests the radical break with the dominant tradition of cognitive theory on organizational learning that aesthetic understanding entails.

3.5 Conversation in practice and conversation on practice

A practice is not only learnt with the hands, and through observation; it is also learnt through systematic discursive procedures. Accordingly, I now discuss the difference between talk in interaction – conversation *in* practice – and conversation *on* practice, that is, when the practice itself become the object of the talk.

Conversation *in* practice is a decisive factor in the circulation of knowledge. When instructions are given and followed, a collaborative action is performed which posits tasks of shared understanding as practical problems and brings out the relevant domain of ignorance to be remedied. In other words, on a building site where, for the sake of argument, reinforced concrete has never been used, there would be no need (nor opportunity) to learn how to distinguish among the various types of reinforcement, or to recognize the quality of a cast (does it need finishing? should it be 'vibrated'? has it been made too quickly?), the compactness of the cement, and so on. What the novice learns depends on the actual practices in which he may be involved and on the quality of his participation in them. Instructions and micro-explanations are dispensed absolutely at random, in the sense that they depend wholly on the situation at hand.

In other words, the statement 'you should always (emphatically) keep the delivery docket when a lorry leaves' is also a signal that the 'docket is important', to be committed to memory as 'try to remember to ask for the docket and keep it', as well as a warning that 'when a lorry delivers, make sure that you ask for and keep the docket, and that it is within reach when the bookkeeper asks you for it; otherwise you are committing a transgression and there will be consequences'.

Generalizing operators – 'always', 'never', 'generally'; 'you must', 'one must', 'you mustn't' – are much used in the transmission of practice. And they are often employed to transform events into 'memorable events', i.e. they are used at the same time to code events and transform them into knowledge objects, and to highlight their salience. They are therefore knowledge pointers which engender learning because in part they induce sedimentation in the memory and in part commit the hearer to remembering. They also signal 'accountability': that is, they mark a point at which things are expected to happen in a certain way and at which it is possible to make mistakes or blunder – a point, therefore, at which account must be given of one's actions.

Descriptions are often given without emphasis and without using knowledge pointers – that is, they are 'naturally' embedded in the discourse – and often simply because the expert by definition does not think them worth spelling out. Thus the expert calls an iron girder a '120 UNI IPE' (from the H-shaped cross-section of the girder (IPE) with a fixed ratio between the 'core' and the 'flanges'; UNI refers to the international standard classification). This helps the novice see not a girder but a girder with a specific cross-section, and it reveals a small world of differences among girders in terms of thickness, cross-section, composition and use. These micro-descriptions are capitalized within a system of codified knowledge objects and positioned within a hierarchy of saliences which are then used to abbreviate all subsequent actions and indexical references.

Since the relevance of accounts depends upon the developing course of the organizational occasions of their use, Garfinkel (1967: 3) writes that 'whenever a member is required to demonstrate that an account analyzes an actual situation, he (sic) invariably makes use of the practices of "et cetera", "unless" and "let it pass" to demonstrate the rationality of his achievements'.

The presence of the researcher alongside Gianni was at times an opportunity to make explicit in words what was implicated by an act of categorization or the indexical meaning of an expression. When the assistant site manager gave instructions to one of the workers when the researcher was present, he always altered his explanation or added to it so that he could be sure that both the novice and the researcher had understood, and at the same time so that he could display his competence as an instructor fulfilling his institutional duty.

Made explicit in the 'et cetera' is both the knowledge related to 'doing' and that related to 'being'. In the following interaction, witnessed by Gianni and the researcher, the assistant site manager intervenes in the work of a labourer, Luigi, a man of around 60, a pensioner, who worked on an hourly basis:

> A doorway was being knocked through one of the thick stone walls. Luigi was carefully breaking a last protruding stone, taking care not to hit it too hard and make too big a hole. The result was that he was banging too softly and achieving nothing. The assistant site manager intervened, somewhat pedantically, and explained to Luigi that 'if you want to be a builder . . . and not just a labourer . . . you must use this' (getting out his folding rule). He measured the opening already made and with an air of self-satisfaction declared that the problem did not exist because the protruding stone was clear of the aperture in any case.

Thus, using his hierarchical position, the assistant site manager 'gave a lesson' to Luigi and to the two novices present. Although the lesson was probably more useful to the two spectators than to the labourer, for all those concerned it was an occasion to learn not only the usefulness of an artefact but also the difference between being a builder or a labourer and its associated value system. When learning workplace practices, a novice also learns how to enact an identity, and this kind of knowledge is more often transmitted in indirect talk and idle conversations.

Moreover, when the assistant site manager assumed his role as instructor, he turned the practice into an object of discourse and inserted a distance between himself as 'knower' and the object of his knowledge. The practice was no longer a *practising* but rather the object of the discourse. While conversations *in* practice are structured by a specific grammar in which various subjects and points of view confront each other, conversation *on* practice constitutes a different discursive practice.

During observation in the field it was possible to overhear conversations on practical ways to solve problems, where observations were given and obtained, confirmation received and assessment made, as well as apparently purposeless conversations. Conversations prompted by problems – that is, ones initiated to deal with some form of difficulty – often took the form of collective debate in which there were those in favour and those against. Sides were taken according to norms that obliged the participants to express views according to their hierarchical position, or on the basis of their acknowledged professional competence, or again on the basis of their position in the informal group. These conversations were sometimes joined by 'dummy participants' – that is, by parties who were not actually present ('If the engineer were here, he'd say', 'If the USL[8] were here, it'd say'). The distinctive competence reinforced by these conversations was in part sustained by differentiation from the points of view of the others. During the debate, different options were considered in so far as they concerned both solving the problem and recasting it. The adversarial format always comprises the possibility that a solution will be found, as well as negotiation of the solution best suited to the circumstances. Participation revealed that conversations *on* practice were occasions to take one's measure with others and to self-reflect on one's own competences, both for those entitled to speak and for those only entitled to listen (the novices, for example, who had to keep quiet lest they make fools of themselves). For the latter, these conversations were useful occasions to gather 'hearsay', given that argument on practical matters often relies on stories.

Another type of conversation *on* practice witnessed during the ethnography was 'purposeless' conversation, which always had an important social function (by conversing one expresses respect or interest and creates social bonds) and often enriched the knowledge shared in the community of practitioners about practices in which some of them were not directly involved. For example, the bulk of the information gathered by the researcher on the aims, functions and norms of book-keeping derived – apart from the accounts directly furnished by various actors – from his overhearing of a 'time-killing' conversation between the architect and the accountant. During one visit, they conducted a dense dialogue lasting at least five minutes with apparently no other purpose than to agree on the importance of book-keeping, thereby confirming, at least in principle, the type of documentation and methods to be used for the rest of the project.

As in the other conversations, the enrichment derived both from comparison with other positions and from the consequences of the implicit self-dialogue. During their conversation, in fact, while the architect and the accountant exchanged impressions and opinions, they also celebrated the importance of their competences.

We may conclude that discursive practices are the medium for the conveyance of knowledge, both for what language does and for the social relationships that it constructs. As we have just seen, naming something 'knowledge' presupposes a coding practice within a domain of scrutiny and the practice of coding is a collective achievement of a naming subject, which in naming knowledge objects also names knower subjects.

3.6   Knowledge mediated by social relations, artefacts and norms

A good example of how learning is mediated by social relations is provided in Becker's article (1953–4) 'Becoming a marihuana user'. In contrast to traditional social psychology, which attributes a predisposition for drug use to individual traits, Becker explains the process of 'getting high on marihuana' as a group process and indicates workplace culture as the main interpretative factor. He finds that an interactional process is needed in order to become addicted: 'thus, the motivation or disposition to engage in the activity is built up in the course of learning to engage in it and does not antedate this learning process' (Becker, 1953–4: 235). The steps in this coaching process have been listed by Star (1996: 301) as follows: (a) learning to smoke the drug properly; (b) learning to connect bodily sensations with the use of the drug (learning to get high); (c) learning how to enjoy those sensations. Star comments on how both recognition and redefinition are part of the situation of learning and points out that the one cannot be extracted from the other. Each step involves a different kind of knowledge: smoking properly involves the development of a technical competence; learning to get high involves the social competence of trusting the social relation through which the specific know-how is transmitted; and learning to enjoy it requires the development of an aesthetic competence. In learning a trade these three competences must be mastered, and social relations are the medium through which they are acquired.

Quotidian life on the building site was, in fact, a resource which offered the occasions necessary for comprehension, and the redundancy necessary for certain attitudes to become habitual. The learning of workplace practices was mediated by numerous sources and occasions, but mainly by social relations and by the artefacts in use.

First, when a newcomer starts a new job, his/her learning is mediated through his/her relation with a reference figure. As one of our informants said:

> ... on all the building sites where I've worked I've always had a site foreman who I could ask how to do a job. He told me how to do it and I did it as he said.

For Gianni, like all his colleagues, the primary reference figure was the person doing the job for which they were preparing:

> I got my orders from the surveyor and from the owner. I was really under them. I won't say equally, but almost. And then there was another surveyor, an older man, I don't know, quite how old, about fifty, and he too ... but he ... more than anyone else I was looked after by this young surveyor enrolled on the professional register; let's say he's the firm's surveyor.

The importance of the quality of this relationship was acknowledged by many informants on the basis of their personal experience. To exemplify his statement that 'it's important that the workers, especially if young, should be stably placed alongside suitable persons', a site foreman told us the story of Lapo, which was a 'paradigmatic case' in the firm:

> Lapo had done his builder's course, and he started off well, working with me. But then he fell in love with the tricar, and today he drives, tomorrow he drives, he's spent six months only driving the tricar around the building sites. So his employment relationship has ... 'deteriorated'. [Then] he's worked on scattered sites, a week here, a week there, in contact with different people not always able to look after him, and he's turned into a layabout.

However, the site foreman defended Lapo against building-site gossip by asking to have Lapo assigned to his team, because they had previously worked well together. His comment: 'he's not a bad lad . . . he just needs guidance' expressed the conviction that a trade is learnt mainly through a relation with a mentor, not through participation in the activities of the community of practitioners.

It should be added that the assistant site manager was valued in the firm not only as an excellent builder and a trusted figure but also as an 'educator' of those who worked with him. In that community of practitioners there was social recognition of the importance of having a mentor in order to become an expert, and of reputation for competence in mentoring apprentices.

Observations in the field, however, showed that the resources with which to increase one's competence went well beyond the initial reference persons: learning was not traineeship alone. The assistant site manager once told Gianni:

> you should always try to learn from everyone, even a hod-carrier can teach you.

The primary sources of knowing are the relationships with the persons close by, those who do the same or a similar job in the same workplace. Yet occasions for the learning and sharing of practice do not necessarily reflect hierarchical relationships. In the workplace, when experience is recognized by those concerned, it takes priority in practice:

> It was raining. Work was going on inside the building. The timbers to sheathe the lift shaft had to be cut (to construct the wooden casement into which the cement was to be poured), but the bench-saw was outside the building. What was to be done? The site foreman and the assistant site manager were called. Everyone present took part in the conversation, and everyone had a solution to offer. Some were examined and then discarded: the crane couldn't be used, because that would mean removing the temporary roof covering; the saw was too large to pass through the door, and widening the aperture was too costly. A labourer came up with the answer: 'We can use the circular saw, I've seen it done before'. Hence who knew, led, and even if he was only a labourer, at that moment he was the source of knowing and had the power to say how things should be done.

This is a clear example of how hierarchy and competence are the two main organizing principles which shape power relations in the workplace according to the situation at hand, although those power relations are quickly restored as soon as the 'exceptional situation' is over. On this occasion Gianni saw that competence can become authoritativeness without a disruption of authority relations. With the relative positioning of each worker within a peer group known, their differences in terms of status, competences and distinctness are formed in a context of apparently irrelevant interactions. When we work we bring with us an ability to assess social relations developed outside work as a social practice of recognizing and celebrating social stratification; and once in the workplace we use this tacit knowledge, adapting it to workplace practices.

Finally, practice is learnt not only from direct relations with people present in the workplace, but also from sources in a wider professional community. For example, it is possible to learn, or simply to find out, new things from other operators, both colleagues and people engaged in similar activities, who perhaps unintentionally convey experience. When asked how news circulated in the building trade, one of the site foremen told us that:

> I find things out through the workmen . . . It's not that I go and ask, but a workman whose been on another site comes here to work and perhaps finds himself in difficulties . . . then we talk and he sees the difference in the way we work here . . . he sees that here we expect a type of work that elsewhere isn't expected.

Other figures, who by the nature of their work are constantly in contact with other practitioners, transmit and spread experience as well as technological innovation. As one of our informants noted:

> since the site foreman puts in the orders, he's in contact with the warehousemen, with those who've got the cement, the bricks, with those who have special stock, and so on. Sometimes you hear that a new material has arrived, a new resin which you mix with water. The word spread that there was a new product which worked well, so we got it.

The mechanism referred to is 'word of mouth', and the example gives the impression that the community of practitioners is embedded in a web of social relations which do not halt at the border of the specific construction site, and that the community is embedded in the industry and the local society. Thus, by word of mouth, people and artefacts are conveyed into the situated practices.

Practice, moreover, is mediated not only by the social relation with people but also by the artefacts used in practice. This applies to all the artefacts employed to perform work, not only those that embody an element of 'new knowledge' as technological innovation. Thus, occasions for learning are provided both by 'experimentation' – i.e. use in the field of a new fast-seal resin to fix planking with a new injection method – and by the use of a second-hand register. When the accountant had given Gianni a used notebook in which to record measurements, he did not fail to point out 'not only do you save money, but you've got examples'. The notebook was an old measurements register from another site with numerous unused pages. We may consider this an artefact of memory, one of the many memory artefacts used in workplaces to produce and articulate material representations. Their role in the preservation of procedural memory[9] has been highlighted by Cohen and Bacdayan (1994). Procedural memory is memory of how things are done, and it involves skills or routines such as behavioural routines, procedures, tools or programming, which assume material and textual forms.

To the extent that the acquisition of practical competence is based on the ability to use diverse and multiple resources, it is possible to view aspects usually neglected or apparently unrelated to learning as a 'source'. For example, crucial for safety is the knowledge conveyed by norms, especially as the source of attention rules. An elderly site foreman described this very well:

> . . . If it's something new you learn it from books. Once, all you needed . . . with the old system thirty years ago, there was no need to lay an earth [connection] tube . . . that's changed. Once there was one switchboard for the whole site, not today. Everything's separate, everything must have so much safety. Now one rod's not enough . . . you sink one every fifteen metres . . . [whereas] previously one was enough. These things the regulations tell you . . . now there are the new safety rules to study and apply, then on-site they are changed a bit. If there's an inspection, if something happens, then we're responsible, not the firm.

Norms are regarded as repositories of knowledge and not just as constraints. Scholastic knowledge of safety regulations is recognized as a valid source of information, and the novice is a human intermediary of institutionalized knowledge which reaches the field via the school. At the same time the obligation to abide by the rules and be accountable for infringements tacitly alters practice, because it shifts attention to aspects that would otherwise be neglected. It is not the repressive nature of the rules but their content of practice that makes the change, as suggested by the following extract from an interview with one of the site foremen:

... the rod ... you put that where there's an electrical bridge to make. You measure ten metres from the bridge. This is a rule because you're really close to the bridge, perhaps around the walls there's the problem of the tube, one thing or another. That's part of the risk, because around the walls there's always the risk of finding a tube, when you plant a rod. If there's a garden ten metres away, then you go into the garden, because there sure are no tubes there. This depends on the person doing the work because there's no rule that tells you. But there's a rule that tells you that every ten metres there must be a bridge, that yes. The distance from one bridge to another must be fifteen metres. This is what's said by the agency that sends the books. If it was up to us, I'd put a four-sided wire clamp on the bridge and make an arc, all hooked up.

The dynamic here is still an interaction between everyday practice and the abstract practice institutionalized in the norm. The norm is interpreted so that the prevailing practice is adhered to, but this practice is also modified, more or less imperceptibly.

3.7   How 'you learn nothing at school!'

The practitioners on the building site used this expression rather frequently. Even if they had not read Becker's article (1972), 'A school is a lousy place to learn anything', they seemed to share its thesis. But contrary to Becker they did not need arguments to support it: their statement 'You learn nothing at school!' has a strong pragmatic meaning which is now illustrated.

One of the main features that distinguishes the transmission of practice in the workplace and the methods used in traditional educational settings ('classrooms') is that in the former case the 'context' – that is, the lived situation – is used as a constitutive resource (Rogoff, 1995). This is even more evident in situations like building restoration where the non-standardizable nature of the object on which work is being carried out means that many activities are rooted in the context of the action. The difference between 'scholastic' and 'situated' knowledge emerges clearly from activities like measuring, as attested by the following example collected during the fieldwork.

'Gianni is very precise and meticulous. Which is certainly appreciated, especially in relation to the tasks assigned to him.' However, immersed as he was in his role as measurer, he was not flexible in rounding up or down, unlike the assistant site manager and the foreman. In fact, in very many situations there is a threshold of detail above which the advantages of precision are outweighed by the loss of precious time. In these cases the expert uses short cuts in his calculations and systematically rounds down – that is, to the benefit of the customer.

When measuring paint, Gianni used a gauge designed on the drawing board (in the office) and he stuck to it even when there were numerous short cuts that he could have used. In order to comply with the design, he measured walls and surfaces of the same size again and again; to follow the design he repeatedly added up and subtracted the same amounts.

In the example observed, shown in Figure 3.1, Gianni had to measure the surface area of a vault (b) with a small fillet at the sides (a) (c) and a small fascia in the middle of the vault, which was not to be included in the calculation (d). Gianni could have used two methods: one rapid and based on computational short cuts, the other more accurate but much more laborious.

Short method used by the assistant site manager: consider the whole of the arch as a single strip and then measure c, measure a, measure b, measure d (measurements that can be made without moving around the room), then calculate 2(a + b + c), add d and multiply by 1.57 (coefficient used to calculate the curved surfaces of the arches by considering them as semi-circles).

Long method used by Gianni: measure a, put down the tape measure, pick up paper and pencil and then perform the following operation: [a × 1.57]; pick up the tape measure again, then measure b and perform the following operation: [b × 1.57]; then measure c and perform the following operation: [c × 1.57], repeat for e, f and g; finally measure d and calculate [d × 1.57]. Finally, add up all the products.

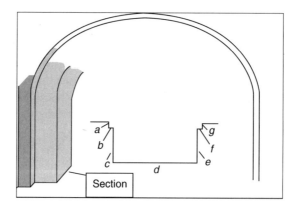

Figure 3.1 The area of a vault

The novice, conditioned by recent training to apply canonical scholastic patterns, used pre-packaged methods and logic even though there were obvious short cuts that he could have taken. He repeated calculations, he performed useless operations. The expert, by contrast, was able to identify local resources and use them to obtain satisfactory results with a marked saving of energy (or time, or money). Situated activity therefore uses existing conditions as resources to carry out an operation in the manner deemed most economical.

Conversely, the 'scholastic' mode was used, for example, by the novices fresh from their courses, who ignored the resources available in the specific situation and employed as their appropriacy criterion the one learnt at school, which required completeness, precision, adherence to formalized rules, and which facilitated explanation and justification of the steps taken. The strategy used to perform the task or action was thus decided *a priori*, or it was imported from the school and instilled in the situation, which in this case was reduced to the mere condition in which the formula or method was applied, and was therefore stripped of the opportunities that it offered.

However, it should be pointed out that the content learnt from school instruction was in fact utilized, although not always in the manner foreseen by the teachers.

First, the information learnt at school served as a template, as a linguistic background (knowing what you are talking about, what is happening). Gianni's vocational training course had provided him with a set of references, perhaps in the form of mere notions learnt or 'picked up' in a classroom, which served him as an initial stock of tacit references on which rapidly to build practical competence.

Secondly, the school served to expand the horizons of practice, as an extended form of talking-in-practice. As acutely pointed out by the director of the building school and other informants, those who receive explanations (which are ways of seeing what has already been done in a formal context) after they have learnt how to do things in practice, are illuminated and profoundly enriched. They acquire a sense of completeness and the sensation of a heightened capacity for abduction (extension of a particular case to other similar but not identical cases). Thus is confirmed by the following fragment from an interview:

> To set an arch, if you go to school in two minutes you can do it. Instead before you had to go off and look for . . . the section, the vein. Now you don't, with schooling you already know the system, and I've noted this with the old builders, old site foremen, and those who've been able to

attend school. I've seen this when doing vaults, how to set a vault, which now . . . those who do it by practice try to do the abutment and then the span, those who've been to school set it up differently.

The distance between the academic and situated modes of learning was clearly perceived by both novices and experts, who expressed themselves on the matter with such expressions as 'at school you learn nothing [about all this]'. The use of this utterance had a specific pragmatic meaning. It was not intended to devalue the school, but rather to encourage the novice to abandon the school experience and acquire confidence in the tricks of the trade and in so doing sustain the processual acquisition of expert identity. Short cuts were symbols of mastery and the utterance was a way to celebrate the community expertise.

In order to interpret the pragmatic meaning of the utterance 'You learn nothing at school' we must reflect on the relation between an expert's knowledge and a novice's. We know from the literature that experts differ from novices in task performance, in the amount of knowledge that they have and in the organization of this knowledge, but not in cognitive abilities. The main difference between the two rests on the fact that, unlike experts, novices are unable to link problem situations to principles, and that they use domain-independent knowledge rather than domain-specific knowledge. Therefore, in pragmatic terms, when the expert suggests short cuts and mocks academic knowledge, the action that he is performing should be read as an encouragement to the novice to leave a domain in which he has gained mastery and venture into a new one in which he is not yet expert, and to trust both the mentor and the community. In teaching short cuts and similar 'tricks of the trade', the practitioners are supporting the novice's effort to acquire a new identity, giving him trust and support only if and when the novice proves worthy of them.

Learning the trade means also developing one or more social identities. An occupational and an organizational social identity build upon individual identity, but they have highly significant social referents because individuals' definitions of their selves are based also on the group or other social categories to which they feel that they belong and on the situations in which they find themselves. The relationship between social identity and organizational learning is still largely unexplored, although we know that the social identities of organizational groups are 'vested in the systems and bodies of knowledge that they perceive they own. Their members attribute symbolic value to that knowledge and regard themselves as having a right to arbitrate over this value' (Child and Rodrigues, 2003: 540), but 'since the ways social identities and organizational learning interact are complex they have to be examined at different levels: individual, group, organization and network' (Child and Rodrigues, 2003: 553).

3.8 To sum up: becoming a practitioner

This ethnography – based on the shadowing of an apprentice – has provided an opportunity to describe some of the processes involved in the learning of safety practices.

We learned first that safety is not a separable form of knowledge. It is not something that is learnt as such. Novices learn to master safety because they are allowed to take part in a local culture of practice. Learning to become a competent member within a culture of practice is a process by which novices appropriate – within a context of unequal power relations – the 'seeing', 'doing' and 'saying' that sustain this practice. The process is not a passive act of 'being absorbed' but an active, reciprocal endeavour undertaken by both the novice and the community of practitioners with hegemony over the learning resources. If the fundamental tenets of the local culture of safety prove to be incompatible with those of the novice, the latter may interrupt the socialization process and leave. Quitting a less safe firm for a safer one may be a skill acquired in practice, as well as an indicator of a wider societal process of firm/worker matching.

Learning the trade involves becoming a competent member of a community of practitioners and mastering the appropriate material and discursive practices. This process has been described in terms of discursive practices activated by the community in order to shape the knowledge objects and the knowledge subjects within the domain of their occupational scrutiny:

- *Highlighting.* The objects of knowledge should be marked and made salient within a field of situated 'doing'. When socializing a novice, practitioners employ a series of 'knowledge pointers'. Novices learn first by watching, looking, seeing and listening to others as they carry out meaningful activities; in so doing they become able to understand and appropriate the knowledge pointers used by the community to code their activities. Language plays a fundamental role both by providing a 'scaffold' for the unfolding activities and by furnishing the elements that enable the novice to make sense of situations and contexts. Linguistic productions, such speech acts and narratives, enable the novice to learn how to see, listen and feel on appropriate occasions. Moreover, by attending to, and becoming part of, conversations during practice and about practice, novices discover the tacit map of the distribution of power/knowledge and learn who knows what, and who can be asked what in which circumstance. Not only does the novice acquire knowledge of what is said, s/he also comes to know through what is silenced, and what is silenced by whom and why. Suppressed discourses are discursive practices as well.

- *Shaping aesthetic feelings.* Occupational knowledge is acquired also at the sensory and aesthetic levels: 'knowing how' is inherently also 'feeling and sensing how'. The bodily abilities are developed by the individual, but the community elaborates and transmits the codes of appropriateness for a disciplined body and the criteria of aesthetic evaluation of work performance (the 'aesthetic' pleasure produced by a 'job well done'). Developing a sense of safety relies on ineffable subtleties derived mainly from repeated exposure to clues and sensory experiences provided by the unfolding activity, as well as on the linguistic productions which take place during the activity.

- *Talking in practice and talking about practice.* While people are 'doing', their talk is part and parcel of the ongoing activity and has mainly a performative character. When practice became the topic of discourse it occasions the possibility to make explicit some of the 'et cetera' of practical talk and thus renders them negotiable and open to scrutiny.

- *Weaving the texture between the social and the material.* Work is mediated by social relations and by material artefacts. Social relations such as that between mentor and mentee are deemed important for the transmission of craft knowledge. As this belief is 'practised', a model of training is supported while celebration is made of the community's identity and of the social bonds within it. Other mediations — through material artefacts and norms — are embodiments of processual memory.

- *Supporting the enactment of the new identity.* As the object of knowledge is shaped within a domain of 'doing' and 'knowing', the identity of the 'knower' is positioned by means of discursive practices. Mastering a domain of craft knowledge requires enactment of the identity associated with it, and the apprentice's acquisition of domain-specific knowledge in terms of 'tricks of the trade' is encouraged (or discouraged) by the other practitioners, who also help him to shed school experience and scholastic knowledge.

In conclusion, cultures, organizations and society are constantly reproduced in practices describable as practices-as-work (as regards the transformation of a given work process), practices-as-language (as regards professional language and interaction within a given work process), practices-as-aesthetic (as regards the perceptive faculties and aesthetic sensibilities used by individuals) and practices-as-morality (as regards the politics and power of the various groups or social classes involved in a given work process).

NOTES

1. A previous version of this chapter has appeared as Gherardi and Nicolini (2002a). The fieldwork was conducted by Davide Nicolini. The material in section 3.7. derives from the unpublished research report. The reasons for the choice of a young male researcher was both age (as we shall see later) and sex. A woman researcher on an Italian building site would probably have had a hard time of it given that women who actually work in construction have to cope with a highly male-dominated environment, as I have documented in a research project on organizational cultures in male-dominated professions (Gherardi and Poggio, 2003).

2. We wish to thank *Scuola Edile* for giving us access to the field, the firm where the ethnography was conducted, and all the people who gave up their time and energy to help us understand their world.

3. Shadowing is a methodology by which the researcher intrudes into an alien setting and uses the various difficulties and incidents provoked by this intrusion to study the setting itself (Bruni, 2004). In Sachs's (1993) view, shadowing is a set of methods used to gather data about 'on-the-ground' phenomena within predetermined periods of time. At whatever level of observation, it yields a combination of documentary data on how people engage in their everyday activities, individual and collective.

4. It was not always easy for the researcher to play the role of assistant to the novice (among other things, Gianni was very young – 23 years old, 10 years less than the researcher). The temptation to impose age-related differences, and also differing abilities to cope with situations, raised a constant risk of potentially damaging consequences for both Gianni's future and the results of the observation. This required constant self-control during the work which, at least in comparison with the experiences recounted by Gianni's co-trainees interviewed at the end of the training period, kept the level of disturbance introduced by the presence (in incognito) of the researcher to a low level. The quality and type of the relationship between the researcher and the trainee, the attitude towards them of the workers and owners of

the firm, the opportunities for learning and the tasks assigned, in fact, did not differ substantially from those of the other trainees.

5. Knorr–Cetina (2001: 181) characterizes objects of knowledge (epistemic objects) in terms of 'a lack in completeness of being'. Objects of knowledge have the capacity to unfold indefinitely.

6. Goodwin's discussion of professional vision is based on research conducted in a field school for young archaeologists and in a courtroom. He defines professional vision as 'socially organized ways of seeing and understanding events that are answerable to the distinctive interests of a particular social group' (Goodwin, 1994: 606) and he uses videotapes as his primary source of data to illustrate how the two professions learn and teach how to see. My use of the term 'professional vision' is broader since it includes both the physical act of seeing, and the outcome of a vision as a cultural practice.

7. For a short and clear review of the literature on tacit knowledge see Ambrosini and Bowman (2001) who summarize the main features of the concept. Tacit knowledge is taken-for-granted, action-based, context-specific, experience-based, difficult to express; it generates causal ambiguity; it can be both a benefit and a hindrance; it is awkward to research. Given the difficulty of using the term unambiguously, I shall avoid employing it as far as possible, and if I do so I shall explicate what its use signifies.

8. USL is the local Italian Health Agency.

9. Declarative memory correspond to Ryle's (1949) 'knowing that', and procedural knowledge corresponds to 'knowing how'. Declarative memory concerns facts, knowledge of concepts, individuals and events. Its knowledge can be reported and is not tied to the situation in which it can be used. Procedural memory is memory of actions, skills and operations; it refers to knowledge about how to do things (Stevenson, 1993: 26).

CHAPTER FOUR

Knowing in a Community of Practitioners

As far as the moral engagement goes, 'tasting' the world seems to offer a considerable advance on 'handling' it.

(Bauman, 1995: 125)

4.1   Community of practice or the practices of a community?

The concept of community of practice has been acritically introduced in previous chapters. It evokes the community of scholars that has formed around this concept and has had the great merit of innovating the study of organizational learning. While recognizing this merit, however, I want nevertheless to offer some reflections on how – in being used – the concept has changed. I propose to turn it upside down.

The scholars who first developed the concept had backgrounds in anthropology or in educational or social psychology. However difficult and ultimately restrictive disciplinary distinctions may be, it is important to locate the historical and disciplinary provenance of a concept in order to understand how it has been transformed by being transferred to different contexts, and also to bring criticisms against it which are constructive and not pointlessly iconoclastic.[1]

If we re-read the book by Lave and Wenger (1991) which first systematized the concept of community of practice, we find that the concept is based on the empirical study of five types of apprenticeship in crafts or craft-like forms of production. These are ethnographic studies of trades in contexts which were not always organizational, and not always in industrialized societies. Lave and Wenger examine apprenticeship learning among Yucatec midwives in Mexico, among Vai and Gola tailors in Liberia, in the work-learning settings of American navy quartermasters, among butchers in American supermarkets, and among 'non-drinking' alcoholics in Alcoholics Anonymous. They describe the trajectory by which a novice becomes an expert, with an interest in knowledge distinctive of ethnomethodological studies, and of symbolic interactionism and the concept of moral career. In fact, Lave and Wenger describe the learning process as social and situated participation, using the concept of 'legitimate peripheral participation' in settings where the technologies employed, the forms of recruitment, the relations between masters and apprentices and the organization of learning differ. They take little account of these differences, not because they are unaware of them or deliberately seek to conceal them, but because they are much more interested in the shared features that enable them to describe how new-comers actively utilize the work setting in their search for learning resources, and to discuss how identity and motivation are generated as newcomers move towards full participation.

The organizational dimension of learning is absent from their analy-sis because midwives, tailors and alcoholics anonymous participate in organizational practices which do not relate to formal organizations, and because the quartermasters and butchers were studied in their work practices from a pedagogical rather than an organizational point of view. And, in fact, the main theoretical contribution by Lave and Wenger's study, as synthesized in masterly fashion by William Hanks in his fore-word to the book, is its development of a social theory of learning which stands in opposition to the cognitive theory. The differences between the two theories are set out in Table 4.1.[2]

The term 'situated' provides the basis for claims concerning: (a) the relational character of knowledge and learning; (b) the negotiated char-acter of meaning, and (c) the concerned (engaged, dilemma-driven) nature of learning activity for the people involved (Lave and Wenger, 1991: 33).

Lave and Wenger view learning as situated but they assume a realist ontology of learning: although it is situated in social relations and not in the heads of individuals, they have no doubt that learning 'happens' even when asserting that 'agent, activity, and the world mutually consti-tute each other' (ibid. 33). Their concern is to distance themselves from a model of scholastic and cognitive learning in which persons receive a body of factual knowledge about the world, and to introduce a more active and more global conception of learning. But the fact remains that – as Stephen Fox (1997) stresses – their study is situated within a mod-ernist project. Consistent with a modernist project is the view of context as pre-given, although the effects of objective social structures are not determined but take shape within socio-economic relations. On the

Table 4.1 Learning in a cognitive and in a social perspective

Learning in a cognitive perspective	Learning in a social perspective
Question: what kinds of cognitive processes and conceptual structures are involved?	Question: what kinds of social engagements provide the proper context for learning?
Where? Learning takes place in the minds of individuals.	Where? Learning takes place in a participation framework.
Who? The individual learns.	Who? The community learns because learning is mediated by the differences of perspectives among co-participants.
How does reproduction of knowledge take place?	How does reproduction of knowledge take place?
Through doctrine and enactment of pre-given codes of action.	Through the maintenance of certain modes of co-participation in which the knowledge is embedded.
What is the role of language? Language is the medium of knowledge transmission.	What is the role of language? Language is a means of acting in the social world.
Learning is a way of knowing the world.	**Learning** is a way of being in the social world.

other hand, the concept of context as 'emergent' is more in keeping with a postmodernist project. 'In the postmodern view, "context" is no longer "out there" in the messy, complex surface of an objective world; rather, that very surface complexity and confusion are a projection of language itself, the inconsistencies of its classifications, taxonomies, dichotomies, and more' (Fox, 1997: 741).

Both Fox (1997), Fox and Grey (1999) and other authors like Contu (2000) and Contu and Willmott (2003) have pointed to an ambiguity in Lave and Wenger's work: the ambiguity between realist and constructionist assumptions, for example, with respect to consideration of the context as sometimes pre-given and sometimes emergent (Fox, 1997), or as a two-faced Janus (Contu, 2000) which contemplates both possibilities, and which shifts analysis to what Contu calls 'semiotics of practice'. This is discussed in more detail below; for the time being, I point out that Janus's 'realist' gaze becomes more explicit in the work of Wenger (1998, 2000), where he is concerned to show how a community of practice can be identified and consequently developed, while his 'constructivist' gaze merges with a practice-based approach (Gherardi,

2000a; Contu and Willmott, 2000). The difference can also be expressed as a question of emphasis, depending on whether use of the term 'community of practice' gives priority to the 'community' or to the activity comprised in the 'practice'.

In his book of 1998 – *Communities of Practice* – Etienne Wenger defines these communities as social units of learning even in the context of much larger systems forming constellations of interrelated communities of practice. However, the subtitle of the book – *Learning, meaning and identity* – shows that Wenger is most interested in the dimension of the community which comprises identity, belonging and boundaries. In a subsequent article entitled 'Communities of practice and social learning systems', Wenger (2000: 229) is even more explicit when he writes that communities of practice are the social containers of the competences that make up a social learning system. Three elements define competence:

- the sense of joint enterprise: to be competent is to understand the enterprise well enough to be able to contribute to it;
- mutuality: to be competent is to be able to engage with the community and to be trusted as a partner in these interactions;
- a shared repertoire of communal resources: language, routines, sensibilities, tools, stories, etc. To be competent is to have access to this repertoire and to be able to use it appropriately.

In a community of practice, knowing involves two components: the competence that the community has established over time, and the subjective experience of the world as a member.

Wenger distinguishes among different forms of participation according to three modes of belonging:

- engagement: doing things together – the way in which we engage with each other shapes our experience of who we are;
- imagination: constructing an image of ourselves, of our communities – these images of the world are essential for our sense of self and for our interpretation of our participation in the social world;
- alignment:[3] making sure that our local activities are sufficiently aligned with other processes so that they can be effective beyond our own engagement. Alignment has to do with coordinating perspectives, interpretations and actions.

Wenger gradually leaves behind the more anthropological task undertaken with Lave of describing participation as a means of learning. He now explores a declaredly prescriptive dimension which comprises a framework with which to identify what can be done in organizations in regard to communities of practice, boundary processes among communities and identities as shaped by participation in social learning systems. Moreover, the empirical base for his book of 1998 is more organizational. Indeed, the examples in the book refer to a community of claims processors working in an imaginary organization called 'Alinsu'. Wenger – together with two other authors associated with the Institute for Research on Learning – therefore reply in the affirmative to the question whether communities of practice can be subjected to an explicit organizational design and to managerial intervention. The management practices of constructing a community employ a discourse of 'community' as a rhetorical device to mobilize support for community building (Swan, Scarbrough, and Robertson, 2002).

Assumption of the concept of community of practice in management studies, and with applicative and prescriptive intent, is evident in Orr's (1996) empirical study – an organizational ethnography of the community of Xerox photocopier repair technicians – and even more so in the theoretical analyses of Brown and Duguid (1991) and Stucky (1995). If and how communities of practice constitute an organizational reality which traverses formal structures, and whether and how such communities are social learning systems, are still unresolved issues. But it becomes increasingly evident that communities are conceived as social objects or as collective subjects.

Exemplary in this regard is the article by Bobrow, Cheslow and Whalen (2002), in which the authors reflect from within the Xerox Palo Alto Research Center on the experience of the Eureka Project – which Orr studied – and the development of RAPPER, a model-based expert system designed to help repair technicians in the diagnosis of problems and the memorization of solutions invented *ad hoc*. Their story begins when the engineers charged with designing the expert system follow the technicians in the field and 'discover' the ways in which they share knowledge on how to deal with unusual problems not covered by the repair manuals. Practical knowledge is shared by means of informal communication – the 'war stories' recounted by the technicians when they meet in the canteen, for example – trust relations internally to the community, and all practices defined non-canonical. The authors make it clear from the outset that Xerox was interested in canonical practices, and not in those of the technicians, because it wanted to replace the 'expert' technicians with less skilled ones, given that the former were difficult to recruit and presumably cost more.

This first study in the United States directed the attention of the Xerox engineers to the importance of a spontaneous and voluntary social system (which, note, already existed before they set out to study it), and it furnished the entire community with knowledge produced by some of its members in the solution of problems. It was then followed by projects to transfer the model and the relative information technology to other areas. Thus born was the Columbus Project in France, which should have convinced Xerox's Worldwide Customer Services to extend the system to all the organization's technicians. Xerox in France was an average or low average service performer, but after the experiment it considerably improved, which prompted Xerox to introduce Eureka in Canada. Bobrow, Cheslow and Whalen conclude their article with discussion of the organizational barriers to change and how to remove them. Perhaps the most striking aspect of their discussion is its laconic comment on the difficulty of moving a new practice into an organization: 'the usual mechanism for diffusion of a program was really unsuited for the socio-technical nature of Eureka' (ibid. 27). I am certainly not the first to have emphasized that the managerial use of the concept of the community of practice underestimates the interweaving of power and knowledge, which Foucault (1977) described with such efficacy.

A similar concept – 'community of practitioners' – was used in the same years, but in the community of scholars who studied technology and innovation.

In determining how technological knowledge is transferred, one may consider the following quotation:

> The fraternity of mechanics who invented the machinery of the Industrial Revolution was a small cache of men, on the order of a few hundred, who over the course of about three hundred years (roughly 1600–1900) made the great mechanical improvements that preceded the electrical age.
>
> **(Wallace, 1982: xi)**

Historians of technology who study the ways in which practitioners develop and diffuse technological knowledge define technological change as a change in knowledge. They describe the group (or groups) responsible for generating new technology in terms of 'communities of practitioners' and hypothesize that revolutions occur in technology when a new technological paradigm and a new community of practitioners become dominant. When technology is studied as knowledge, knowledge diffusion and knowledge institutionalization (Laudan, 1984), then scholars become aware of how shifts in the practitioners' knowledge play a crucial role in knowledge development, and of how technological knowledge can easily be lost.

John Fitchen (1961) gives a fascinating account of his effort to reconstruct the methods used by medieval masons to construct vaults. In technological knowledge, he stresses, there are losses as well as gains, and technological knowledge frequently shifts, rather than expands, with the appearance of new technologies.

Historians, for instance Edwin Layton (1974), or sociologists like Barry Barnes (1982), have helped promote studies of technology as systematic knowledge of the useful arts and sciences and as an activity related to other forms of human activity. This interest has prompted questions about the social structure that sustains practitioners in their development of new knowledge, or in transmitting already codified knowledge through canonical practices.

Illuminating insights are afforded to those interested in the relationship between social structures and practical knowledge by the literature on technology as knowledge. Scholars like Ferguson (1977) and Laudan (1984) who have set out to define the unique character of technological knowledge from a cognitive point of view stress that technology differs from science in that it is a highly visual activity, and that technologists are not inclined to verbalize. Since scholars in the traditional scientific disciplines are ill-equipped for analysis of knowledge expressed in visual form, the myth has spread that technological knowledge is quintessentially tacit.

I prefer to reformulate this observation, putting it not in the terms of a property intrinsic to technology and to those who study and develop it, but in those of the practical knowledge transmitted with the support of a social relation that teaches novices to look, and the knowledge of what to look at and where. Such knowledge is comprised both in verbal communication and in aesthetic understanding, and it is transmitted within a community of practitioners. I shall show that the social relations which tie a community of practitioners together constitute the locus of technology as knowledge. Although Edward Constant (1984, 1989) did not emphasize social relations as the vectors and custodians of technological knowledge when he coined the term 'community of practitioners' as the central locus of technological cognition, he nevertheless declared that:

> All technological practice is dominated by well-defined communities of practitioners which are tautological with equally well-defined, well-winnowed traditions of technological practice.
>
> *(Constant II, 1984: 28–9)*

Community and tradition are the *loci* of technological knowledge. In Constant's view, the concept of technological community 'applies equally well to a handful of identifiable corporate entities or to some aggregation of properly acculturated individuals' (ibid. 30).

I prefer to relate the concept of community of practice to that of community of practitioners, and my reason for citing Constant's work is that he has shown extremely clearly that a practice and the tradition of a practice do not respect organizational boundaries but instead traverse several organizations. Constant aptly points out that a car is a car, and that there are many more conceptual and technical similarities between a Honda and an Oldsmobile than there are differences. The technological knowledge of how to make a car (or a computer or a toothpaste) is comprised in practice, while the identities of Honda (of IBM or of Colgate) are comprised in their corporate logos, not to mention the differences between Japanese and European or American cars, i.e. those which Thomas Hughes (1983) has called 'distinctive national styles in technological practice'. Constant (1989: 232) singles out the locus of technological knowledge as the community of practitioners, with its associated professional societies and educational programmes, while the locus of technology as function is embodied in and mediated by organization and knowledge. Function, community and organization are the building blocks of the 'culture of technology' at the institutional level.

These authors on the sociology or history of technology describe the interplay among the social relations which sustain knowledge within a community of practitioners, the culture of technology which crosses organizational boundaries, organizational cultures and society at large. Cultures are not only values, assumptions, beliefs or behaviours; they also have a material base consisting of tactile, functional but also symbolic artefacts (Gagliardi, 1990).

I argue that it is practice, with its materiality, its technological knowledge and its transorganizational character, that organizes a community. I maintain that practice 'performs' the community (Gherardi and Nicolini, 2002) in order to emphasize that the terms of the causal relation have been reversed: it is not the community as the acting subject that somehow precedes the action and has ontological primacy over it; rather, it is the process of doing, the course of action, which aggregates an incipient community in a process of reciprocal definition. A community does not exist before the practice that brings it into being as a community of practice, nor does a practice exist outside or prior to its 'performativity' (Law, 1999).

In what follows I shall stress that in various disciplinary fields (educational anthropology, social studies of technology and management), the concept of community of practice (or of practitioners) denotes slightly different things and serves divergent knowledge-gathering interests.

In social studies of technology, the term 'community of practitioners' is used to focus on the community as the locus of technology as knowledge, and to discuss: (i) the relationship between science and technology, rejecting the definition of the latter as the applicative appendix to the former; and (ii) the industry-wide creation and diffusion of technical knowledge. Thus recognized is the independence of community from organization. The intent of these studies is not to be prescriptive, but rather to describe how the development of technical knowledge in communities is determined by the form taken by the presentation and solution of problems, and by the construction of artefacts which incorporate the new knowledge. The role of power is recognized not only among human actors and organizations but also among non-human entities: indeed, the title of a well-known article asks 'Do artifacts have politics?' (Winner, 1985, to which the rejoinder by another article is 'Do politics have artifacts?' (Joerges, 1999).

Among ethnographic studies (educational, sociological or anthropological) interest in communities of practice concentrates on the social processes by which knowledge is transmitted from experts to novices and on the mobilization of the learning resources present in work settings (i.e. where working, learning and innovating are co-present but neither the experts nor the novices are aware of it). Reflection on the structuring of power within the community is not entirely lacking, but these studies tend to be concerned more with the social processes by which values, behaviours and goals are shared, conflicts are resolved and social structures are protected against change. The intent − in these studies − is to found the subjectivity of a collective social subject, where the term 'social' is used mainly in contrast to the term 'individual'. Cognitive studies on learning assume that the individual is the knowing subject. According to these studies, it is the community that learns, and the individual learns insofar as s/he belongs to the community and becomes a competent member of it. In other words, learning in a community of practice is a process of active socialization which changes both the person and the community.

Finally, scholars in management studies who use the concept of community of practice mainly concern themselves with empirical investigation of communities and with problems of knowledge management at the level of both organizational structures and technologies to support knowledge work, and also with industrial relations, although this term does not belong in the explicit vocabulary of these studies – rather, the issue of power and conflict is avoided or concealed by the 'performative intent' (Lyotard, 1984). This latter is the expression which Lyotard uses to denote the intent to develop and celebrate the knowledge which contributes to the production of maximum output for minimum input. It involves inscribing knowledge within an instrumental frame of means-ends calculation.

The foregoing explanation of the pedigree of the concept of community of practice now allows me to make some of my methodological choices explicit, as regards both research design and theoretical analysis. I believe that locating the concept solely in the managerial literature, accusing authors of reifying it and/or of obscuring power relationships, is to throw the baby out with the bath water, so to speak. Yet it is only intellectually honest to recognize the historical importance of the contribution of the concept of community of practice to development of a situated learning theory as an alternative to dominant cognitive perspectives on learning and as a forerunner of the practice-based theorizing of knowing and learning in organizations.

Consequently, I prefer to use the term community of practitioners instead of 'community of practice' with a shift of emphasis which highlights the concept of 'practice' rather than 'community' so that I can argue that the community is an effect, a performance, realized through the discursive practices of its members. In this chapter, after presenting a view of the community of practice as the locus of technical knowledge, as knowledge mediated by social relations, and as an instance of reflexivity, I shall propose the concept of the 'situated curriculum'.

I now return[4] to the description of the building site as a community of practitioners in order to show how technical knowledge is constituted as a domain of transferable knowledge, how the novice proceeds through this 'programme' according to his/her ability to seize learning opportunities, and how technical knowledge and social knowledge are indistinguishable. Learning how to do and learning how to be are part of the same social process, and a community of practitioners can be read as the enactment of a locus not only of identity, belonging and engagement but also of socio-technological knowledge. Therefore in the next section I shall understand the link between learning a practice and learning as a practice, situated in a web of other working practices and in a nexus of politico-economic relationships and institutions.

4.2 The situated curriculum

The notion of 'situated curriculum' derives from the related concept of 'learning curriculum' introduced by Lave and Wenger (1991) in contrast with the 'teaching curriculum'. When they investigated the kinds of activities in which the Vai and Gola tailor novices were involved, they found that both the order of the garments produced, and the segments of work that they performed, served as a general curriculum for apprentices. Tailors' apprentices first learn to make hats and drawers, informal and intimate garments for children: progressively they move backward through the production process to cutting jobs and:

> under these circumstances, the initial 'circumferential' perspective absorbed in partial, peripheral, apparently trivial activities – running errands, delivering messages, apparently trivial activities – takes on a new significance: it provides a first approximation to an armature of the structure of the community of practice.
>
> *(Lave and Wenger, 1991: 96)*

Generalizing from various studies on apprenticeship, Lave and Wenger suggest that every community has a 'learning curriculum' which consists of a field of learning resources and opportunities situated in everyday practice as viewed from the perspective of the learners. The learning curriculum is characteristic of the specific community and it cannot be considered in isolation, nor can it be analysed separately from the social relations that shape 'legitimate peripheral participation' in that community. It is important to stress – as Contu and Willmott (2003: 285) do – that this notion directs attention to the power-invested process of bestowing a degree of legitimacy upon novices, since power relations enable or impede and deny access to learning resources and learning practices. As Lave and Wenger (1991: 42) write:

> Hegemony over resources for learning and alienation from full participation are inherent in the shaping of the legitimacy and peripherality of participation in its historical realizations.

Hence, the social space in which a community is embedded already contains the institutionalized power relations for its reproduction in terms of unequal access to resources. Some novices will find their possibilities truncated while others are enabled as they move along their learning trajectories.

Lave and Wenger use the notion of 'learning curriculum' in antithesis to that of teaching curriculum. Their purpose is to emphasize the

contrast between two different ways of conceiving the process of learning: one based on legitimate engagement in actual activities and on co-
participation with other members of the community; the other based
on mediation through an instructor's participation and relying on an
external view of what 'knowing' is about. Aside from their argumenta-
tion, however, the terminological difference underscores (beyond the
authors' own intentions) the fact that learning also takes place through
basic and technical instruction in the anticipatory socialization phase.
'Anticipatory socialization' has been defined as the phase comprising
socialization to work prior to actual encounter with the organization
(Porter, Lawler and Hackman, 1975; Van Maanen and Schein, 1979;
Depolo, 1988).

   Accordingly, the learning curriculum includes all the learning opportunities offered to individuals pursuing the same occupation in their
work careers. These opportunities include the teaching curriculum
during the schooling phase, the situated curriculum of the community
(or communities) to which they belong during their occupational
careers, and all the other formal and informal occasions of learning
offered in the day-to-day lives of organizations.

   In order to address the specific aspect of the organizational access
related to the learning opportunities offered in the process of engagement, I introduce the concept of 'situated curriculum' to denote the
pattern of learning opportunities available to newcomers in their
encounter with a specific community within a specific organization.
While the learning curriculum focuses on learning opportunities related
to a specific occupation, the notion of the situated curriculum emphasizes the fact that its content is closely related to the specific set of local
material, economic, symbolic and social characteristics of the field of
practices and work activities.

   Thus, whereas the notion of legitimate peripheral participation suggests that gaining acceptance in a community of practice entails entering a domain of activities and relations with a distinctively constituted
order, access to this ordered world of relations and activities takes place
in a context of unequal distribution of learning resources, and it is always
marked by some recognizable pattern of power/knowledge combination. Characteristic of entry into the new social setting is the fact that
individuals are often given a specific set of assignments and activities
which enable them to participate in the ongoing social interaction and
to learn while they become competent members of that specific social
context. It is this ordered set of activities and tasks that I term the 'situated curriculum'.

The status of legitimated participant granted to novices is thus associated with a 'situated curriculum', a set of activities governing the process of becoming a member. Every community shapes the specific trajectory of activities that the novice must learn in order to become a full member, but it is not a rational plan; nor in craftwork is it the outcome of a formal agreement. It is better described as a set of situated opportunities offered to newcomers in a more or less defined order, dependent both on those who have hegemony on the learning resources and on the novice's capacity to recognize the opportunities when they are granted. Although it is possible for an external observer to describe a general set of activities and tasks characterizing the process of admission into the community, the situated curriculum is more the variable outcome of ongoing workplace practices, social interactions and power relations than an invariant precondition of thought, action and learning: a situated curriculum is embedded in the working practices of a community and it cannot be considered apart from those practices.

Taken together, the concept of situated curriculum and that of legitimate peripheral participation aid understanding of both the socialization of newcomers and the reproduction of the community itself. Through its acceptance and cultivation of novices the community of practitioners reproduces itself by perpetuating and transforming the specific modes of acting and co-participation that define it.

A general feature of the situated curriculum is its tacit nature. The situated curriculum is embedded in the general habits and traditions of the community, and it is sustained and tacitly transmitted from experts to novices, but while it is reproduced elements of change are introduced. Social reproduction is not a mechanical process of photocopying; it is more similar to physiological reproduction which retains elements of similarity while introducing diversity. Our ability to recognize a practice – like 'doing a seminar' – derives from the fact that even when the context changes (local academic habits) or a contingency occurs (the technology does not work), we continue to see the pattern in the activities done. The situated curriculum is one of the ways in which new knowledge, both cultural and material, is institutionalized in the community of practice. As such, it is one of the most important mechanisms of organizational learning.

A further general characteristic of the situated curriculum is its increasing economic impact. This is associated with legitimate peripheral participation: at the beginning of their paths, novices experience fewer demands on their time, effort and responsibility; their tasks are shorter and simpler, the costs of their potential errors are small, and they are usually held minimally responsible for the results of the activity as a whole. However, as their learning process proceeds, more advanced novices are given more challenging tasks with greater economic impact. These tasks provide them with an unstated opportunity to demonstrate their preparedness and skills.

4.3   Gaining access to a situated curriculum

The fieldwork on the construction site suggested that the attribution of tasks to the novice(s) followed a well-defined and established pattern. This finding was confirmed by the fact that all those working on the site, as well as other people in the construction industry, apparently considered the assignments to be entirely acceptable and reasonable. The researcher then compared the tasks assigned to the apprentice during the observation period against those given to other novice construction site managers undergoing training in other companies (Gherardi, Nicolini and Odella, 1998). This comparison revealed a regular pattern in the order in which the tasks were assigned. This pattern was then cross-checked among the novices, and completed on the basis of other field data and a small number of specially designed interviews administered to individuals occupying different roles in the occupational community.

The regular pattern emerging from the research indicates that, in order to become a site manager, and in order to win the acceptance and confidence of the significant others in the industry (bricklayers, subcontractors, engineers, etc.), a novice must be able to perform successfully, to show proficiency and to become progressively independent in the execution of a certain number of specific work practices. These activities and tasks, summarized in column 1 of Table 4.2, are assigned to him during different phases of his apprenticeship. They constitute the general contents of the situated curriculum of the community of practice of construction site managers, a general theme recognizable throughout the whole community. Column 2 indicates the learning content of the various tasks, while column 3 describes the competences that novices start to develop as they perform the activities described.

It should be noted that what I have termed 'task' is the result of the community of practitioners' coding process, which categorizes a domain of practical knowledge into individual practices and in so doing constructs a vocabulary for talking *on* practice and *in* practice.

Assignation of the tasks listed in column 1 of Table 4.2 begins with the activities in the first group at the top of the table and proceeds

Table 4.2 The situated curriculum of the construction site manager

The tasks of the apprentice construction site managers The order of assignments proceeds from top to bottom according to an increasing level of responsibility; blocks indicate set of activities assigned at different levels of experience	Task-related learning	Legitimate peripheral participation: competences that novices start to develop through these activities
Taking care of the daily report on tasks completed.	Gaining an overview of the general work flow.	Becoming a good apprentice; behaving like an insider; gaining legitimization as a peripheral participant; knowing the company, its history and who the relevant actors are.
Keeping track of employees' work hours (to be notified to the central administration). Helping to measure work completed for reporting purposes. Measuring and reporting all work completed.	Recognizing, interpreting the clues that the experts use in their day-to-day practice (tacit knowledge); appreciating the economic dimension of any decision, action and mistake; using the language, the jargon and learning the ropes of how to behave as an insider; learning the basic routines of accounting; grasping the basic issues related to the management and control of personnel.	

Table 4.2 *Continued*

The tasks of the apprentice construction site managers The order of assignments proceeds from top to bottom according to an increasing level of responsibility; blocks indicate set of activities assigned at different levels of experience	Task-related learning	Legitimate peripheral participation: competences that novices start to develop through these activities
Ordering the necessary supplies of building material and technical equipment.	Understanding the relation between work flow and supplies; appreciating the role of artefacts in daily practice; building a map of different sources of provision, information and innovation in the industry negotiating and establishing durable trust ties	Gaining recognition as a good learner (showing readiness and busyness); establishing positive formal/informal relations with other members of the community and of the organization; acting as a representative for the company; establishing and maintaining business relations.
Managing the flow of supplies, managing the providers' network, including negotiating for prices and keeping track of technical innovations.		
Planning the job process (what comes next and when).	Gaining a systemic perception of the work site; acquiring responsibility for the work flow; understanding and coping with task interdependence; recognizing and estimating the constraints in the specific work context; translating constraints into working time and into economic figures.	Gaining recognition as a manager; negotiating with the workforce and with other parts of the company; collaborating with other professionals; motivating and controlling workers; designing and supporting coordination of activities.

Estimating the time and the work hours necessary to complete a job. Making estimates.	Recognizing the logical order of the work flow; coordinating the complex web of tasks, people and external constraints; facing the problems of managing people and competences.	Managing business relations with subcontractors; learning the ropes about personnel legislation and regulation.
Assigning tasks to teams and individuals.		
Establishing the composition of work teams.		
Negotiating prices, costs and planning changes in course of the process.	Negotiating with customers; managing business relations; acquiring a profit-oriented perspective; taking care of the entrepreneurial aspect of work (acquiring and retaining customers, providing customer satisfaction, dealing with complaints, etc.).	Adopting an entrepreneurial perspective; gaining respectability outside the company among competitors as well as establishing contacts in different administration offices; developing a network of relations with actual and potential customers; looking around for better jobs.
Managing the billing process (which includes negotiating the value of the work included in the reports).		
Negotiating with subcontractors.		
Managing customers and customer satisfaction, looking for new contracts.		

downwards. The logic underlying this situated curriculum is therefore fundamentally linear and incremental: the different blocks of activities are assigned according to a criterion of increasing responsibility in relation to the preparedness of the novice, thereby minimizing the economic impact of potential mistakes. The apprenticeship of the construction site manager requires that the novice must learn to perform all the activities specified, with some exceptions as regards those in the last block, as discussed below.

The first two blocks of activities from the top are assigned at the very beginning of the work career of the construction site manager, and in close sequence. According to our informants, they give novices a broad overview of both operations on the site and of the different aspects of the job. Thus the situated curriculum of the construction manager does not follow the ordering of everyday practice. In order to provide the necessary peripherality, activities are learned in sequences different from those that production usually follows. Construction site manager apprentices do not start by negotiating the overall budget for the work, or by planning the workplace set-up, or by deciding the composition of work teams and the division of labour – three activities that constitute the preliminary operations of any construction project. In fact, as Table 4.2 shows, their first assignments are usually reporting activities and the management of supplies, i.e., the final stages in the production process. Each step provides an unstated opportunity to recognize and appreciate the contribution made by previous activities to the present one. Column 3 of Table 4.2 also shows that, at the beginning of their work socialization, novices not only have to acquire technical competences regarding the job, they must also learn how to perform their new role of legitimate peripheral participants, developing all the strategies necessary to fit in with the specific social characteristics of the new work context. They have to gain legitimation.

The following two blocks of activities are assigned at a later stage in the socialization of the novice. As emphasized by many of our informants, the order here is relatively fixed: the novice site manager must show proficiency in directing the technical aspects of the work flow before starting to manage the workforce. The reason for this is the fact that new assignments are set in such a way that both the economic impact of potential mistakes and the risk of their hampering the work of other employees are minimized. In the construction industry most technical mistakes are usually easy to detect, given that the operations are limited in number, and they are often repeated. As an informant put it:

you always start from the floor and if the novice does something wrong, there'll be enough time for his supervisor to discuss the matter and correct a possible mistake; you always start under the supervision of a senior site manager.

By contrast, putting the wrong work team to work results in an immediate economic loss; as the same informant put it:

at the end of the day, when you finally realize that you have chosen the wrong people for that specific job, it is too late to make up for the mistake.

The unfolding situated curriculum is also characterized by several progressive and regressive moves: that is, it proceeds in a forward-and-backward mode (Lave, 1988). Two learning phases apply to each of the new tasks performed by novices: the 'way-in', a period of observation of the operations performed by a senior site manager, and the 'actual doing', in which apprentices start to take responsibility for some or all the tasks, even though they may be more skilled at some than at others. Whereas in the observation phase the novices are provided with strong support (scaffolding) by seniors, this support is progressively reduced as the quantity of their output increases, and as they gain confidence and are able to win the trust of the senior workers. Authors refer to this style of guidance as 'scaffolding' (Wood, Bruner and Ross, 1976) in evident analogy with construction industry vocabulary.

Yet, whenever the newcomer moves to a new and different activity or set of activities, the pattern is repeated and the scaffolding is provided again. Accordingly, the path followed by the novice is not a linear and progressive movement towards a higher level of autonomy and expertise. It is better understood as a shuttling back and forth between areas of autonomy and dependency that can last for a long time.

The final block of activities is assigned very late in the novice's career, when the new site manger is recognized as an expert and a reliable member of the organization. This last block is in a sense 'additional', because the assignments are closely dependent on the specific organization and management culture of the company (level of decentralization and empowerment, division of labour), and they become dependent on the quality of the individual site manager (so that good new site managers will be given a chance to perform some of these activities, while others will not).

The chronological ordering of the sets of tasks is not as strict as the use of a table might suggest. Indeed, the pattern is not rigid, but is related to the opportunities offered by the specific activity. The nature of the situated activity may alter any orderly pattern, producing innumerable variations on an original theme and rendering the progression apparently chaotic and ambiguous. It may happen that the novice starts his career on a site where the same tasks are performed for months and months (e.g., restoring all the facades of a castle, a job that may take up to two years); as a consequence, the apprentice will be asked to repeat some of the tasks of the first groups again and again.

The specific character of the curriculum of construction site managers may become clearer if it is compared with another example described in the literature.

The curriculum of the Vai and Gola tailor's apprentices studied by Lave and Wenger (1991) differed in that it followed two seemingly opposite logical paths at the same time. In its overall design, the tailors' curriculum moved from the general back to the particular: the production stages were reversed, and the apprentices began by learning garment finishing first, and then proceeded to the earlier, more critical operations involved in producing a garment, such as cutting the material. At the same time, however, within each phase of the production, the novices operated according to the opposite logic; they started by performing the simplest and less critical tasks, and then moved to the most complex and central ones.

While the Vai and Gola apprentices followed a 'holistic' path, so that they first obtained an overview of the job as a whole and then returned to its individual parts, the situated curriculum of the quartermasters studied by Hutchins (1993) followed an opposite, more instruction-like, step-by-step path which gave them full knowledge of the entire spectrum of navigation practice. As a result of their work socialization, they achieved a general perception of all aspects of the job, not a background introduction.

As I have shown, the novice construction site managers seemed to follow a different pattern, one somewhere in between the previous two. They started with activities that gave them an overview of the different aspects of the production process, and they then returned to specific tasks, being assigned integrative functions only later in the course of their careers.

The quartermasters' curriculum differed from the other two also in terms of the individual versus team nature of the work, and the specific distribution of expertise among the various members of the team. Although both tailors and construction site managers work with others, their occupation is fundamentally an individual one. By contrast, quartermasters work as a team, and their performance is based on specific processes of collective cognition. In this case, in order to guarantee a high level of reliability and minimize the chance of misunderstanding, all members must be able to perform all the tasks of those on whom their own operations depend. The step-by-step linear curriculum provides the system with enough redundancy to prevent errors that might jeopardize the safety of everyone.

We learn from authors writing within 'activity theory' that analysing work as culturally mediated activity means questioning the social intelligibilities of mindful practices (Engestrom and Middleton, 1996; Star, 1996) and accepting a view of 'expertise as ongoing collaborative and discursive construction of tasks, solutions, visions, breakdowns, and innovations' (Engestrom and Middleton, 1996: 4).

4.4   How power relations shape opportunities to learn

The specific characteristics of a situated curriculum relate to specific aspects of the work practice in the industry as well as in the organization.

In the first place, the nature of the industry, which consists to an overwhelming degree of very small firms with only a handful of workers, restricts the possibility of developing a rigid internal division of labour and specialization, so that site managers are required to be 'all-rounders'. The situated curriculum provides them with the necessary know-how: novices start with activities that give them an appreciation of the different aspects of the production process, and then they revert to specific tasks.

The specific work-related lines of communication and the limits on observation deriving from the spatial setting of the activities of others have consequences for the learning process and for the structuring of the situated curriculum. This is particularly important for the site manager, who performs the supervisory role. On-site work operations are conducted in distinct and separate settings, so that the site manager must develop a particular form of expertise based on the capacity to 'see in practice', that is, recognize the quality of individual jobs and their relations to the whole. Accordingly, the tasks assigned at the beginning of the apprenticeship process require a great deal of mobility within and without the site: measuring, reporting and managing the supply of stocks all require ceaseless travel on and between sites. By contrast, later assignments, namely those of the third block in Table 4.2, require advanced novices to follow longer segments of operations on the same site in order to obtain a deeper understanding of the technical nuances of the construction process. Finally, whenever a novice has acquired a substantial level of background knowledge, he may be asked to supervise numerous sites at the same time, a task that requires him to draw on the reservoir of clues and relevancies accumulated in the course of his apprenticeship.

The time framework of the work practice has also a significant impact on how learning opportunities are structured: it may take years for a building to be restored or finished. If the site manager curriculum required the apprentice first to acquire thorough understanding and appreciation of the completed work, the period during which he was kept idle would be too long to be economically viable.

Situated curricula differ in the contextual and relational factors that combine to shape situated curricula as actually experienced by novices. At this level, therefore, contextual constraints and individual discretion interact to shape organizationally and individually situated paths of socialization. The difference can be described in relation to: (a) the individual's skill in appropriating knowledge; (b) the quality of social relation with co-workers; (c) the economic context.

At the level of individuals, the situated curriculum is influenced by the style and strategies adopted in their process of participatory appropriation (Rogoff, 1995). Participatory appropriation is the process by which individuals transform their understanding of, and responsibility for, activities through their own participation. The notion is thus used in contrast to the term 'internalization' employed by the cognitive approach to learning and cognition, which suggests some form of transfer of knowledge. Novices play an active part in their learning process and differ in their ability to see and in their willingness to seize learning opportunities. The mentors offer no further opportunities when they judge that the previous one has not been taken up or fulfilled properly. In other words, the individual novice may or may not actively seek out learning opportunities and thus shapes his own situated curriculum. The individual's active role in the learning process was most clearly expressed by an informant in our fieldwork: an elderly and expert construction site manager who claimed that the fundamental distinction between a good and a bad novice is the 'effort applied to stealing workmanship with the eyes'.

At the level of social relations within the community of practitioners the situated curriculum is shaped by patterns of interpersonal engagement and by arrangements between co-workers. The ways in which interpersonal relations structure situations, facilitate or limit access to activities, artefacts and social relations profoundly affect the individual situated curriculum. Novices start their careers with the support of a reference figure. The first steps in the community are taken under the supervision of a senior worker, who may simply be the person most willing to 'waste' time explaining to the newcomer things taken for granted by experienced workers. The pattern of relation and communication between the two is crucial. We noted that whenever the site manager realized that we were paying attention to his conversation with a colleague he would modify his rhetorical style: he would switch from a strictly coded mode of conversation to a more open one. In a way, he was explicitly translating a message that he would otherwise have left implicit because it could be taken for granted. Other informants, however, used communication styles which were much less conducive to learning, ranging from the very common 'authoritarian style', where no effort was made to help the novices learn from what they did, saw or heard, to a less popular 'neglectful style' whereby the novices were largely forgotten and left at the margins of ongoing practices. Accordingly, different styles and arrangements in the social relationships between the novice and senior figures shape which events and situations counted as learning opportunities.

At the same time, the importance of power relations for the development of a novice derives from the fact that socialization into a community of practitioners involves more than dyads. Novices relate to a number of other actors besides their 'mentors': senior apprentices, expert workers and other occupational figures operating in connection with the community of practices, all constitute potential learning opportunities for the novice. The arrangements between these people and the novices, together with complex interpersonal involvements among them, define the segments of activity and social interaction to which the novice gains access, and they therefore shape the horizon of learning opportunities.

For instance, once the novice has gained sufficient 'experience', he may start to learn from interaction not only with but also between experts. The novice starts to draw lessons from the stories and anecdotes told in his presence, or he may 'steal' professional tricks and techniques by watching others doing something in a certain manner, without further explanation being necessary. As novices accumulate a sufficient stock of background knowledge, they can also begin to learn from other members of the community doing different jobs in the same professional field. For example, apprentice site managers are able to learn aspects of their work from bricklayers, architects, machine operators and technicians. Individuals related in other ways to the activity of the community become sources of learning. In our case, dealers, commercial representatives and officials all provided the novices with opportunities to learn specific aspects of practice.

However, the process of gaining membership is by no means an invariably easy and pleasant experience for a novice. Social relations in the workplace include not only coordination, support and friendship, but also rivalry, conflict between generations, jealousy and competition among peers. In our fieldwork we found that one of the most conspicuous factors interfering with legitimate peripheral participation, one which systematically limited the span of the situated curriculum, was the seniors' jealous custodianship of their expertise. They were loath to relinquish the influence associated with their hard-won expertise.

Finally, the distinctive task environment also shaped the field of learning opportunities for the novice. It impacted on the novice's career insofar as his supply of learning opportunities was shaped, and very often made convoluted, by the need to follow two different logics of action at same time, namely the 'logic of learning' and the 'logic of giving a real contribution' ('because we pay your salary'). The exigencies of production may shape the individual curriculum so that some areas of expertise are ruled out for the novice. For instance, we observed a case in which the novice was asked to take over the management of supplies on his arrival. He performed the same task (together with a few others) over and over again, to the point that it became his overriding preoccupation throughout the training period. This was going to affect his possibility of learning other aspects of practice. Contrary to what happens in a formal instructional setting, in the workplace the subversion of order is of little immediate consequence: while theory has to be taught sequentially, practice can be learned in many different patterns according to the nature of the opportunities offered by the actual situation. However, bearing in mind that an expert construction site manager is respected especially for his breadth of experience, limitations on the range of an individual's situated curriculum may have repercussions on his career.

The use of different technological artefacts also modifies the range of learning opportunities available both at the general level of the community – as already discussed – and at the local level. Some tools are 'open' to the novices in the sense that their purpose is obvious from their appearance; while others are not. Using charts to plan the work, or paper and pencil to log jobs on a construction site, teaches an apprentice more about what is to be done than watching someone doing the same task or inputting data on a computer keyboard. In our research, for example, building plan charts were posted on every available surface in the site manager's office, providing easy and open reference during his discussions with employees; in similar fashion, an old register was handed to the novice so that he could use it as both scrap paper and as an example of how to file the daily report on tasks completed. Had the company used an automated report system, in which the records of some operations might have been lost, the artefact would have provided fewer learning opportunities.

4.5   Practising, teaching and talking about them

For the members of a community of practice, what I have called the 'situated curriculum' amounts to nothing more than one of the many taken-for-granted aspects of daily workplace activity. Once socialization to work has produced its effects and newcomers have moved on from the role of peripheral participants to the status of fully legitimate members of the community, the learning they have acquired, together with its patterns and implicit complex logic, becomes part of their tacit knowledge. Such knowledge is not retained in the form of any sort of cognitive structure or plan of action, and it is best understood as a custom or 'habitus' sustained collectively by the community.

One consequence of acquiring some form of knowledge, skill or competence by being socialized into a 'habitus' is that it renders this background invisible to the people who live in it and sustain it. This happens to the situated curriculum as well: the path of learning opportunities unreflexively followed during the period of legitimate peripheral participation is cancelled once the former novice becomes an insider. The situated curriculum thus remains tacit. As a result, uncovering the situated curriculum becomes a problem in that the experts who have undergone the learning experience are unable to translate it back into a communicable form. When asked to describe the situated curriculum, experts are forced to use communication modes alien to that of their practice, so that their accounts are usually unsatisfactory.

This is well exemplified by the results of our attempt to substantiate our findings by returning to the field to test our understanding of the situated curriculum. After uncovering the situated curriculum through participant observation in a community, we contacted one of the site managers observed in action and asked him to outline a 'practical' cur-

Table 4.3   The curriculum suggested by the expert site manager

---

Knowledge of available building materials and technologies.
Building construction methods and techniques.
Practical legislation on construction (mandatory paperwork, role of the
   various bureaucratic agencies, responsibilities and legal consequences of
   mistakes and failures to comply with regulations and norms).
Organization and management of construction sites/safety techniques and
   legislation.

---

riculum which would help a novice to become a site manager. In
response, he declared that 'he would teach' the items listed in Table 4.3.

The expert provided a meagre list of only four items which referred
generically to technical competences (knowledge of available materials
and building techniques), legal and bureaucratic information and knowledge about logistics and safety procedures. The site manager's response
is nonetheless of interest, for several reasons.

In the first place it leaves out many of the 'things to learn' shown in
column 1 of Table 4.2, which are very much part of his everyday practice. Indeed, he even failed to indicate the tasks that he had assigned his
apprentice to do for months. Secondly, he uses an abstract language, and
a disciplinary organization of topics, so that his 'curriculum' resembles
more an impoverished version of a teaching curriculum than an account
of the rich and varied learning opportunities observed in the field.

This aspect is put into relief if the current official teaching curriculum used on the course for assistant construction site managers is compared with the previous two. It appears that the site manager's proposed
programme comes closer to the teaching curriculum than to the situated one, although he had never been involved in teaching or training,
nor had the teacher ever received training.

Table 4.4 shows the headings, culled from official documents and
public reports (Cantiere Scuola, 1995), of the curriculum followed at
building school by the novices observed during our research. The list is
very broad and complete and covers a number of topics ranging from
the most basic and general (how to read and draft a construction project,
construction and diagnostic methods for building and restoration, construction and environmental planning), to the most specific (environmental analysis, hydraulic systems construction and methods, landscaping
techniques, computer-supported mapping techniques). The list also
makes some references to construction and safety standards and regula-

Table 4.4   The teaching curriculum

Headings of the teaching curriculum used in the SME construction site
manager training course

Introduction to personal computer and computer graphics techniques
Building methods and techniques
Diagnostic methods for building restoration
Environmental analysis and map reading
Computer-supported mapping techniques
Restoration theory and techniques
How to read and draft a construction project
Construction and environmental planning
Installation planning methods and legislation
Hydraulic systems: construction and methods
Landscape design and maintenance
Construction-related norms and legislation
Organization and management of construction sites/safety techniques and
   legislation

tions, which are of fundamental importance in the work of construction site managers.

   I would stress that both the teaching curriculum and the one suggested by the site manager embody a perspective on learning which is
substantially different from that of the situated curriculum. The content
of Table 4.4 fits the traditional definition of curriculum as the systematic description of the teaching activities planned for a specific and
limited period of time and understood as a well-defined system comprising several sectors aimed at the teaching, accomplishing and optimal
assessment of a study course (Frey, 1977). Its implicit logic is based on
the notion of a linear, ordered, consequential and complete path, while
the learning contents are articulated according to a strict disciplinary
tradition. The instructional curriculum starts from what we have called
a cognitive perspective on learning, and it reflects the conventional
wisdom that the curriculum is a form of teaching plan (ISFOL, 1992).
By contrast, the situated curricula described above exhibits an erratic,
context-dependent, redundant, event-based and largely non-linear
sequence, where, what to do, how to do it (and how to do it skilfully)
are taught on an experiential basis, and, as described in Chapter 3, the
novice 'learns the ropes' of the trade by imitation and contact with the
practitioners.

The difference between the situated and the teaching curriculum can be also be framed in terms of Bernstein's (1975) distinction between invisible and visible pedagogy.

Bernstein introduced the idea of invisible pedagogy in order to describe situations in which learning takes place within a weak framework and with weak forms of classification. He suggests that an invisible pedagogy is characterized by the fact that control over the pupil is implicit; that the 'teacher' arranges the context, which the learner is supposed to rearrange and structure; that the learner regulates his/her own movements and social relationships; that there is a reduced emphasis on the transmission and acquisition of specific skills; and that the criteria for evaluation are multiple and diffused. The main difference between a visible and an invisible pedagogy resides in the fact that while the first emphasizes states of knowledge and solutions to received problems, the latter emphasizes ways of knowing, and the activity of problem setting and construction. Accordingly, in a visible pedagogy the learning progress can be evaluated by explicit criteria, while the main criterion of evaluation in an invisible pedagogy is busyness and readiness to perform new, more challenging activities. In a visible pedagogy, learning is solitary and structured into fixed time sequences; by contrast, an invisible pedagogy is based essentially on processes of tacit learning rooted in doing by imitation and social interaction with a variable and flexible time structure. In the case of invisible pedagogy the organization of space and the setting have little significance, whereas they are of fundamental importance for a visible pedagogy, where visibility is fundamental for both the learner and the teacher. It should be pointed out, however, that an invisible pedagogy still provides a strong form of social control, one all the more powerful because it is not based on formalized rules but vested in the process of interpersonal communication. We may state that learning in the workplace takes place within a community of practitioners according to an invisible pedagogy, as opposed to training activities based on a more visible pedagogy.

The community of practitioners is thus strongly regulated by power patterns of social order that are also effectively perpetuated because they are implicit and invisible, not only to the novices but also to the experts. The fact that these patterns are 'absorbed' through socialization limits occasions to dispute the principle on which they are based.

When asked to 'abstract', i.e., to summarize his everyday practice in formal terms, the site manager failed to give an account of his scaffolding efforts. Instead, he reverted to a scholastic logic, using an impoverished version of the logic that he apparently thought appropriate for the researcher. Consequently, he unintentionally applied the scholastic class-room model of learning and the related conceptual categories that he had absorbed tacitly when he went to school. As other authors have noted, the school should not be thought of as a special place where people can acquire formal, universal and easily transferable knowledge; it is better conceived as one of the specific contexts of daily activities in which they learn specific practices deeply rooted in that specific context (Becker, 1972; Resnick, 1987). In the classroom, we mainly learn to become full and proficient participants in the school community, learn-ing how to solve academic problems and do tests, acquiring the appro-priate language and style of thought, and doing all the right things in order to become 'expert' pupils.

When asked to become 'a teacher' (this seems to be how the site manager interpreted the researcher's request to explain or describe the situated curriculum of his community), he re-enacted his own experi-ence as a pupil, and used the classroom logic he had absorbed at school. In doing so, however, he ventured into a different professional commu-nity, the community of training specialists, where he was obviously not an expert. In fact, professional trainers form a community of practition-ers in its own right, operating with similar mechanisms, although it is one based on practices different from those of the jobs for which they provide training. Training experts follow rules, they use language and concepts, and they adhere to values and validity criteria specific to their own community. The site manager, unable to describe the situated cur-riculum otherwise, adopted a logic different from, and incommensurate with, the one used in his own work context. He consequently failed to convey the richness of his own practice, which could not be captured by the schooling framework. Nor was he able to provide an account in a 'foreign' language – one that he could handle at the same level as the professional training specialists who had devised the curriculum used for the novices' training course.

The concept of situated curriculum may be of interest to all those working at the boundary between the instructional and the working environments. The notion of the situated curriculum and the reported difficulties in bringing it to the surface emphasize the limits of the process by which knowledge is institutionalized and transferred among different communities of practitioners. Any form of general knowledge is the result of some process of abstraction of the practices of a specific situated context of activities in which knowledge is embedded. The process of generalization and of abstraction constitutes a form of trans-lation that, like all translations, transforms, modifies and mutilates the object of the translation. There is a price to pay for institutionalizing knowledge through abstraction and generalization. Instructional agents learn to work in the awareness that in any learning endeavour there will be a component of idiosyncratic knowledge that cannot be transferred to other contexts, and, at the same time, they are delegated to legitimate the participation of the novices on behalf of the community of practitioners.

4.6   To sum up: the incorporated 'known' and the enacted 'knowing'

While in the previous chapter I gave priority to description of procedural knowledge, of 'knowing how', in this chapter I have concentrated on declarative knowledge, on 'knowing what'. My intention has been to show how the recursive process by which what is 'known' and embodied in the members, artefacts and discourses of a community of practitioners becomes knowing 'enacted' in the performance of practical activities and an learning opportunity for those novices able to take it.

I began the chapter with a historical reconstruction of the concept of 'community of practice', both to distance it from its origin in managerialese and to acknowledge an intellectual debt to the situated learning theory which opened the way for a practice-based approach. I criticized the idea that it is the community which constitutes the collective learning subject, and consequently argued that the expression 'community of practitioners' should be used, thereby shifting the emphasis to practices, and to how working practices are collectively performed to produce material as well as epistemic objects and social relations. Practices tie the activities of practitioners together and generate the set of communitarian, not institutional, social bonds that I call 'community' and which do not exist prior to the practices themselves.

Practitioners establish a discursive body of practice – so-called 'technical vocabulary' – which distinguishes and classifies the activities that they undertake (they employ a coding process similar to the one used by researchers) and the expertise inherent in them. The ethnographic analysis began with observation of activities and the recording of their vocabulary in order to reconstruct the tasks over which a novice should gain mastery to gain acceptance as an expert. I use 'should' to emphasize that the process is not linear, but rather an encounter between opportunities to learn and the subjective capacity to identify and seize such opportunities.

On a theoretical level, the situated nature of the curriculum reveals that knowledge is relational and that learning is based on forms of involvement and participatory appropriation. Accordingly, the situated curriculum enables novices to become competent members in the way defined by the specific organizational setting, connecting them with the historical dynamics of that setting. By performing the tasks set out in the situated curriculum the novice learns not only the specific skills of the occupation, but also its criteria of accountability, the specific set of values sustained by the community, and the situated pattern of power relations, together with the proper strategies to cope with them.

I would emphasize the paradox whereby the expert performs his/her role as mentor according to a progression of relatively well-defined tasks (which are common to the occupation) but is not explicitly aware of it. We may consequently conclude that the situated curriculum is a body of tacit knowledge in that the expert knows more than s/he is able to explicate. This finding also shows clearly that teaching is a practice that takes place in a field of other practices – working – and to perform it, expert and novice must activate and co-produce bodies of knowledge in some way already codified, and enact them in relation to the situation and the relationship between them. Setting all these elements in relation with each other resembles the activity of building a nest, which when completed, is a tangle difficult to unravel.

Taken together, Chapters 3 and 4 enable us to reflect more generally on the meaning of 'situated knowledge' and on the multiple uses made of the expression. 'Situated' has a multiplicity of meanings, all of which are present when we consider the knowing process as embedded with the performance of a working practice:

• Situated in the body. The materiality of the knowing subject is primarily anchored in the body; and a body is sexed. The feminist critique of science and feminist work in the sociology of science and technology have helped to show that even 'universal' knowledge is situated, while feminist objectivity simply means bodily-situated knowledge (Fujimura, Star and Gerson, 1987; Harding, 1986; Mol, 1999). The advantage of a 'partial perspective' – the term coined by Donna Haraway (1991a) and taken up by Marilyn Strathern (1991) – is that knowledge always has to do with circumscribed domains, not with transcendence and the subject/object dichotomy. Moreover, the material body – the body that works – assumes shape and location within the set of practices that constitute the work setting. The knowledge acquired via the five senses is aesthetic, not mental. It often forms the basis for specific competences. Craft trades require trained bodies – ones, that is, which have incorporated an expertise or a connoisseurship (Turner, 1988). It is through the body that 'an eye' (or 'a ear' or 'a nose') for something is acquired, so that aesthetic knowledge (Strati, 1999) also comprises the ability to develop a professional 'vision' in the broad sense.

- Situated in the dynamics of interactions. Knowing in practice articulates the emergent – *in situ* – nature of knowledge from interactions. The situation of an action can be defined as the set of resources available to convey the meaning of one's own actions and to interpret those of others (Suchman, 1987).

- Situated in language. This specification highlights that all expressions change their meanings according to the subject uttering them and according to the context of use. The situation, therefore, not only defines the circumstances of an action, it also produces them through language. I prefer to talk of 'discursive practices', rather than communication or language, in order to emphasize that talking is doing, and to shift attention from the subject that talks and his/her communicative intent to the fact that situated talking practices have a form of their own (*qua* 'practices') and relative independence from the subjects that perform them.

- Situated in a physical context. Space is not an empty container for situations, nor is it a passive receptacle for the organized activities of actors-in-situation. On the contrary, subjects actively engage with space and establish relations with it. An organized space – a workplace – is a 'situational territory' (Goffman, 1971b; Suchman, 1996) in which objects remind subjects of what they must do, prevent humans from doing things that may harm them, guide action according to intentions inscribed in their design, and make work and life comfortable, both materially and socially. Because the materiality of situations enters into relations, objects can be conceived as materializations of knowledge, as tangible knowledge which 'steers' and sustains a set of practices.

NOTES

1. One of the main criticisms made of the concept of community of practice is that the term 'community' evokes ideas of social cohesion, harmony and sharing as the absence of conflict, especially in American culture. In European sociology of Weberian derivation the term 'community' carries the connotation of consensus, but it principally evokes the idea of a dialec-

tic between community and society, between movement and institution. When we talk of 'sharing' we should bear in mind its two meanings of common access and division into parts, conceiving it in terms of Hatch's (1997: 205) apt definition as 'doing something separately together'. A culture is shared when everyone participates in it and endorses its general models, but this does not signify that everyone's contributions and experiences are the same. When talking of culture a set of meanings, interpretations, values, systems of shared beliefs or knowledge, therefore, it must always be remembered that this definition is based on both commonality and difference.

2. The table is based on Hanks's introduction and follows its line of reasoning. However, I alone am responsible for the final schematization.
3. Note that the term 'alignment' used by Wenger does not explicitly relate to actor network theory. It refers not so much to coordination in classic organizational terms as to a subjective 'tune' or harmonization.
4. A previous version of this chapter has appeared as Gherardi, Nicolini and Odella (1998).

CHAPTER FIVE

Knowing across Communities

*It is by organizing experience that we transform
experience into power.*
(Mary Parker Follet, 1942: 258)

Shadowing a novice – Gianni – enabled us to shed light on the working
practices of a community of manual workers. As we followed Gianni's
learning trajectory, we found that learning-as-practice situated within a
set of working practices consists in establishing the appropriate connections among what is known, the actions that are in the process of being
realized, the vocabulary appropriate to those actions and the social relations which sustain activity-directed saying and doing. We now leave our
novice and turn our attention to what happens at the boundaries
between one community of practitioners and another. It should be
borne in mind that several communities of practitioners (builders,
plumbers, carpenters, engineers, project managers and others besides)
interact on a building site, and it is from – and within – their interde-
pendencies that workplace safety arises. Our ethnographic observations
convinced us that the relations between one community and another
are of particular importance. We noted that in the course of certain
interactions, people behave not as single individuals but as members of
a community and speak on its behalf. We, as others before us (Clegg,
1975), noted the existence of a plurality of discourses which competed
with each other to define what safety is and to gain hegemony over it.
Intrigued by this verbal contest, we asked ourselves how several communities could cooperate in practical activity while clashing over the
reasons, modes and goals of the cooperation itself. Understanding and
joint action require a certain consensus of views, but what is the
minimum level of consensus for cooperation to be possible, and how is
it achieved?

We came to the conclusion that the harmonization of several communities within a constellation resembles more the production of dis-

sonances than accord on a canon (Gherardi and Nicolini, 2002). This musical metaphor[1] conveys the image of positioning one's voice while listening to others without necessarily joining them. In fact dissonance is a combination of discordant tones producing a harsh effect; it is also a note which in combination with others produces this effect. By contrast a canon is a musical composition in which the different voices take up the same melody one after another, at either the same or a different pitch, in strict imitation. If the discourse among communities were to produce music, it would not be harmonious, nor would it resemble Bach's *Golden Canon*.

How do the continuities and discontinuities among communities of practices help or hinder the circulation of knowledge?

The most accredited answers in the literature describe this process in terms of negotiated order (Strauss, 1978), the negotiation of meanings (Wenger, 1998), alignment effects (Law, 1994; Suchman, 2000), or processes of collective sense making (Weick, 1995). These replies emphasize the consensual and prevalently harmonious aspect of the process and, in my view, they more appropriately describe the production of knowledge within a single community. But they underestimate the discontinuity among interconnected practices, and they fail to describe how knowledge remains isolated and not communicated from one community to another.

I shall argue that conversation among communities is a specific discursive practice whose aim is not only to reach understanding and/or produce collective action but also to foster learning by comparison against the perspectives of all the co-participants in a practice. It requires examination of the harmonies and dissonances that may coexist within the common performance. Groups of people who work together for a period of time create a discursive community that produces a situated discursive identity which enables them to compare different perspectives but also makes them realize that they may remain isolated, juxtaposed, non-communicating, and even in conflict. In such exchanges boundaries between the communities may or may not shift, or be traversed. Learning may be just as much about how to negotiate current relationships as about changing them.

The focus in this chapter will be on discursive practices among communities of practitioners where they involve explaining why accidents happen or how to prevent them, or how to attribute responsibility for them. The concept of 'discursive community' (Vaux, 1999) is used to convey the idea that, in a constellation of interconnected practices, the boundaries of the speaking community, the character of the audience and the identity of the object under discussion – safety in our case – are all, in principle, open to negotiation.

The idea of several communities of practitioners forming a discursive community presupposes, not that a unified object or a shared set of values or beliefs exists, but that the identity of the community is maintained through the negotiated performance of community, where each community maintains its own voice while listening to that of the other, and where communication is both negotiated order and disorder. The first question to be answered, therefore, is whether each single community studied had a single voice.

In order to obtain an answer, we drew up a simple research design: an analysis of the causal accounts of different communities to the same two questions. Why do accidents happen? How can they be prevented?

5.1   Practices of accountability

In everyday organizational life, it is not 'problematic' that members recognize, demonstrate and make observable to each other the rational character of their actual practices. The 'non-problematic' is a practical achievement and a situated 'doing' which perform accountability through the mobilization of appropriate accounts. The main focus of ethnomethodology is on the procedures whereby members make a setting 'account-able', i.e. 'available to members as situated practices of looking-and-telling' (Garfinkel, 1967: 1).

For ethnomethodology, the relation between activities and accounting practices is reflexive. That is to say, it considers the description of social activities to be an integral part of the activities described. In this light I analysed how diverse practitioners, engaged in interdependent actions, produce reasonable explanations of the causes of accidents. Garfinkel (1967: 7) writes:

> practical circumstances and practical actions refer for them (members) to many organizationally important and serious matters: to resources, aims, excuses, opportunities, tasks, and of course to grounds for arguing or foretelling the adequacy of procedures and of the findings they yield.

It is in this way, through practices of accountability, that people show to each other that they belong to the same moral community (Fele, 2002) and maintain an ordered, banal and normal set of beliefs and motives.

Collective beliefs are part of the culture of practice on the one hand, and an explanation of that culture on the other. Beliefs are a form of discourse on organizational referents: they predefine a semantic space in which facts and accounts are interchangeably mixed. This applies in particular to accounts concerning events that the organization views as problematic: namely accidents. The gravity of accidents is of little importance in this case, since both serious disasters and minor workplace accidents violate the social order (Leplat, 1982). Their occurrence signals a problem within the organization, and they both directly involve and indirectly question its management.

The causal accounts that explain, justify or criticize accidents are therefore an important source of information on the belief systems and models of organizational behaviour underlying the safety culture of a particular work setting. The mutual accounts of different communities of practitioners, in explanation, justification or criticism of accidents, are a discursive practice which makes the organizational phenomena 'accountable' to oneself and to others. Causal accounts predefine a semantic space in which facts (what happened) and beliefs (why it happened and the meanings of what happened) are interchangeably mixed (Antaki, 1985) and made accountable to the speaker as well as to the listener (Antaki and Fielding, 1981). One may therefore suggest that the diversity of interpretations among communities of practitioners stems not only from their positioning within the organizational hierarchy but also from the different logics and conceptual frames that they use to handle problems.

Two distinct and functionally complementary (in terms of skills and hierarchical position) occupational groups share responsibility for safety on a building site: the engineers and the site managers. The assumption, therefore, was that the similarities and differences between the two groups' conception and management of safety would have a direct bearing on the safety measures adopted in the workplace.

The accounts of workplace accidents were collected by means of interviews[2] conducted with the members of the two communities (five engineers and five site managers employed in the same firm). The interviewees were asked for their opinions concerning the causes of accidents and actual or potential measures for their prevention. In order to focus on the various aspects of the safety cultures of the two communities, the interview transcripts were analysed using the following two methodologies:

1. An analysis of causal explanations couched in ordinary language. The interviewees' explanations of workplace accidents were analysed in detail using Antaki's (1985) technique, and for each of them a causal scheme was plotted.[3] These diagrams provided a visual representation of the reasoning followed by the interviewee in

explaining the accident: that is, they summarized their explanation and its content. Direct comparison was made between the structural values of the explanations furnished by the two groups and then three different models of causal reasoning were identified. The hypothesis that they were used differently by the two communities of practice was tested by comparing rhetorical style, underlying causal logic and content.

2. A semiotic study of organizational discourse, in particular semiotic analysis by semantic groupings (Manning, 1987; Feldman, 1995). Accordingly, a taxonomy of the principal meanings attached to the concept of safety was extracted from the interview transcripts. These meanings were grouped according to their contents and relations, giving rise to two semantic schemes (one for safety and one for prevention) for each community of practitioners.

Analysis of the explanations suggested that the causal schemes plotted from the interview transcripts belonged to three ideal-typical models of causal explanation: a linear model, a co-occurrence model and a ramified or factorial model (Figure 5.1).

Starting with the same set of possible causes of an event, the linear model took the form of a sequential chain of causes; the co-occurrence model assumed the synchronous action of several causes; and the ramified model explained the event in terms of a single factor (or latent cause) which encapsulated other antecedent causes.

These causal reasoning models were based on different cognitive styles. The first model reconstructed the causal sequence that was

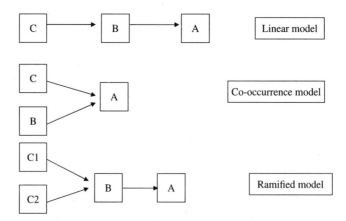

Figure 5.1   Three causal explanation models

chronologically most logical, determined and founded on explicit rationality (e.g. the probability of events, their plausibility). The co-occurrence model, by contrast, combined causal situations which differed despite their reciprocal relations. The ramified model distinguished between two components of the causal dynamic: the direct component of the event (expressed by the relation between the latent cause and the eventual outcome) and the antecedent component (the specific causes that constituted the latent cause).

Preliminary analysis suggested the existence of a relationship between community membership and use of one of the various accident explanation models. This relationship was corroborated by qualitative analysis, and it was also tested quantitatively using a statistical data-processing program which performed calculations on a limited number of observations (StatXact, 1992). The tests were selected according to the indications set out in Siegel and Castellan (1988). Specifically, it showed that level of schooling (in this case coincident with community membership) was a crucial variable in determining preference for a particular explanatory scheme. In fact, the ramified model was associated with membership of the community of the engineers;[4] the co-occurrence model was associated with membership of the occupational community of the site managers,[5] and the linear model was not significantly associated with either of the two communities of practitioners.

Joint use of these two methodologies brought out two principal features of the causal accounts offered by the two communities of practice. First, it revealed the 'causal theories' of accidents specific to the two safety cultures; that is, the assumptions which underpinned both cognitive models of behaviour (Schank and Abelson, 1977) and decisional models (Tversky and Kahneman, 1974). Second, it highlighted the presence of different conceptions of safety and different types of commitment to accident prevention in the cultures of the two groups. The following two sections briefly outline the interpretative perspective from which the engineers and site managers observed reality and discursively constructed their safety cultures.

The engineers explain

The explanations of accidents furnished by the occupational community of engineers drew on a causal reasoning model which, although linear and logical, was also rather inflexible and uniform (see Figure 5.2).

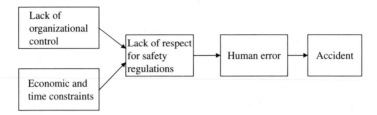

Figure 5.2   The engineers' explanation – plotting of a causal scheme

The engineers tended to conceptualize problems in abstract terms, and they rarely provided concrete descriptions and examples. Typically, their reasoning model distinguished between the immediate and latent causes of accidents and universalized this distinction, so that a deterministic and mechanistic perception of events was adopted.[6] Furthermore, the engineers preferred to give precise and definite explanations of the causes of work accidents, and they were more concerned with the quality than with the variety of these causes. The engineers, in fact, gave fewer explanations on average than did the site managers, and they more frequently cited global or systemic causes stemming from the broader organizational context. For example, they mentioned the following with particular frequency: the absence of a safety culture in the workforce, scant organizational concern for safety and the high cost of accident prevention to the firm.

When the engineers offered explanations they tended to concentrate on accident prevention. Oddly, the rhetorical form taken by their examples resembled that of a 'problem-solving' script. They began by providing an 'objective' description of a situated problem to be dealt with (typically 'How can accidents be prevented in this case?'), and of situational constraints. They then illustrated their own solution to the problem. Implicitly, therefore, the engineers depicted safety as the outcome of a problem-solving strategy which sometimes involved negotiation over institutional constraints (for example, laxly applied safety regulations) and sometimes direct intervention by authority (economic sanctions on subcontractors failing to comply with safety regulations).

Analysis of the engineers' interviews revealed that they defined safety in three different ways: as the organization's responsibility, as an attitude to adapt and as a cultural product.

Safety as the organization's responsibility is a variable deriving from the firm's concern for quality of workmanship and product; quality expressed in the form of decision-making choices and the careful checking of work performance. According to the engineers, the purpose of this concern was to increase worker commitment to accident prevention measures.

Secondly, the engineers saw safety as the ability to adapt experience and knowledge of the environment and the production process to the organizational context via a process of problem setting and problem solving. This obviously affected decision making because it promoted innovative managerial attitudes and focused the entire organization's attention on safety.

Thirdly, safety was viewed as a cultural product made manifest as greater emphasis on collective welfare. According to the engineers, this conception of safety derived from greater professional awareness among the workforce, as well as from greater awareness of risk at the institutional level, and it was made explicit in the workplace safety measures and regulations implemented by the company.

The engineers' conception of accident prevention linked closely with the interpretation that they gave to safety, which they believed to have the following three aspects: (i) managing safety requires planning skill as manifest in accident prevention measures; (ii) accident prevention has an economic aspect to it because efficient safety precautions yield long-term benefits for the firm; (iii) accident prevention is of importance to the organization because improving a firm's safety record – by means of controls and special training – involves all its members.

The engineers' use of an explanatory model embodying a deterministic view of reality and problem solving, coupled with a non-participative conception of safety, enabled them to assert their occupational group's position and to posit their safety strategy as the 'one best way'. Moreover, by assuming responsibility for safety promotion, they enhanced their professional status within the firm and avoided confrontation and therefore conflict with the other communities of practitioners.

The pragmatics of their communication, in terms of power/knowledge, reveal their effort to secure hegemony for their discourse, both by enacting responsibility and by couching their explanations in 'scientific' language and abstract knowledge. Even when they mentioned concrete situations, they did so in a way that the knowledge gained from the single case was generalizable (Figure 5.3).

(a)   (b)

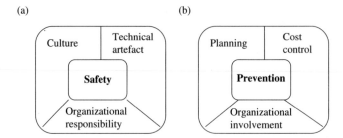

Figure 5.3   Semantic scheme of safety and accident prevention in the engineers' community

Figure 5.4   The site-managers' explanation – plotting of a causal scheme

The site managers explain

The explanations of workplace accidents provided by the site managers were based on a causal reasoning model which focused on the relations among the various components of the work context (Figure 5.4).

An 'unsafe' working environment, for example, was defined not in abstract terms, but by furnishing examples and by emphasizing the immediate causes of accidents. Moreover, the site managers employed a reasoning model which focused on the synchrony of events and the co-occurrence of several causes in determining accidents. It was a model, therefore, which paid close attention to situated and concrete phenomena.

The site managers provided numerous concrete examples which, as the interviews proceeded, developed into full-fledged narratives. Recounting an episode typical of that context served to illustrate and justify the dangerousness of the working environment. But it fulfilled another purpose as well. The site managers' examples, in fact, justified the occurrence of accidents and depicted them as a routine aspect of the building industry. Their community was therefore exonerated from blame and, at the same time, their identity was portrayed as both professionally and personally deeply concerned with the problem of on-site accidents.

The site managers regarded the problem of safety as crucially important as regards their work role and the area of the organization that they administered. This central importance of safety was evidenced by the plethora of meanings attached to it. For the site managers, in fact, the concept of safety had four different dimensions, each of them connected with specific individual, relational and organizational aspects of the work setting.

First, safety was regarded as a social variable based on trust among several actors who shared the same working environment (but not the same jobs). According to the site managers, this trust relation sprang from the co-presence of two features: practical experience and professionalism. Practical experience (on-the-job training), they declared, had taught them to place greater importance on the relational aspects of work, which they sought to enhance through mutual reliance and cooperation among colleagues. Professionalism induced them to identify more closely with their work roles, and therefore gave rise to autonomous and responsible performance of the tasks assigned to them. A greater amount of 'responsible autonomy' and an ability to enhance professional relations, in fact, were regarded as most important for coordinating one's work with that of others and therefore for solving the everyday problems arising on the building site.

A second aspect to safety was the ability to predict variations in the production process and their consequences. Planning for safety promotes a global vision of the organization of work and its goals. It therefore fostered the more efficient coordination of different work tasks. This view of safety derived, according to the site managers, from practical knowledge of the firm and its dynamic aspects, but also from abstract knowledge of the firm's operational logic (i.e. from vocational training).

Third, safety was defined as the ability to monitor one's own performance and that of others, and to alter the environment accordingly. This ability derived from the individual knowledge possessed by each worker, but it was also determined in part by the standards of workmanship demanded by the firm. Moreover, according to the site managers, this monitoring had effects on decision making because it required priorities and deadlines to be set which were appropriate to the context.

Fourth, safety was viewed as a hierarchical responsibility. That is to say, safety depended on the hierarchy – organizational but also informal – that operated in the workplace. Safety, therefore, was not the sole responsibility of those with most authority and influence; it was also the product of greater concrete and practical experience of work. Evident in this assertion is its pragmatic meaning *vis-à-vis* the community of engineers as a claim for participation in decision making by virtue of experience deemed to be 'different' from, if not 'superior' to, abstract knowledge.

Prevention (i.e. the 'management of safety in practice') was invested with fewer meanings than safety. It was in fact viewed as comprising three aspects. The first, as with the engineers, was knowledge of the work context and its risks. Prevention was therefore the reduction or containment of these risks by the organization. The second aspect was the reduction in the economic and organizational costs that accrued to the firm from efficient accident prevention. The third aspect of safety management, according to the site managers, was training. To this, however, they were hostile, because they viewed the imposition of a safety culture different from their own as indicative of the power that the firm exercised over its employees' workplace behaviour, and therefore as the indirect attribution of responsibility. The site managers' concern with the concrete and situated aspects of safety, in fact, was not matched by the safety management model that the organization proposed to them. And this also applied to the causal model that they utilized in their explanations of accidents. A conception of causality based on synchrony is extraneous to the formalized and explicit culture of many organizations, and it is often dismissed as pure 'sensation' because it does not comply with the criteria of scientific rationality (Figure 5.5).

The difference between engineers and site managers recalls the contraposition between a 'check-list mentality' and an 'on-site complexity'.

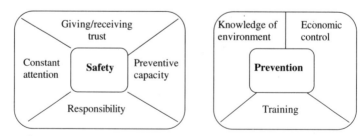

Figure 5.5 Semantic scheme of prevention and safety in the site managers' community of practice

Turner and Pidgeon's (1997: 57) concept of 'on site' can help us syn-
thesize both the site managers' mentality and the main characteristics of
a building site. It is an intriguing concept because it refers to the fact
that any concrete or material system possesses numerous properties, all
of which are potentially evident when the system is directly encoun-
tered. A 'site' represents the concrete aggregation of whatever abstract
systems have been imposed upon it, and its planners or users become
involved at that site in a multiplicity of systems, some designed, some
unpredictable. Large-systems planning encounters difficulties in organizing precisely because of this 'on-site' situatedness. For example: 'the
design of subways as means of separating pedestrians and traffic over-
looks the opportunity created "on site" for these subways to be used by
teenage gangs or by exhibitionists'.

The planning rationality may be represented by a check-list: if all the
items on it are under control an accident should not happen, if one does
happen it is due either to mistake or fate. But the other community
would sceptically reply that accidents are 'normal' because of the 'on-
site' situatedness.

For the researcher seeking to define and develop the idea of an organizational safety culture contradictions arise. These contradictions stem
from the presence in organizations of diverse 'causal theories' of
accidents, and therefore from the different interpretative perspectives
adopted by communities of practitioners when they address problems of
safety and risk. Comparison among the form and content of the explanations for accidents provided by the members of two communities of
practitioners – building engineers and site managers – showed that this
diversity did not derive solely from the division of labour within the
organization. The causality models employed by the two groups to interpret phenomena, as well as their conceptions of safety, gave rise to highly
specific attention rules and forms of knowledge which each group activated as it responded to risk.

For the site managers, who viewed safety mainly in relational terms,
risk should have been dealt with by protection-oriented organizational
behaviour, while for the engineers, who viewed safety mainly in terms
of planning, it should have been dealt with by organizational behaviour
oriented towards worker's co-responsibility. How then did conversation
come about between these two communities of practice, given that they
were interdependent?

Wenger (1998: 129) provides an answer to the question by pointing
to two elements: styles (which spread as people in a community of practice, borrow, imitate, import, adapt and reinterpret ways of behaving) and

discourses (which travel across boundaries and combine to form broader discourses as people coordinate their enterprises, convince each other, reconcile their perspectives and form alliances). However, Wenger writes, 'styles and discourses are not practices in themselves. They are available material – resources that can be used in the context of various practices'.

I disagree with Wenger on the latter point: discursive practice is a practice in itself, which is not performed to produce negotiation over meanings, nor to convince, to form alliances, or to coordinate, even though these outcomes may arise and be visible. Discursive practices in a constellation of interconnected practices comprise a plurality of discourses and legitimate their co-existence. Discursive practices create – in the first place – a conversational space and actualize potential conversation; in the meantime every other outcome of conversation is left open and it emerges from conversation, from alternation between the participants, from the energies unleashed in conversation, from its emotional force, and so on. Discourses are not solely the means to produce social relations like understanding, negotiation, conflict; they are also autonomous practices of sociability. People talk in order to talk and not solely to do something.

In what sense, therefore, can one speak of an organizational culture of safety if there are as many cultures of safety as there are communities of practitioners sharing tacit knowledge on workplace safety and accident prevention? It seems that, on the one hand, a safety culture is a self-referential discourse developed by the members of a community, while, on the other, it is a dialogue with other communities with interdependent working practices. Communication and self-communication (Broms and Gahmberg, 1983) are processes internal to a community of practitioners, but they are also processes which operate among the communities internal to an organization and between these and the external communities that constitute the organization's institutional environment. The concept of self-communication emphasizes that, in communicating with others, we also communicate with ourselves. Not only does discourse directed at Alter retroact on Ego, but it is a moment for the construction and public representation of the identities of the talker or talkers.

One may therefore say that an organizational culture of safety is an open conversation which may be joined by the communities that constitute an organization. By 'open conversation' I do not mean just an even-handed dialogue based on an endeavour to convey meanings. Instead this conversation is structured on and by power, and it is fundamentally ambiguous and fragmentary. It is a conversation that goes beyond the distinction between the interior and exterior of an organization. For it is both a local discourse[7] with the members of that organization within a geographically and culturally circumscribed setting, and an institutional discourse involving such interlocutors as the normative system and the great agencies of socialization, control and prevention which operate at the national and also international level. Knowledge and power, then, structure every discourse on safety. It is this that will be described in the next section as a 'mirror game'.

5.2 Mirror games

The concept of the 'game of mirrors', together with that of 'typification', has been formulated to describe the texture of organizing (Gherardi and Strati, 1990) and originates from phenomenology. From the outset, observes Alfred Schutz (1962: 347–8) subjects find themselves in situations already designed for them by others; they are already 'premarked', 'preindicated', 'presignified' and even 'presymbolized'. Only a small part of knowledge originates from direct experience. The rest of it is a socially derived 'social heritage. It consists of a set of systems of relevant typifications, of typical solutions for typical practical and theoretical problems, of typical precepts for typical behavior' (Schutz, 1962: 348).

These are all forms of knowledge (Strati, 2000: 81) distinguished by the fact that they are taken as 'beyond question' by participants in organizing processes, and that they constitute socially approved organizational knowledge. They are intended to help the organizational members to define their situations in everyday life, and to do so in a form which is 'typical'. In everyday life each organizational member designs his/her action and expects it to be understood by other actors and to provoke their reaction. That is, a 'game of mirrors' occurs whereby:

> to the natural aspect the world has for group A belongs not only a certain stereotyped idea of the natural aspect the world has for group B, but included in it also is a stereotype of the way in which group B supposedly look at A. This is, on a major scale – i.e. in the relationship between groups – the same phenomenon which, in respect to relations between individuals, Cooley has called the 'looking-glass effect'.
>
> *(Schutz, 1964: 247)*

As typifications structure themselves, and as reciprocal typifications are created in the course of shared stories, therefore, the social struc-

turation of knowledge is configured. This process is sustained by discursive practices which are apparently paradoxical because they are not
directed towards reaching an agreement but instead are intended to assert
one's own point of view over the points of view of others. I shall now
analyse the mirror games of three communities: the engineers, the site
managers and the contractors.

The engineers' knowledgeability

Conflict or simple differences of view are givens additional to the complexity generated by space and by a multiplicity of events in the same
space. As we have seen, the site managers viewed and narrated the
accountability of on-site safety on the basis of their practical experience
by citing examples, going into details, interrogating themselves on what
else they could have done – in other words, locating safety at the level
of relations among practices. The engineers, by contrast, recounted safety
in terms of events that should not have happened, of failures of foresight or regulation. For the former, accidents were part of 'the order of
things' and whether or not they happened depended on circumstances;
for the engineers, accidents symbolized the disorder that interferes with
and upsets an ideal order. In the community of engineers:

> You study the site plan on paper, which means deciding where to put
> the equipment, the junction boxes, the crane [. . .] When you prepare the
> cement mixers you already know that they've got to have safety protec-
> tion [. . .] so you're aware of a set of regulations. At the planning stage
> you're in control of what the safety requirements should be so that the
> various work phases can go ahead (interview with an engineer, paragraph
> 2/2)

> The basic problems of safety are always the same, and the rules to obey
> are always the same. But then it's easier to enforce them on one site than
> another, for objective reasons [. . .] Some things you can generalize, others
> you have to look at case by case (interview with an engineer, paragraph
> 1/3).

> Good information management on a scientific rather than a voluntary
> basis [makes] the information available to everyone, and then it's infor-
> mation not interpretations (interview with an engineer, paragraph 3/6)
> Formalizing means clarifying what the objective is, and how corporate
> resources can be deployed to achieve the declared objective, rather than
> everyone acting according to what they think is right or most important
> (interview with an engineer, paragraph 3/6).

Evident in the above reasoning is how control over actions is embedded in practices. Safety is therefore accountable by virtue of norms of technical rationality and managerial rationality. The reverse case is constituted by rules which are inadequate and disobeyed. This is the perspective expressed by 'check-list logic', where the check-list symbolizes the practice that made the engineers accountable to their community.

Although the engineers declared that they had not learnt safety at university but on-site, their professional knowledge enjoyed a social legitimacy – and therefore an authority and authoritativeness – that the site managers' knowledge did not. The former was abstract knowledge and it bestowed qualities like generalizability, codifiability or transferability; the latter was practical knowledge, and it was contingent, situated, implicit and did not confer social authoritativeness. The former informed the technical rules and legal practices of ascribing responsibility, as well as scientific 'risk analysis'; the latter was good practical 'housekeeping', and it was codified only as a practice code. The former belonged to the symbolic universe of the male; the latter to the female.

The site manager experience

The site manager is responsible for the day-to-day running of small building sites. He knows that he is the 'node' at which numerous practices intersect. Indeed in our research, a site manager described himself as:

> a traffic warden supervising the pieceworkers, the crane-drivers, the carpenters, and those with lorries to unload. I act the warden and give urgency to the work as I want (interview with a site manager, paragraph 3/2).

This image of the 'warden' shows how the site manager's explanations of the causes of accidents related to the simultaneity of events. A building site is a relatively confined physical space, which becomes the theatre for action by numerous groups of actors who are both independent and closely interdependent. This is why the site manager described accidents in terms of:

1. Temporal interdependence. One team got further ahead with the work, and those that followed were endangered. The pieceworkers did not bother to keep the site tidy, and those that came after them worked in dangerous conditions.

2. Spatial interdependence. Everything happened at the same time. The
    work was never perfectly synchronized, although management of
    the physical space should have been a collective task.
3. Cultural models. Specific working conditions like piecework or
    'black' work created a lack of concern with personal safety which
    jeopardized the safety of others. Conversely, the 'trusties' personified
    control delegated by the site manager.

Yet a shared perspective could be identified, and it was constructed
by participation in shared practices, by experience of similar situations
and above all by taking active part in discursive practices centred on the
practice itself:

> When it's a scattered site, I have to be everywhere at once. So there are
> five or six people working, and it may happen that one of them does
> something that endangers someone else who comes later and doesn't
> know about it. There has to be a bit of cooperation (interview with a site
> manager, paragraph 1/5).

> The site's in order the evening before, but when the men start working the
> problems begin. If they need a piece of wood, they take it from the scaf-
> folding and don't think about the consequences. When they're plastering
> and the scaffolding gets in the way, they remove it. They always act as if
> they were in the jungle (interview with a site manager, paragraph 3/13)

These situations were inhabited by numerous actors who coordinated,
or otherwise, their actions. They therefore also produced an occupational
identity centred on the image of the traffic warden and the analogy
between road traffic and the danger-generating intersection of specific
practices – each with its own 'safety' criteria – in the same physical space.
Unlike a traffic warden, who possesses a highly codified gestural vocabulary, the site manager constantly wandered around the site, looking for
danger and pointing it out to the others. To do so he used discourse,
persuasion and the linking-up of non-communicating practices.

This activity has been termed 'brokering' (Eckert, 1989; Wenger, 1998),
in that a broker personifies the ability to transfer and translate certain
elements of one practice to another, to understand and appreciate the
differences in perspective between one community and another, and
authorization to influence the practices of one or more communities.
Brokering is often associated with innovativeness, or the creative copying
that results from exporting elements of a practice developed in one particular community to another. This may be the case, for example, of a site
manager who moves to another firm and persuades his new community

to adopt elements of his former community's practice. But brokering is also what the site manager does in his day-to-day work, when he acts as a living intermediary to synchronize the practices of a plurality of actors, each with a specific body of knowledge. His own competence consists in an ability to understand the others' knowledge to the extent necessary to get them to communicate, and it involves translation, mobilization and alignment (Latour, 1986; Law, 1992) among perspectives. His brokering practice constructs a social structure that reflects shared learning and which, although it may utilize non-human intermediaries in the form of technological artefacts, is prevalently a discursive practice based on the ability to translate from one language to another.

To be noted is that as the two communities talked about 'doing safety', they implicitly offered a different understanding of what a practice is. While the engineers stressed the normative vision of 'good practice', and therefore saw practice as a support for control over action, the site managers portrayed practice as the locus of action emergence.

The main contractor's economic rationale

The main contractor as a professional, full-time manager and employer – as opposed for example to the traditional artisan, who was both an expert practitioner and owner of the business – is a relatively new figure in Italian small and medium-sized building firms. The main contractor embodies the economic rationality which now flanks, and/or conflicts with, the technical rationality of the engineers and the relational rationality of the site managers. The main contractor's point of view is overtly biased towards the economic aspects of safety:

> If you're sorted out [with the law], things go better, then you avoid fines and also accidents, because accidents cost you. The insurance companies make you pay more if you've had a certain frequency of accidents (interview with a main contractor, paragraph 2/3).

> I have to work out immediately what my difficulties are going to be in running the building site. But it's not that I can alter the project; I must only decide how to get it done well and in the least time possible, and safely. Time is money, and I always have to keep an eye on accident prevention (interview with a main contractor, paragraph 1/6).

As to be expected, the main contractor's discourse concentrates on economic considerations. And yet it 'enters into conversation' with the discursive positions of others, acknowledging their situated legitimacy:

Usually most sensitive to safety are the persons legally responsible for it, who in certain cases are our in-house engineers (interview with a main contractor, paragraph 2/6).

I've got fifteen building sites and not all the site foremen are equally safety-aware. Even we technicians, we're not all the same, we don't see things in the same way (interview with a main contractor, paragraph 2/4).

As a group it's the carpenters who make on-site safety (interview with a main contractor, paragraph 1/4).

For the sake of simplicity, I have restricted discussion of participation in the conversation on safety to the three communities comprising the engineers, site managers and main contractors. But, of course, other communities with different positionings could have taken part in the same conversation. First, the three communities analysed were those with most authority and responsibility *vis-à-vis* safety, but also present on-site was the community of workers from the subcontractor firms:

[Compliance with the law] doesn't concern only our workers, who are under our control, but also the other people who work on the site for us [. . .] who are outside the company's jurisdiction, external and distant from company headquarters (interview with an engineer, paragraph 3/7).

The employment relationship distinguished participation in a discursive community on safety between the workers employed by the firm and the pieceworkers from the subcontracting firm – even though they participated in the same practice.

To summarize, I have described three of the main voices that contribute to the discourse on safety in a building site and also suggested that other, distant and yet present voices are continuously referred to (e.g., the institutional voice). Participating in a community of practice means being able to understand the boundaries of the speaker's community and, at the same time, the discourses on practice of other communities. To explain these communication dynamics Boland and Tenkasi (1995) use the concepts of 'perspective making', to refer to communication that strengthens the unique knowledge of a community, and 'perspective taking' to refer to communication that improves its ability to take the knowledge of other communities into account. While this approach is very useful for practical purposes like designing communication systems to support perspective making and perspective taking, its exclusive focus on integration undervalues the symbolic and expressive role performed by discursive practice in identity building and in positioning identity within a discursive community. The notion of the mirror game expresses entirely the opposite point of view, namely that the purpose of discursive practices is not to construct a shared discourse in which differences are mediated and dialogue serves to achieve understanding. On the contrary, communities talk to each other in a dialogue of the deaf, as if their discourse bounces off the other community (the mirror) and returns in the form of self-communication which refuses to consider the other's point of view. Is this foolish? Only if one interprets communication as instrumental and as intended to achieve a goal; because if one regards the symbolism of communicating as construction of one's own voice, and of legitimation to have a recognized/recognizable voice, then one realizes that dissonances arise from a community's desire to affirm a distinct and distinctive voice. Realized in discursive practices are understanding *in* practice and contending, negotiating and dissenting *on* practice intended to create 'voice' for each participant and to form a domain of knowledge in which each community is able to exercise its mastery.

The mirror game between the engineers, site managers and contractors therefore yields an interpretation of activities, both expressive and material, which:

- express a specific logic – technical, relational and economic – which is pragmatically intended to affirm an occupational identity and an organizational role;
- sustain specific attention rules (March and Olsen, 1976) and are therefore intended to legitimate the criterion used prevalently by a community to take decisions or to legitimate/give accountability to the decisions taken;
- socialize the members of other communities to the logic of one's own, as well as to the values and aesthetic and moral criteria underpinning its professional vision. By means of this activity (also known as 'boundary crossing'), knowledge of one's own community and of others is created, and comparisons are possible without it being necessary to negotiate or seek compromises.
- celebrate membership of an occupational community, the distinctive features of the community's mastery as specific competence, and therefore domination over it; they affirm a reputational scale and distances among roles.

The mirror game is used to establish and maintain a social relation of crucial importance for social cooperation in workplaces: antagonism. The paradox is only apparent. Consider, in fact, that the division of labour, the essential principle of organizing, divides the organization's overall goal into sub-goals and assigns these to individual units in the organization/community of practice. Achieving this overall goal thus becomes the coordination principle, the one that restores unity to what was previously divided. The former principle expresses the need to produce a canon, a harmonic composition, the latter the need to produce dissonance. As it compares different voices, as it acquires the ability to hear the voice of the other, the community produces a shared knowledge base. This base enables divergences of view to be resolved; but it does so, not by producing a complete fusion but by rendering *action intelligible to both sides*. The importance of antagonism should not be underestimated, not simply because conflict is a physiological rather than pathological phenomenon, but because antagonism between several or different expertises and practitioners is the necessary condition for negotiation and the sharing of knowledge.

In the next section, the mirror game, as a discursive practice, will be analysed as a 'positioning' activity which enables the speakers to position themselves and their community of practice within the network of power/knowledge relations, and to legitimize that positioning. Co-participation in a practice implies taking one's own perspective on it and being able to see and understand other perspectives and relate them to the domain of knowledge over which each perspective has mastery.

5.3 Positioning: the discursive production of subjectivity

The concept of positionality originated in gender studies (Alcoff, 1988; Davies and Harré, 1990; Gherardi, 1995) and it has been used mainly to examine the problem of the production of subjectivity. For Davies and Harré, the concept of positioning belongs to social psychology, and their use of the term 'positioning' contrasts with the concept of human agency as role performance. It is therefore useful for the analysis of the production of self as a linguistic practice within the dynamic occasions of encounters. Whereas Davies and Harré employ the concept of positioning to illuminate the social level of interaction, Alcoff uses it to shed light on a politics of identity understood as choice from a plurality of selves and as positionality in a social context. I prefer the latter definition of the concept because it affords insights into the politics of representation of a subjectivity in a public space; that is, to a constantly shifting context, a situation that includes a network of elements involving others, objective economic conditions, cultural and political institutions, ideologies and so on.

It is within a particular discourse that a subject (the position of a subject) is constructed as a compound of knowledge and power into a more or less coercive structure which ties it to an identity. A discourse is an institutionalized use of language and of other similar sign systems. It involves a 'positioning' of the participants (i.e. a statement of identity and an involvement in power relations).

A subject position incorporates both a conceptual repertoire and a location for persons within the structure of the rights pertaining to those who use the repertoire. A position is what is created in and through conversations as speakers and hearers construct themselves as persons: it creates a location in which social relations and actions are mediated by symbolic forms and modes of being.

As people assume discursive positions for themselves, they also attribute – explicitly or implicitly – discursive positions to possible audiences.

An example taken from the field concerns the practice of 'getting the site ready for an inspection'. The engineer and the site manager were conducting an internal site review in preparation for an imminent inspection:

> **Engineer**: how about the way in which the scaffolding is anchored . . .
> **Site manager**: I think it's all right . . . it's safe, I checked, it isn't moving and the anchors are really solid.
> **Engineer**: Yeah, but if the inspector were here he'd say that the law requires that . . .
> **Site manager**: Yes, but the law also says that we should install that special scaffolding under the roof . . . for three days of work . . . it would cost us a fortune . . .
> **Engineer**: . . . The old man at the office [the main contractor-entrepreneur owner of the firm] would have an heart attack if we spent all that money . . . you know him . . . he's happy for us to take the risk, otherwise how are we going to make any money . . . (reconstructed from field notes[8]).

This brief interaction shows how engineer's check-list mentality is not just a matter of 'saying' or a legacy from his university training; it is also a situated 'doing' based on his legitimacy to pose such a question because it is part of the structure of rights pertaining to his position as a member of an occupational community; a position enacted in the context of a practice in which the site manager co-participates, positioning himself as the actor with mastery over that 'doing'. But at the same time, as they consider the scaffolding, both of them know, and recognize that the other knows, that the scaffolding is 'problematic'. The engineer positions the

object as 'a problem' by introducing 'a virtual participant' – the inspector – into the discourse. Also to be noted is that the unproblematic object
becomes a troublesome one only if it is associated with an absent troublesome human. The inspector is an indirect decision-maker: he represents the logic of formal requirements and his presence is anticipated in
the discourse. What is the effect of making the absent inspector 'present'?
To answer we must ask who takes responsibility for the troublesome
object.

The site manager enacts his 'on-site complexity' competence and puts
forward his practical reasons: the scaffolding is under the roof, to install
it in accordance with safety regulations would require three days of work
and the cost/benefit ratio would be too high. The engineer backs up
the site manager's reasoning by introducing the figure of the owner into
the discourse and constructing it as a decision-making rationale which
gives priority to economic rationality. In doing so, he implicitly nego-
tiates the site manager's co-responsibility in the event of a critical report
by the inspector. Note how the subject 'we' is introduced into the
exchange first to signify the co-responsibility of the engineer and the
site manager for spending money, and then to identify the owner's
interest with the general interest. In five lines and a few seconds of conversation we have the positioning of two 'present' subjectivities, two
absent ones, a negotiation, the construction of a third 'common' subjectivity and the outline of a narrative for the potential observation of
the inspector.

Through practices of mutual accountability, speaking subjects not
only make the world more intelligible but also choose a discursive position for themselves and for others. Learning in constellations of interconnected practices is mediated by comparison among all these different
perspectives and by power relations. As in some of our examples, these
perspectives do not necessarily blend to produce a single and harmonious safety culture. On the contrary, the fact that they are situated in
material and social relations means that they assume discursive positions
that may equally well be unintelligible and antagonistic, as in the
following exchange between a safety consultant (an engineer) and a
(trade) site manager:

Engineer: According to the law you'll have to fence off that area while
you take the beam down . . . safety regulations, you know . . .
Site manager: But that doesn't make sense . . . this isn't how we usually
do it . . . it'll get in the way . . . We'll have to walk all around it . . . doesn't
make sense . . .

Engineer: Yeah, I know, but you'll have to do it anyway . . .
Site manager: OK, but it'll be a pain . . . this is ridiculous. (reconstructed from field notes)

In this case the rights pertaining to the repertoire of the person who takes the responsibility are not under discussion or negotiation, and the acknowledgement of the 'good reason' that the site manager brings into the conversation ('the usual way of doing things here') is merely lip service.

Our findings here are similar to those of Bechky (1999), who studied (mis)communication across occupational communities in an electronics firm. She noted that engineers and assemblers manifest their different ways of understanding things in their use of different languages (the former, as in our case, have an abstract understanding of things, the latter a concrete one). Because they engage in different 'language games' (Wittgenstein, 1953), the members of the two communities use homonyms (same signifier but referring to different material objects) and decontextualization (different terms for the same item). Very often, artefacts are utilized as 'tangible definitions' (Bechky, 1999), material ways to define problems through discursive practices by exploiting the power of indexicality. As a result, they are able to talk successfully about something understanding each other by means of misunderstanding.

By means of positioning, the speaker creates statements of identity, repertoires of rights and involvement in power relations. By means of words people in interaction also create a material world.

5.4   Doing things with words

Discursive practice among interconnected communities of practice comes about in the form of both discourse *in* practice and discourse *on* practice. When the engineer and the site manager were deciding how to set up the site or to solve a problem, they were united in a shared practice: doing and saying were the same things.

The engineer and the site manager were walking around the site to double check installations in view of an imminent inspection by the safety enforcement officials. The engineer looks up at the scaffolding:

Engineer: We'll have to move that rail there, it's not legal . . . it's too low.
Site manager: That's fine . . . I'll tell C. to do it . . . We should also move some of these brick piles . . . but then the workers will have to walk quite a bit . . .

Engineer: Yes, but they give a bad impression . . . officials in this area are nit-pickers . . . also move that piece of machinery there, I'm not sure we've got all the paperwork . . . better if it's out of sight. (reconstructed from field notes)

Words were just as instrumental as drawings or any other artefact. The two practitioners were *de facto* setting up the site by means of words.

Instead, when they were talking about practice – for instance, when they were trying to understand why an accident had happened, or at any rate working out the reasons for some or other on-site episode – this was a reflexive discourse which interrupted the flow of the practice to make space for the social activity of mutual accountability. Consider the following episode.

A group of workmen were gathered around a long steel beam that should have supported the new ceiling. The beam was too short, it did not fit. Men sat on other beams with their legs dangling, or stood on the floor below looking up at the beam. A bottle of water appeared from someone's lunchbag and was passed around. The site manager was called in. He too stood and took a drink of water. He was the first to break the silence, speaking in a low voice, as if talking to himself:
Site manager: We'll have to notify the engineer, he's going to have a fit . . . Who on earth measured this thing . . .
A worker: We followed the drawings . . .
Site manager: But can't you see that the room is crooked . . .don't you know you always have to measure things again! The architect just draws a straight line, he doesn't know what this old building is really like . . . (reconstructed from field notes)

Situated practices are both pre-reflexive (they depend on unstated assumptions and shared knowledge for the mutual achievement of sense) and reflexively constitutive of the situated members' contexts from which they arise. Reflexivity is used to create a sense of orderliness for action but it reflexively creates the context itself (Garfinkel, 1967). Reflexion on practice makes the world comprehensible both to oneself and to others. It may modify the practice or it may leave it unchanged, but in both cases talk about practices performs a function at once material and symbolic. It creates a material world but also attests membership and competence in discursive practice among different communities (apart from one's own), and it celebrates identity. Discursive practice about practice puts the community on stage, producing it culturally, materially and symbolically. Consequently, participating in a discursive community means being able to *relate to* the discourses on practice of other communities.

I have described the discourse on safety as a practice which engenders conversation in a discursive community internally to which various communities of practitioners assume their positioning.

It is widely acknowledged that different communities of practice have different explanations of how an organization works. Schein (1996), for example, identifies three different types of extremely common management culture: (i) an operator culture, or a line organization which views work as involving interconnected systems and cooperation among people; (ii) an engineering subculture which values technical, error-free solutions; and (iii) an executive subculture which focuses on the financial bottom line. Our site managers, engineers and main contractors can be straightforwardly related to Schein's three occupational subcultures. If we consider the set of ideas that they express, their beliefs indubitably induce coherent predispositions towards action (safety prevention). That thought precedes action is a belief widely held in Western culture, with its profound trust in rationality, although one could equally well argue the opposite and maintain that the linkage between thought and action is almost non-existent, as in hypocrisy (March and Olsen, 1976; Brunsson, 1982, 1989).

The theoretical problem that Schein's model does not address is how coordinated action in the presence of an incoherent thought system is possible. Schein's definition of culture, in fact, emphasizes the ideational elements that come to be shared. Consequently, everything that is not harmonized or sedimented inevitably ends up in a residual category which we may call 'noise'.

A further example – one very close to our research experience in that it concerns an incident review programme in a nuclear plant, and a root cause analysis at a chemical process plant from a learning perspective – is provided by Carroll (1998). The article begins by quoting the words of a station manager at a nuclear plant with an excellent safety record: 'What we do around here doesn't always make sense'. The question that Carroll asks is therefore why should effective behaviours and activities not be explicable and perhaps not discussible? The answer is that the difficulty lies in the available 'mental models' (Senge, 1990) or understandings of organizations, people and technologies.

Carroll explains the difficulty in terms of four categories of logic obtained by cross-referencing two dimensions: anticipation versus resilience (or fixing orientation versus learning orientation) and concrete versus abstract. He finds that design engineers work with logics that help them anticipate and therefore forestall problems in concrete objects. Their world is visual, and their natural reaction is to fix the problem and restore everything to its original state. Also executives are focused on anticipation, models and strategic plans, but their world is numerical rather than visual. By contrast, operators and craftspeople, who have their hands on equipment, are concerned with resilience, and their world is manual or tactile. Finally, there are the social scientists, management consultants and human factor experts, with their long-term view of experimentation and learning in the abstract. Theirs is a verbal world of ideas, written publications and persuasive conversations (Carroll, 1998: 711).

Carroll's article is convincing in its description of two research projects in which groups of people from different communities of practitioners come together to produce knowledge on the theme of safety. Carroll's argument is that learning in groups is actuated by a feedback cycle (observing, reflecting, creating, acting), and that 'mental models' create difficulties for both learning and organization. His interpretation rests on a conception of learning as a mainly cognitive activity, and on an idealist conception of knowledge and knowing.

This is a legitimate representation of learning, knowledge and knowing in organizations, but it is antithetical to our system of representation, which conceives learning as intrinsic to every form of practice and emphasizes the material character of knowledge and the social character of knowing.

Our interpretation of what happens in groups of people with various organizational and cultural backgrounds, who meet for a period of time in order to analyse a problem or to draw up a project (Gherardi, 2000b), is that they create a discursive community and activate a situated discursive identity which enables them to compare among different perspectives but also brings them to the realization that they may remain isolated, juxtaposed, non-communicating, and even conflictual. Comparing among perspectives means both comprehending and not comprehending, accepting diversity as well as rejecting it, understanding and misunderstanding. To assume a discursive position is a political move in that it involves positioning oneself in a network of social relations structured by power, interestedness and the mobilization of interests.

When examining the practices that weave other practices together, the image of 'heterogeneous engineering' (Law, 1992) 'in which bits and pieces from the social, the technical, the conceptual, and the textual are fitted together', may prove useful. However, the term 'heterogeneous engineering' also denotes that this alignment is by definition precarious and incomplete. It is the contingent and unstable result of the work performed by the local discursive practices. Change in one or more of the constellations of interconnected practices is a likely outcome of this weaving bits and pieces of knowledge together through language and communication. However, the change in question amounts to subtle shifting, 'rubbing', pollution, contamination, drawing and redrawing boundaries, translation and misunderstanding between knowledges – all figures that are substantially different from those used in the rhetoric of, say, 'knowledge management', which uses a message-transmitting framework.

Discursive practice is central to organizational knowing and acting because it performs the ephemeral and unstable alignment which preserves the arrangement of materials, persons, technologies and knowledges in a form recognizable as a practice. In this sense one may argue that discourse is a practice generative of other practices, a mode of ordering distinguished by its capacity to handle both coherence and incoherence, harmonies *and* dissonances, consonance *and* cacophony.

5.5   To sum up: practices which perform communities

Safety has been defined as an organizational competence that arises from a constellation of interconnected communities of practitioners, and in this chapter I have argued that the learning of safety in a constellation of communities of practitioners is mediated by comparison among antagonist perspectives of the world embraced by the co-participants in the production of this practice.

Comparison among perspectives is made possible by a discursive practice intended to create associations among elements, mental and material, within mutually accountable discursive positions. These associations are provisional and unstable because the practices of each community are situated within specific views of the world (and of safety) and power relations *vis-à-vis* other communities. They therefore generate tensions, discontinuities and incoherences just as much as they produce order and negotiated meanings.

Discursive practices among interconnected communities of practitioners are modes of ordering which produce a body of knowledge shared by the communities involved, but not only in the form of stable, cumulative knowledge institutionalized in routines. Indeed, the distinctive feature of a building site is that it is a temporal organization which is usually born and dies within a year and cannot rely on structuring processes akin to organizational memory. The discursive practice that I have described does not rule out the processes of harmonization, negotiation of meanings and the integration of local forms of knowledge; nor does it rule out the complementary ones of competition, conflict, dominance and exclusion, although it should be stressed that all these processes take place through discourse and in the materiality of talk.

Communities of practitioners – in our case, the engineers, site managers and main contractors – assume their respective positionings within the situated discourse on safety. The engineers conducted conversation in order to accredit a technical and error-free conception; the site managers emphasized the contingency and impermanence of concomitant events, and the main contractors highlighted the compatibility/incompatibility of safety costs with other parameters. In their shared discursive practice, these actors compared their perspectives both during discourse *in* practice (i.e. in the course of collective action) and during discourse *on* practice (i.e. when the narrative concerned accountable action).

In summary, discursive practices within each specific community and among a constellation of interconnected communities are mediated by objects, artefacts or tangible definitions. But discursive practices are not only instrumental to understanding and negotiating; they are the expression and the means for positioning a community identity within a subject position in a discourse. Voice, knowledge and power legitimate a subject position within a discursive community, and if consonance is necessary for understanding each other positioning, dissonance is necessary for asserting identity. Antagonism in principle is the basis for cooperation in practice.

NOTES

1. I am grateful to Attila Bruni and Katrin Gilbert for their comments on musical metaphors.
2. The fieldwork was conducted by Francesca Odella, to whom I am indebted. Parts of this chapter have appeared in Gherardi, Nicolini and Odella (1998) and in Gherardi and Nicolini (2003).
3. In order to prevent distortions due to interviewee preferences for particular narrative styles, the explanations provided by each individual were checked.
4. The significance of this association for a sample of 12 cases was 5 per cent – Fisher exact test – and the value of the coefficient of association chosen – Goodman and Kruskal tau – was 0.466 with 10 per cent significance.

5. The significance of this association for a sample of 12 cases was 13 per cent
    – Fisher exact test – and the value of the coefficient of association chosen
    – Goodman and Kruskal tau – was –0.800 with 0.8 per cent significance.
6. The values relative to the frequency of numbers of paths, steps and rami-
    fications for the two occupational groups were as follows: 78.9 per cent of
    the engineers' explanations followed a single path (with a 16.2 per cent
    over-representation relative to the column marginals); the engineers' expla-
    nations were over-represented among those with three or more steps and
    among those with branches (15 per cent over-representation and 12.3 per
    cent over-representation relative to the column marginals). As regards the
    site managers' explanations, these more frequently displayed a multiple path
    (with a 7.5 per cent over-representation relative to the column marginals),
    and no more than two steps (with a 13.3 per cent over-representation
    relative to the column marginals).
7. According to Foucault (1984), a discourse is a historically situated set of
    thoughts, expressions and practices. A discourse of safety is a predominant
    mode of thinking about and acting within the world as regards safety,
    danger, prevention and all the concepts belonging to this symbolic universe
    of meaning.
8. The fieldwork for this part of the research was carried out by Davide
    Nicolini, to whom I am indebted.

CHAPTER SIX

Knowing within an Organization while Mending its Texture

Our description will be in words or figures or pictures but what we describe is going to be in flesh and blood and action.

(Batenson, 1979: 27)

How do organizations respond when their members are injured or even killed? Workplaces in the building industry are rich sources of information on breakdowns related to safety and accidents. In previous chapters we have seen that knowing about safety is:

- situated in the texture of ongoing practices;
- rooted in a context of interaction, acquired through some form of participation in a community of practitioners, and kept within a situated curriculum;
- relational and mediated by artefacts and discursive practices;
- continually 'translated into practice', i.e. reproduced and renegotiated, and hence always dynamic and provisional.

Safety can therefore be viewed as a situated practice, an emerging property of a sociotechnical system, the final result of a collective process of construction, a 'seeing', a 'doing' and 'saying' which involves people, technologies and textual and symbolic forms assembled within a system of material relations. In the case of breakdowns, especially, it is also possible to observe how emotions are collectively handled. Although I have not expressly emphasized the connection between emotions and learning, we have repeatedly seen how the emotions are present in interactions: recall, for example, the silence of the organization on safety, and the emotionality that narratives convey, and as they do so transfer knowledge as well. The breakdown of a practice is also an emotional breakdown. As Fineman (2003: 569) writes: 'not only is emotion a learning "product" in many personal and organizational displays, it also lies at the heart of the building of trust, competencies and the political and moral order of the enterprise'. All these elements are involved in a constant process of generation and translation rooted in organizing activities and contained within the texture of a field of practices.

I shall show in this chapter how repairing the social order following a workplace accident is not only an interpretative activity of account-ability and sense making, but also a social and emotional practice of engi-neering the heterogeneous elements that make up the texture of a field of practices. Three types of repair processes are illustrated: darning, patch-ing and quilting.

I propose to portray the circulation of knowledge within an organi-zation as continually 'translated into practice', i.e. reproduced, negotiated, changed and also neglected; and hence three processes of knowledge translation are described: invisible learning, mock learning and catch learning.

In the following sections I shall examine the production of safety as a process of knowledge translation which takes place within a learning network, and memory work as a collective practice which translates experiential learning into code for remembering and a guide for future actions in specific workplaces and learning nets.

6.1   Breakdowns in a texture

In order to illustrate how knowledge is translated into practice (i.e. how it circulates and in circulating is transformed) I shall analyse accidents that have occurred in building firms during the same time period and in the same geographical area. These were accidents subject to investi-gations by the supervisory institutions and in one case by the judicial authorities as well. Many of the actors involved therefore shared the same safety culture and institutionalized ideas of what is 'safe', 'dangerous' or 'risky', which they themselves had helped to create and establish.

The accidents will be analysed from a sociological perspective, which defines them as breakdowns in the texture of practices. The analysis will focus on the processes of repair and reconstruction of the ordering modes of so-called 'normalcy' described as mending activity. The fun-damental processes of repair and reconstruction of social order after a breakdown represent processes of knowledge in translation.

The normalcy of organizational life arises from relations of connect-ing in action, and this connective texture is taken for granted when the alignment of ideas, persons, materials and technologies holds together. But this texture is subject to rips and tears which require skilful mending work. With this view, an organization is a blend of different materials that delimit the kinds of choices that actors in that setting may or may not make. For example, a programme for workforce safety in a construction firm involves choices that, once in place, can become long-term fixtures. Having been stitched together with many other choices, they may require significant effort to change or replace them, while in other circumstances the breakdown is sudden and unexpected, as in the cases of an accident or an industrial disaster.

The distinction between natural and man-made disasters (Turner, 1978; Turner and Pidgeon, 1997) has led to the development of a type of scientific inquiry which considers the organizational factors in the aetiology of accidentally caused disasters. With the expression 'man-made disaster' Turner marked out a type of disaster previously undistinguished from natural ones. He was the first to conceive disasters in terms of a process of incubation and not as 'bolts from the blue' (his expression). The man-made disasters model (MMD), both as a descriptive tool, and in its later development as a diagnostic and learning aid (Toft and Turner, 1987; Toft and Reynolds, 1994), is about how technical, social, institutional and administrative arrangements can produce safety and/or disasters. It concerns the relationship among information, error and surprise in organizations, 'for we know that responsibility for failure can be just as dispersed and fragmented as responsibility for success' (p. xv). Turner (1978: 22) recalls that the two Chinese characters used to express the word 'crisis' signify 'danger' and 'opportunity', the purpose being to show that crises – like those induced by MMD – may constitute a threat but they also ' "may, from one point of view, be considered as opportunities for pursuing social change within an organization, or even as a means of aiding personal growth for individual managers'. Breakdowns may or may not be learning opportunities.

Turner and Pidgeon view a sociological definition of disaster as raising a challenge against existing cultural assumptions in this field of study. In fact the sociological literature on disasters has been enriched in recent years by a further shift away from organizational factors understood in the mainly structural or socio-technical sense towards the cultural factors used in interpretation of safety problems (Gephart, Steier, and Lawrence, 1990; Wright, 1994; Pidgeon, 1995; Gherardi, 1998). The main assumption is that organization is concerned with intention and the execution of intention, and disasters always represent a failure of intention, a failure of foresight. We can conceive a disaster as an 'an event, concentrated in time and space, which threatens a society or a relatively self-sufficient subdivision of a society with major unwanted consequences as a result of the collapse of precautions which had hitherto been culturally accepted as adequate' (Turner and Pidgeon, 1997: 70). The advantage of this definition is that it covers instances where the amount of physical damage is not great but the mishap reveals a gap in defences, which were regarded as secure, and a need for cultural readjustment.

Thus, by adopting an MMD model of analysis, we may follow Turner and Pidgeon by formulating a definition that does not refer to the physical impact or scale of the event. Instead, in sociological terms, an accident can be defined 'as the overturning and disruption of cultural norms and expectations for dealing with risk and safety matters' (Turner and Pidgeon, 1997: 74). The MMD model suggests that 'technical, human, managerial and cultural dimensions interact in a contingent open-ended process that precludes deterministic analysis' (Horlick-Jones, 1996: xx).

Moreover, to the first conceptualization of disasters in socio-technical terms we may apply notions drawn from the actor–network theory and see in the disappearance of the hyphen from sociotechnical systems the demise of the distinction between the social and the technical (Law, 1999). In this case, the boundaries among the technical, human, managerial or cultural vanish, so that an accident can be defined simply as a breakdown or dis-alignment in what hitherto has been a way to order heterogeneous materials.

This case study began with the consideration that a workplace accident (especially when it involves serious injury or death) is in various respects a trauma for an organization, as well as being a situation of enacted sense making of the event (Weick, 1988). On the one hand, there is the emotional impact on the victim's workmates, added to which is the civil and criminal liability of the technical and managerial staff and the employer. On the other hand, there is the economic impact taking the form of administrative sanctions and higher insurance premiums, and also the indirect costs arising from the reduced productivity consequent on the accident (due to the non-usability of the equipment and facilities, and to the absence of the injured worker or workers). And then there are the collateral effects at the public level, in relationships with the workplace safety authorities, and especially with workers and trade unions.

Reasoning on accidents as learning opportunities starts from the hypothesis that, given the impact of every accident on the organization of work and the management of resources (economic, emotional and symbolic) within a firm, it is of a certain interest to reduce its effects. This can be achieved in various ways, only some of which bring improvements to the general situation as regards safety.

The comparative case-study research[1] examined six cases of workplace accidents in an equal number of construction firms in Trentino-Alto Adige.[2] The information was collected by means of document analysis and unstructured interviews conducted both within the firms, at various levels of responsibility (workers, technicians, administrators, proprietors), and in the firm's institutional context (institutions affected by the accident). The number of interviews varied according to the size of the firms and the number of the institutions involved in the investigation, from a minimum of 10 to a maximum of 22 per case study. The qualitative analysis of the data was conducted on the bases of an analytical scheme based on MMD, the same scheme that was used as an outline for the interviews and document analysis.

From the MMD model, and from Toft and Turner (1987), we borrowed the idea that accidents can be analysed in processual terms. We consequently elaborated a scheme for their qualitative analysis. The MMD model divides into six stages:

1. notionally normal, when precautions and assumptions are considered to be adequate;
2. incubation period, when unnoticed errors and events accumulate and problems become highly ill-structured;
3. precipitating or trigger event, when the final critical error or abnormal operating condition appears;
4. onset, when the immediate physical impacts begin to bring cultural disruption to awareness;
5. rescue and salvage;
6. full cultural readjustment, when the opportunity to learn lessons through inquiry and the implementation of recommendations arises.

This model delineates a six-phase process of development which was used for the field research. Here I shall use a version of the model reduced to three stages for my description of the process:

- Stage 1: 'normalcy', when the texture of organizing is sound, cultural assumptions on danger and safety are solidly ingrained in activities, and precautions are still seen as adequate (stage 1 and 2 in MMD).
- Stage 2: 'the breakdown', when the incident brings cultural disruption (stages 3 and 4 in MMD).
- Stage 3: 'the mending', when normalcy is restored and full cultural readjustment is foreseen (stages 5 and 6 in MMD).

I now describe the texture of practices in which the event assumed the significance of a 'fact' and the drama was enacted. In this operation, the original MMD model is further interpreted in narrative terms by translating the meaning of stage into a theatrical setting. The metaphor of Greek drama is used to emphasize chorality in the process of ordering reality and releasing the tension of the crisis. The Greek word *krisys* denotes the moment of judgement and separation which sows the seeds of recovery, and foresight of the new course of action. When analysing the various accounts of the same accident I shall take care to preserve the element of chorality, giving priority to interpretative homogeneity over dissonant voices.

Of the six cases analysed, I shall describe here only the three that most clearly exhibit the various gradations (high, medium and low) of breakdown.

6.2   Darning: the art of invisible mending

Repair has been studied mainly by ethnomethodology (Schegloff, 1992; Schegloff, Jefferson and Sacks, 1977; Sudnow, 1978), which considers repair to be a technique used to fix breakdowns in language and in conversation. When ethnomethodology and studies of practice are considered together – as in Henke (2000) – social and material forms of order become closely integrated. Henke[3] proposes a sociology of repair to analyse it as an ongoing skill used to maintain workplace order. He writes: 'repair is not at the margins of order, waiting to be deployed if something goes wrong. Instead it is a practice at the centre of social order: repair work makes workplaces normal' (Henke, 2000: 55). Whereas Henke studies repair technicians in order to show that repair work involves more than working on machines and other material artefacts, and that repair workers also fix the social order, I shall seek to show that repairing the social order following a workplace accident is not only a sense-making activity but a social practice of engineering the heterogeneous.

Ethnomethodologists use the term 'remedial' or 'repair' (Goffman, 1971a; Owen, 1983) in relation to the practice of mending the social order. I prefer to use the term 'mending', or its synonym 'darning', for two reasons: firstly to link it with the metaphor of texture, and secondly to emphasize the 'gendered' character of mending work. Darning, in fact, relates more to the domestic sphere, to a manual skill that is disappearing and which has never been noble or extolled in its social representation. The femaleness associated with darning is intended to connote it as a humble activity, one that is not seen or only noted by its absence, like the majority of domestic ancillary and support activities.

The Shelter firm is one of the largest construction companies in the province of Trento and operates in the residential building sector. Founded in the 1970s as an artisan firm it expanded during the 1980s under the ownership and management of its founder and current single proprietor. It has a workforce of 67 employees, of whom 18 form the administrative and technical staff, while the rest are skilled workers and labourers. Because of the size of its workforce, The Shelter is one of the largest building firms in the province. Personnel turnover is quite high, and there are numerous cases of young technicians and workers who have trained in the firm and then moved to its competitors or to smaller businesses.

The company policy centres on a search for efficiency and respect for commitments undertaken as regards both production and the economic treatment of employees, while little attention is paid to human relationships. Nevertheless, The Shelter is one of the few to have an office and a manager entirely dedicated to handling all aspects to do with relations with the personnel, from administrative and social security matters to industrial relations.

The Shelter's accident record reveals numerous minor breaches of the regulations sanctioned by the Labour Inspectorate and two mortal accidents: one in 1987 and one that is the subject of the present analysis.

Act I: normalcy

The company policy at The Shelter had two features of interest for their consequences on safety. First, the firm's concern for its employees was restricted to compliance with technical-legal requirements like medical check-ups, compulsory lessons on accident prevention, and so on. Second, its interest in the relational aspects of personnel management and therefore safety was minimal. Hence safety at The Shelter was considered to be the outcome of regulations and technical knowledge about risks, rather than an individual ability to cope with situations of risk. The emphasis was on technical-normative aspects, so that the technicians were those most aware of the contradiction between the importance (not recognized by the firm) of caring for the organizational aspects of ensuring safety and the firm's assumptions that precautionary measures in full compliance with the law would be enough. In reaction to this contradiction, the safety culture at *The Shelter* took the form of entirely individualized responsibility on the part of both workers and the managers and proprietor.

Act II: the breakdown

While the site foreman was momentarily absent, two workmen and the crane operator were 'tidying up' the site. A number of metal cement moulds were being hoisted from one part of the site to another. Suddenly one of the semicircular moulds uncoupled from the crane, tipped over and fell onto an elderly worker, crushing him to death. The authorities intervened immediately and all work on the site was halted for a month. The inquiry concluded in the first instance with a sentence of criminal negligence passed on the site foreman and chief technician, who lodged an appeal. At the time of the field research the appeal was still in progress.

Act III: the mending

In relation to the operation that caused the accident, the workmen involved had sufficient practical knowledge to move the moulds (which, for that matter, had been shifted around the site on several occasions in previous weeks), but they lacked a critical vision of the risks and the precautions that were necessary. Indeed, certain specific precautions known to the workmen (the use of wedges to hold the unstable moulds firmly in place) had not been taken, nor had notice been taken of a clear warning signal (unstable mould) before the operation began.

From the descriptions provided there seem to have been two factors responsible for the accident. First non-compliance with the safety rules on this kind of operation (use of blocking wedges). Second a lack of coordination between the workmen and the crane operator: the former should have checked that the mould was properly in place; the latter should have supervised what the others were doing and not released the load until it had been firmly wedged. The accounts furnished by the interviewees mention the crane operator, but his role is somewhat ambiguous: his task of supervising the work and therefore of ensuring the safety of all movements of materials seems questionable in the context where the accident happened.

The dynamics of the accident were described thus by *The Shelter's* technical director:

> What they had to do was move a semicircular mould (. . .) These kinds of moulds need special handling, let's say, they're not like normal moulds which stay in place when you put them on the wall (. . .) the semicircular ones have a lop-sided centre of gravity, so there's a special technique for stacking them on the site. This wasn't used, even though the workmen had moved them at least fifty times before, always the same workmen and always the same moulds. That day they moved them on their own initiative . . . or perhaps not . . . the site foreman told them to do it . . . they took the first one, and it was this one that caused what happened: they rested the mould on the wall, and one of them climbed up to release it from the crane hook, and when he was coming down he held on to the outer part of the mould to keep his balance (without putting wedges underneath), he made it topple over, and it fell onto one of the workmen.

The immediate outcome of the accident for *The Shelter* was close down of the site and the crane for around a month, and therefore a compulsory halt on all work, as well as the administrative sanctions on the company following an inspection by the Accident Prevention Service.

When the injured workman died, the authorities prosecuted the site surveyor and the chief foreman, holding them responsible for the organization of work and therefore for safety in the area of the accident. The charge brought against the two employees was that their absence from the site had created a state of danger, and that they had assigned a task to the workmen (one of whom had died) without ensuring that they took the necessary precautions. The court of first instance found both ex-employees guilty, although their defence argued that the inquest had been slipshod (neither the crane driver nor the other workers present at the moment of the accident had been interviewed) and lodged an appeal. *The Shelter* was instead acquitted, and the subsequent dismissal of the surveyor and the foreman severed the connection between the accident and the firm.

Within *The Shelter*, the accident received different explanations. On the one hand it was considered to confirm a lack of safety culture of which the firm was already aware; on the other, attempts were made to explain away the accident as caused by purely technical factors (mistakes made by the two workmen) and individual ones (the elderliness of the deceased worker) or by pure chance.

These factors were offered as distinct and separate causes of the accident with no consideration of the relations among them. Their implicit purpose (especially in the case of the workmen) was to forestall any allocation of indirect responsibility. Attribution of a univocal logic to the accident therefore seems to have served more to deflect analysis of its underlying causes (scant concern for safety among the workmen, negligence by the management) than to foster reflection and learning (or to revise implicit assumptions about safety).

This lack of responsibility, and this neglect of the relational aspects of safety and their management, was remarked upon by the interviewees. In reply to a question about what had happened in the company after the accident, the head of personnel answered as follows:

> Practically nothing happened. I had gone to the site, I know that the surveyor and the chief foreman (though he wasn't there at the time) had gone . . . then they all arrived, of course, the police, the inspectors . . . they closed the site down for days . . . I notified our lawyers, who sent someone to take photographs, so that we'd have some backing if a lawsuit was filed; we had an expert carry out a survey immediately . . . and that was it, everything went ahead quite smoothly: the only one who was a bit worried was me, I wondered how the workman was (. . .).

Consequently, *The Shelter* firm did nothing about the causes of the accident nor about the 'emotional crisis' that it had provoked. The members of the organization had no occasion to reflect on the accident among themselves, except by explaining it away as simple fate, and within a few months everything had returned to the *status quo*.

6.3   Patching: the art of remedial mending

The history of *The Screen* firm is typical of the Italian building industry. It was started up in the 1960s by the present owner (Mr Screen), when he returned to Italy after working abroad as a builder. During the 1980s and 1990s, *The Screen* expanded and its management was taken over by the owner's three sons, who converted it into a joint-stock company owned by the family.

At the time of the research, *The Screen* was going though a period of relatively profound change, with high personnel turnover and a still undefined organizational structure. According to the owners, however, this process was positive because the decision to invest in industrial construction offered good prospects for growth in the future.

Act I: normalcy

The firm's organizational culture was described by all the interviewees in terms of 'benign paternalism': the management sought to foster loyalty to the firm by encouraging employees to participate in corporate life and providing them with fringe benefits like a canteen, transport, medical check-ups and company dinners, besides placing great emphasis on personal relationships with employees and their family members, who also felt that they belonged to the 'company family'.

The participatory style of *The Screen* also extended to workforce safety. The management declared that it participated with great interest in institutional programmes for workplace safety. It cultivated relations with the industry associations; and management had in the past year attended a course on the recently introduced workplace safety legislation. One of the innovations introduced as a result of this legislation was the allocation to each site engineer of a budget to spend on safety equipment and materials. Particular attention was also paid to relationships with subcontractors, and especially suppliers, who were required to supply a safety plan in conformity with *The Screen*'s.

The owners described safety at *The Screen* as part of the trust relationship between employees and employer. Nevertheless, the message implicitly communicated to the workmen was that they were individually responsible not to 'hurt themselves' during working hours. When interviewed, the managers flanked the theme of safety with descriptions of the fraudulent behaviour of some employees, who 'exploited' the safety rules to 'cover' injuries received outside working hours. This ambivalent attitude of the management was also shown by the technicians, for whom the main benchmark for safety was the technical/legal one. In this case, too, safety depended on the individual workman, on his training and on his compliance with the safety rules.

The employees for their part saw safety mainly in the form of managerial responsibility and as a bargaining counter in power relations with the firm.

The ambivalence of safety in the company was also highlighted by its relationship with the institutions (the Labour Inspectorate especially) responsible for its enforcement. The examples cited by the interviewees tended to show, in fact, that safety rules and sanctions were applied in an arbitrary and individual manner. The workplace safety promoted by the institutions, moreover, was seen as a body of distinct knowledge items: knowing safety through the norms therefore meant knowing everything (like a shopping list), not what was effectively relevant to the workplace in question.

Outsiders described the building site where the accident had happened as a 'model' site from the safety point of view. *The Screen* had made major investments, both logistical and economic, so that the site would be 'up to standard'. This concern was due to two specific factors: first the difficulty of the work (deep-level excavations on a site surrounded by residential housing and next to a busy main road), and secondly the site's location in the centre of the provincial capital, so that it was subject to extremely close control by the authorities. The project was therefore described as 'highly dangerous' by the workers and the technical personnel, who recounted how great efforts were made during the initial phase of the work to ensure that it went smoothly, with the constant fear that something might go seriously wrong. The great emotional tension on the site had subsided just under a week before the accident, when in the words of the chief engineer, 'it seemed that our safety worries were over'.

Act II: the breakdown

During work on the roof of a covered car park, three workmen together with the crane operator and the site foreman were moving the first of the roofing slabs into place. Similar operations had been performed in previous days in the same manner. As the slab was being slid along the grid, a workman lost his balance and fell through the mesh. He fell only about two metres, but at first it seemed that he had been critically injured. The accident had great public impact and created panic among the managers until they realized that it was not as serious as they first thought.

Act III: the mending

The site engineer described how the accident happened as follows:

> There was a metal grid on which a workman was walking while a cement slab was being laid in place (. . .) the slab was still attached to the crane and was being positioned, then you stood on it and carried on . . . it was the first slab: I don't say that this was the only way to position it, but . . . (. . .) the first slab always creates this problem, because you haven't

got any support . . . but the workman was walking about on the grid rods, which were stable and didn't have a great deal of space between them (twenty centimetres), so it wasn't easy to fall through . . . and he didn't trip either . . . they saw him fall without the slightest reaction. Perhaps he wasn't feeling well, also because he had problems at home . . . that day he turned up for work at 11, and at 11.15 the accident happened.

The workman's sudden fall had more serious consequences than the circumstances suggested possible: in fact, he was carrying his work tools, and in particular a hammer which caused internal injuries that prevented his breathing. His workmates called the ambulance. At the same moment, one of the firm's owners arrived on the site by chance, intending to check on the progress of work, and then a manager and a technician after the site foreman had summoned them by radio telephone. The panic on the site was heightened by the sudden and unexpected arrival of the police and the provincial inspectors, who sealed off the site and immediately began inquiries. At first, the injured workman seemed to be in a critical condition, and the news from the hospital that he was in intensive care suggested to workers and management that he was about to die.

Immediately after the accident, the workmen on all the firm's building sites paid closer attention to the safety rules. The reaction by the ownership and management was one of shocked silence, for fear that the man's condition might deteriorate, and also because they were unable to understand how such a serious breach of the safety regulations could have happened.

Until the man's injuries proved to be less serious than first thought and his condition began to improve, the situation in the firm was one of great tension and worry over the possible legal and economic consequences of his death.

Thereafter, the firm and the site apparently returned to the *status quo* prior to the accident (end of safety precautions). On the one hand, the management minimized the importance of the accident on the grounds that the outcome was not as severe as had been thought (and had therefore validated the firm's commitment to the workforce and its safety), while on the other the emotional impact of the accident and its damaging effect on the firm's image were emphasized.

The tendency to minimize the importance of the accident is confirmed by the fact that the authorities imposed only minor sanctions on the firm (a fine because height workers were not wearing safety belts), and that the management was only reprimanded for failing to produce a height-break plan, although this (by the Labour Inspectorate) was considered excessive bureaucratic interference, rather than a precaution that could be adopted in practice. However, some innovations were made to the relationship between company and employees in the months following the accident. The discretionality that was previously the rule in safety practices was reduced, and the management introduced an overt precautionary measure (warning letters) with regard to reckless behaviour or breach of the safety regulations by employees.

6.4 Quilting: the art of signalling

The Harbour began operations after the war as a small single-proprietor firm. In the following years it developed into an artisan enterprise until, by the end of the 1960s, it had grown to the size of an industrial company. In the 1970s the owner's sons took over the business and started activities collateral to construction by purchasing a small metalworking firm. At the time of the research, the personnel consisted of 36 employees (including office and technical staff) and five managers (the owners), who divided technical supervision, management and administration. All workers at *The Harbour* were skilled, and 'simple' building and finishing work was subcontracted to small artisan firms and external suppliers.

The accident described arose from relations with a small subcontracting firm working on one of *The Harbour's* construction sites.

Act I: normalcy

The Harbour's personnel policy placed great importance on human relations, which it sought to ensure were not harmed by economic and technical exigencies. Site management and work organization were therefore designed to harmonize these various components (technical, environmental, human, economic). This was evidenced by the fact that the firm saw safety as crucial and as intrinsically bound up with the quality itself of work, and that the firm pursued safety mainly through training provision.

The Harbour's accident record was extremely positive in that there had never been a particularly serious accident at the firm. In recent years, moreover, it had introduced a safety programme, on consultation with a specialist. It had first gradually replaced equipment with new machinery complying with safety standards, and then encouraged its technical personnel to take part in schemes and courses organized by the industry associations, and site personnel to attend training courses.

Such was the background to the accident. Work on a residential building was nearing completion, and the various subcontractors called in by *The Harbour* to do the finishing work were present on the site. Among them was *The Light*, a company specialized in the installation of electrical systems.

In order to plan the schedule of work for the weeks leading up to the accident, meetings were held between the site foreman and the owner of *The Light*. Some days after the first meeting, the owner of *The Light* came onto the site with two young apprentices to start work on the electrical installations. The work proceeded quite rapidly, and soon, after initially being present only occasionally the two apprentices came in almost every day. The owner of *The Light*, who liaised with the site foreman, increasingly absented himself in order to supervise work on another building site nearby, leaving the two apprentices on their own. The young electricians gained increasing familiarity with the site and began to work independently, even without instructions from the site foreman, and in relative isolation from other workers.

Act II: the breakdown

Towards the end of the workday, the two apprentices entered the lift shaft to install the light fittings. One of them dropped a tool and climbed down into the well beneath the lift to retrieve it, while the other raised the platform by manipulating the electrical connections. The manoeuvre went awry and the lift fell on the workman in the shaft, seriously injuring him. The inspectorate opened an inquiry which led to sanctions being imposed on the subcontractor and on *The Harbour*.

Act III: the mending

The young electrician crushed by the lift was immediately given first aid by the workers present on the site, and then, when the lift had been raised, taken to hospital. The day after the accident, a labour inspector examined the state of the site, *The Harbour's* safety measures and the contracts stipulated with subcontractors. His inspection concluded with a fine for *The Light* because of the circumstances surrounding the accident, and for *The Harbour* because the lift shaft had not been fitted with safety barriers. The accident thus seemed to be resolved, because after a month in hospital the apprentice had no permanent injuries and went back to work on another building site, and the judicial proceedings were set aside.

However, the accident had great impact on the site personnel, and especially on *The Harbour*'s management, which realized the riskiness of the situation and the possible damaging consequences of another accident.

The incident was not taken lightly by *The Harbour*, therefore, and in the week following the accident it arranged an informal meeting among the owner of *The Light*, the site foreman and *The Harbour*'s site surveyor in order to determine the causes of the accident and decide on preventive measures for the future. The meeting turned into an occasion to review *The Harbour*'s subcontracting procedures with *The Light*, and generally with other firms, and to revise the organization of on-site work during the finishing phase (i.e. the phase when safety barriers and supervisory personnel are absent). It was decided that, in the future, meetings would be held with all subcontractors prior to the finishing phase. A work schedule would be drawn up at these meetings so that overlaps were avoided and all those concerned were informed about arrangements for access to sites, potentially dangerous situations and the protection and safety measures put in place by *The Harbour*.

An internal inquiry found that the accident had not been due to negligence by *The Harbour*'s personnel, and that the immediate cause had been the reckless actions of the young electricians. In fact, by moving the lift platform they had breached the site regulations, which stated that only technicians from the installation company could use the lift until its completion and certification.

The site engineer described the company's practice as follows:

> Our practice is that as the building goes up we mount scaffolding in the lift shaft (. . .) according to the instructions given to us by the firm installing the lift (. . .) and once the 'rails' (on which the lift slides up and down) have been installed, the scaffolding is removed from the cabin and the doors are installed (so that you work in safety because they're closed) . . . then you can assemble the cabin, and at that point only the lift technicians work on it.

In the weeks following the accident, further meetings took place at *The Harbour* between the technicians and the owners. The purpose was no longer to determine the immediate causes of the accident but to identify the underlying factors responsible for it, so that procedures for the management of external firms working on site by *The Harbour*'s technicians could be changed if necessary.

It was decided that the accident was due to an organizational 'custom' which had implicitly given rise to the situation of danger. Two factors were identified as particularly important. The first was the removal some days before the accident of the scaffolding in the lift shaft, which made it easier for the two electricians to climb down into the well. The second factor was the inclusion in the electrical company's contract of installation of the light fittings in the lift shaft, underestimating the danger involved.

> In this case we included installation of the internal light fittings in the electricians' contract . . . so they should have installed the perimeter lights in the lift shaft before the scaffolding was removed . . . but they said that if they did the work before the scaffolding was removed, we'd break some of the bulbs when we dismantled the scaffolding . . . so they did the work only after the scaffolding had been removed . . . and that's why the accident happened (. . .). (site engineer)

Over the next few months, *The Harbour* introduced controls on subcontractors in the case of particularly complex operations (for example, when several subcontractors were present on site). With specific regard to lift shafts, it was decided that these should be considered dangerous even after the masonry work had been completed, and in the future all work on lifts would be contracted only to the installation company.

6.5   Mending the texture and translating knowledge

The three episodes just described are representative of an equal number of prototypical situations of knowledge translation and its institutionalization (or failure of it) in organizational routines. The perception of the magnitude of the breakdown of normalcy provoked by the accident differs in the three episodes: it was very high in the case of the fatal accident, medium in the case of the workman who fell through the grid and even lower in that of the worker injured in the lift shaft.

Determination of the severity of breakdown is entirely assessed in terms of its emotional impact and it is not set in relation to objective parameters like the seriousness of the accident calculated in terms of days of hospitalization, or attribution of civil liability to the firm. I shall gauge the relative severity of the three breakdowns on the basis of the interviewees' perceptions of it, my purpose being to suggest that there is a possible relation between the perceived severity of a crisis, the ability of the organization to turn it into a learning opportunity and the way in which the texture of normalcy is mended. It is not my intention to assert the existence of a causal nexus among these three variables, since this would require empirical inquiry using a different methodology.

If we now consider the three potential learning situations, we may interpret them by examining the connections that existed before the breakdown, how they changed as a result of the subsequent mending processes and how knowledge was translated.

Corresponding to the first case − that of darning − is an invisible learning situation: an organizational context in which the actors deliberately avoided collective reflection on the accident and change to work practices. If we consider the texture of organizing prior to the accident, we find that the underlying assumption that tied together firm, technologies, people and risk situations consisted of a bureaucratic-formal view of safety and liability: in other words, a belief that the accident-prevention rules on their own are sufficient to prevent accidents, so that responsibility for any that occur attaches primarily to the individual.

The breakdown provoked an emotional reaction consisting in denial of the seriousness of what had happened. Silence was imposed by tacit accord, and it was reinforced by the sacking of the two workmen involved in the accident and by forming the conviction − not without argument and negotiation − that it was due to errors and chance.

The mending of the social order was driven by an endeavour to re-establish the material order and the meaning structures that existed prior to the breakdown, seeking to make both the damage and the darning work invisible. Just as in the art of darning the essential skill consists in concealing the technical operation of sewing the edges of the material together, so in the mending of the social order the desire to restore the *status quo* at *The Screen* gave rise to negotiation over the accident, its minimization, silence as a form of connivance and the avoidance of action that would entail change. Invisibility was therefore the result of a collective process of knowledge translation; a process that was also enacted by the organization's members who actively participated in keeping silence.

Invisible mending is a social practice by which the *status quo*[4] is restored, and it is enacted collectively through discursive and material as well as emotional alignment.

Unlike invisible darning, where the skill resides in its invisibility, when a patch is attached – for example to a pair of trousers – it is obvious that although the trousers are gone at the knees, they can still be worn. In this second type of accident, the organizational texture of safety was made up of a weave where the responsibility of the firm and of individuals was negotiated on a participatory basis and recognized as an 'object of attention', and also as an object of discretionality by the technicians, who could invest in it autonomously by taking decisions situated at the level of the construction site. The emotional and social breakdown was severe until the accident proved to be less serious than was first thought. It is interesting to note in this case that the opportunity for reflection and change intrinsic to the accident was indeed exploited, but in a particular way. In fact, the intention rule that presided over discussion of the accident can be summed up in the formula: 'what can the firm do to show that it complies with safety standards', rather than 'what can we do to make our building sites safer'. Consequently, changes to safety practices took place in the offices and not on the site.

The administrative personnel learnt how to comply more closely with formal requirements, how to show that they were extraneous to reckless behaviour by the workmen and how to give themselves better protection against future inspections. Consequently, one cannot say that the accident constituted an opportunity for knowledge translation focused on safety, and yet this nevertheless took place. I shall call it 'mock learning' in order to stress its lateral or instrumental character in relation to any primary content that it might have.

The term is reminiscent of Gouldner's (1954) concept of 'mock bureaucracy', which stresses formal compliance with organizational rules. Gouldner cites the example of no-smoking regulations to depict a situation in which a number of bureaucratic cues (rules, posters, inspections) call for enforcement of these regulations, but in everyday working life they are ignored by both managers and workers and treated as mere paraphernalia.

Gouldner (1954: 185) writes that 'a rule must be legitimated in terms of the group's values and will be more readily accepted if it is seen as furthering their own ends'. I wish to stress an analogy with practical knowledge and point to the social legitimation required for a form of knowledge to be made effective. With regard to industrial accidents, the concept of 'mock bureaucracy' as an organizational facade has been explored in a study of police bureaucracy (Jermier et al., 1991) and in analysis of mining disasters (Hynes and Prasad, 1997) as situations characterized by overt violations of safety rules in the workplace. However, while it is well known that numerous safety regulations are neither respected nor enforced (they belong to the category of 'bureaucratic paraphernalia'), more ambiguous is the case of mock learning: that is, of situations in which the learning process is deflected to secondary matters. A striking example is provided by the educational system. What are the first things that a child learns at school? Probably s/he learns how to pass muster as a pupil (compliance with what the teachers want), only subsequently does s/he learn what is being taught. The situation in building sites or in an educational context is similar. Mock learning is therefore a way to mend the social order which comprises deliberate reflection on the breakdown, and also changes made to social practices, but the knowledge translation process is focused on secondary matters and driven by a need for legitimation.

Finally, in the third case, the degree of cognitive, social and emotional breakdown was less than in the other two, but greater importance was attached to the accident as an occasion to take precautions and as an opportunity to review organizational practices. The mending of the organizational texture followed the opposite logic to that of invisible mending. In this case, in fact, the mending was intended to be entirely visible and in harmony with the adjoining textures, as when pieces of cloth are fitted together when a quilt is being stitched.

The specific skill involved in quilt making is bricolage: that is, using what is to hand to invent something new and make imaginative re-use of what is old and left over. The metaphor of the quilt brings with it the historical-cultural dimension in which the organizational texture comprises situations of the past, and elaboration of the present is a form of learning from experience.

I call this form of knowledge translation 'catch learning' in order to emphasize the action of seizing an opportunity and of treating even accidents as opportunities.

Note that the texture of practices prior to the accident was already interwoven with values, behaviours and practices which favoured the emergence of safety as the result of the alignment of persons, things and ideas. Repair practices therefore tend to modify organizational routines, but these are modified by repairing the threads, the connections in action, which restore continuity with the past.

When comparing the three cases that I have selected for analysis, one may ask whether the difference among them resides in the degree of breakdown – so that it is more likely that less serious accidents will be opportunities for knowledge translation – or whether it resides in the quality of the texture of organizing prior to the breakdown. What, we may ask, would have happened if the young electrician in the third of our cases had died? Denial or a review of routines? Hypothetical reasoning does not enjoy much credence in the scientific community, yet it can test the plausibility of a story and how a community socially constructs its criterion of plausibility. Although a quantitative study could be used to verify this hypothesis, I shall further develop and test the interpretative framework centred on mending practices. The heuristic potential of this framework consists in showing that the social processes of mending are connected to the quality and configuration of the relations that existed prior to the social breakdown. The image that I have in mind is that of resplicing broken threads; and this can be done by restoring the sense of continuity between before and after a traumatic event. Not only can continuity be restored in a variety of ways but, as the second and third cases show, continuity does not exclude change. Put otherwise, I prefer to hypothesize a relation between the type of organizational texture that views safety as the individual's responsibility and mending processes intended to restore a *status quo* so that the event is forgotten. I also hypothesize a relation between a texture ambivalent towards safety and mending practices which respond more to the form of the law than its substance; and likewise between a texture woven together so that it gives priority to safety and mending practices which set a premium on reflexivity in action.

However, I do not want to discard the hypothesis that the intensity of the breakdown is related to mending practices. Theoretically, a very serious accident may prompt forms of social denial just as much as a minor accident may be dismissed as unimportant, and in neither case are processes of collective reflection and change to the premises for action set in motion. Rather, I offer a suggestion in this regard which I have borrowed from sociologists[5] who have studied memory work in relation to social events like acts of terrorism in Italy (Tota, 2001) or reconstruction after an earthquake (Cavalli, 1997). In the latter case, it has been shown, for example, that reconstruction has been more rapid and efficacious in communities which more actively remembered and celebrated the feeling of continuity with the past. By contrast, in areas where memory work was less intense, or where the tragedy, by introducing a feeling of discontinuity, induced a desire to forget, the reconstruction has taken longer.

I believe that memory work is one of the social processes involved in the mending of the social order, and that the metaphors of the patch and the quilt serve to symbolize the event that must not be forgotten and to historicize the mode of ordering. In fact the processes of social remem-

bering and forgetting constitute a contested terrain shaped by conflicting interpretations of events, and the ways of giving an enduring form
to memories depend on the technologies of memory (Tota, 1999).

The feminist practice that theorized memory work during the 1980s
(Haug, 1987) viewed it in terms of needlecraft and process. The notion
of 'memory work as needlecraft' referred to the analysis of the self as a
historical product, as the trajectory of becoming, and to the self as a *product*
both *cultural* (form of discourse) and *social* (relational practice). With
'memory work' as a *process*, it focused on the way in which awareness
and identity take shape in relation to modes of involvement in a productive activity through:

- identification of the ways in which individuals construct themselves
  within existing structures;
- the ways in which they reproduce the social structures;
- the points/moments at which change is possible, at which our bonds
  are stronger/weaker, at which a new equilibrium has been reached.

These considerations on memory work conclude my analysis with
'ennoblement' of the metaphor with which it began. While the art of
darning relates to a humble activity and to the invisibility of the social
work of repairing the social order, the metaphor of embroidery as
memory work relates to the art of representation and inscribing form
and aesthetics in the social order. Most of all, it emphasizes the difference between the almost unconscious activity of repairing the social
order and the highly conscious one of remembering so as not to forget,
as on a day of remembrance. Memory work therefore symbolizes the
possibility of translating knowledge from experience, but for it to do so
the social facts must be fixed in the collective memory and collectively
historicized and interpreted as lessons of history, whether on a large scale
or on the individual or organizational one.

6.6   To sum up: between the visible and the invisible

Workplace accidents are occasions for translating knowledge from the
place where the 'knowing' crystallizes into a 'known' to the culture of
practice when a network of organizational and interorganizational relations stabilizes their meaning, allocates individual, organizational and
social responsibility, so that accidents may become occasions for learning and changing established practices.

This stabilization is the outcome of a process of engineering the heterogeneous which realigns interpretations, people, materials and organizational practices after an accident. It is not merely the result of an interpretative process. However, the accountability of the accident's meaning is an important part of the almost invisible processes involved in maintaining a social and organizational texture which connects in action the various socially meaningful strands of organizational activity. This texture of connections emerges from action, and the more the action is held together by a mode of ordering the heterogeneity of people, things and ideas, the more it is taken for granted. Yet it is fundamentally fragile and subject to constant negotiation and renegotiation by those involved in weaving its threads together.

A critical event – which an accident usually is – is a breakdown in what was previously taken for granted, and in the situation of normalcy that had been patiently woven together in the microinteractions of everyday life. This breakdown upsets the emotional as well as social order, and also those of decisions and actions. As a consequence, disorder takes over from order, and actors find themselves wittingly or unwittingly engaged in normalcy repair practices. As the damaged texture of normalcy is mended, reflexivity may arise on practices that were previously taken for granted, so that the accident may provide an opportunity for discussion of the previous social order and the introduction of change.

Three ideal-typical situations of translating knowledge in practice have been defined as follows:

- Invisible learning, where the relational network comprising all the organizational actors actively collaborates in the emotional denial of the accident, the intention being to re-establish the previous *status quo* and to make the repair practices invisible. This was the situation in which the accident caused most damage to the previous texture, and this texture was centred on a conception of safety as the individual's responsibility.
- Mock learning, where the accident becomes an occasion for managerial practices but the safety practices actually changed are administrative ones concerning the firm's accountability to the supervisory authorities. Reflection is guided by an endeavour to distinguish the firm's responsibility from those of individuals. The magnitude of the breakdown was moderate, and the connective texture of previous actions centred on the ambivalence between care and deresponsibilization.

- Catch learning, where the opportunity to revise both administrative and work practices is fully exploited in order to prevent the repetition of similar events. The perceived severity of the breakdown is less than in the previous case, although the accident could have been regarded as more serious or more distressing because of its dramatic nature. However, it was interpreted within a connective texture which boasted a tradition of constant attention to safety.

I have proposed a reading of accidents and the learning opportunities connected with them through an unusual lens. An accident, in fact, requires the threads that have been broken to be spliced back together, and this can be done by restoring the sense of continuity between before and after a traumatic event. The various forms taken by the repair practice that I have described reflect various types of weaving:

- darning as a practice intended to conceal the damage so that it is forgotten;
- patching as a practice intended to prevent any further damage;
- quilting as a bricolage and the art of recycling which does not seek to conceal but instead to historicize continuity through change.

A further line of inquiry that might develop from the foregoing analysis of mending practices concerns memory work. In fact, the historical-social dimension implicit in the three kinds of mending relates to different forms of memory work as a social and organizational practice, and implies that if we are to reflect on experience we must first recognize an experience in the flux of becoming, preserve its memory and oppose the forces of oblivion.

NOTES

1. The field data were collected by Francesca Odella and Davide Nicolini, to whom I am extremely grateful. Francesca Odella also processed the preliminary data and wrote the research report 'Si può imparare dagli incidenti? Gestione della sicurezza e impatto organizzativo degli incidenti sul lavoro', Trento, 1999. Responsibility for the interpretations offered here is mine alone.
2. Trentino-Alto Adige is a region in the north-east of Italy and was the territorial setting for the research.

3. I am indebted to Kirsten Foot for directing my attention to Henke's work, and for pointing out the close similarity between my concept of *mending* and that of *repair*.

4. Mindful of Heraclitus' dictum that you cannot step into the same river twice, I do not mean that the *status quo* is the result, rather that is the intention.

5. I am indebted to Annalisa Tota for suggesting a link between our two lines of inquiry during our long summer conversations. Responsibility for transposing memory work to analysis of organizations is entirely mine, although I regard it as a good example of cross-fertilization between apparently distant areas of analysis.

CHAPTER SEVEN

Knowing within a Field of Practices

Language is not meant for telling the truth.
(Lyotard, 1977: 96)

My intention in this chapter is to explore the less evident aspects of network learning, defined here as unintentional learning, and the linkages that arise informally and indirectly among organizations. The focus will be on how knowledge circulates within a network, and as it does so creates that network. Also examined will be how knowledge is conveyed from place to place via intermediaries, which mobilize knowledge and artefacts, and the processes which anchor that knowledge to practices in a field of practices.

Every organization is said to be essentially a social network (Lincoln, 1982), so that networking may therefore be regarded as the activity of giving form to sociality. Networking presupposes competence – both general competence in acting as a socially competent member, and specific competence in whatever is subject to the interaction. But how do knowledge, knowing, networks and networking link together? In recent years an impressive amount of research has been done on networks of knowledge and on networks as knowledge. The main question addressed has been how knowledge and information flow through a network, and the answers have been as diverse as the definitions given to 'network'.

The term 'network' is fashionable because its semantic ambiguity allows its use as an evocative metaphor for numerous collaborative relationships (Van Wijk, Van Den Bosch and Volberda, 2003). While the term may be applied to many configurations of relations, the literature on network and knowledge focuses mainly on environments and relationships, examining the performances of networks formally organized for innovation or product development, and where the interest is more in the exploration than the exploitation or mere circulation of knowledge.

This obviously conditions the way in which the methodology constructs its subject of study.

The state of art, according to Van Wijk and colleagues, of how networks foster the management and organization of knowledge centres around three perspectives: social networks (originating in sociology and anthropology); external networks (originating in economics); and internal networks (originating in management and mainly in international business). While the first perspective focuses mainly on the network as an analytical tool employed by researchers, the other two conceive the network as a governance mode adopted by the organization. Although the three perspectives[1] have contributed to understanding of the facilitatory role of networks in creating and integrating knowledge, I shall focus on the first stream of research, omitting discussion of networks as forms of organizational governance.

Social network research has concerned itself mainly with knowledge transfer through 'ties', following Granovetter (1992), by examining actors' structural and relational embeddedness in networks. Ties have information benefits that accrue in three forms: access, timing and referral (Burt, 1992). This signifies that network ties influence access to the partners, enable actors to obtain information more rapidly and provide information on opportunities. Weak ties are most effective when knowledge is being sought and non-complex knowledge is being transferred, while strong ties more efficiently transfer complex knowledge. The density of a network, its cohesion, its openness or closedness and its structure are the properties that network researchers define with the term 'embeddedness'.

Two views have been put forward on how information and knowledge flow through a network (Van Wijk, Van Den Bosch and Volberda, 2003). The first coalesces into 'structural hole theory' (Burt, 1992) and concerns the brokering of knowledge around the centrality of an actor in the network. The second centres on 'social capital theory' (Coleman, 1988), arguing the thesis that a network is reproduced because of its value in preserving an individual's social capital, which it defines as the set of social resources embedded in the relationship. The social capital perspective emphasizes the cohesion of ties and maintains that actors should be linked as closely as possible, in that many actors in a dense network share the same ties and are therefore structural equivalents. Both views are more concerned with the form of a network and the quality of the ties than with what is exchanged and how the network is formed. To be noted is that the term 'knowledge' is used mainly as a synonym for information. Indeed, many field studies have concerned themselves principally with how firms obtain information, how opportunistic behaviour and imperfect information increase search costs and how trust enables the exchange of information and network formation.

While the main body of field research studies has examined how knowledge and information manifest themselves in networks, Kogut, Shan and Walker (1993) and Kogut (2000) argue that networks should be considered essentially as knowledge. They do so because networks are the outcome of know-how about cooperation (who will cooperate and who has what capability), so that networks constitute capabilities that augment the value of the firm. Hence, knowing how to network is what characterizes network knowledge, and networking can be viewed as the activity of learning in networks (Araujo, 1998; Araujo and Easton, 1999).

To be noted is that the term 'knowledge' is sometimes used in a sense that comes very close to 'information', and sometimes in a sense more closely akin to 'competence'. Two 'capabilities' are ascribed to network knowledge: one is 'absorptive capacity' (Cohen and Levinthal, 1990), the other 'alliance capability' (Lorenzoni and Lipparini, 1999). The former is built on prior knowledge (the more knowledge the firm has in a certain domain, the easier learning will be), the latter is the ability to interact with other firms which improves learning. Are these competences properties of the network?

I maintain that there is a 'blind spot' in the literature on networks and knowledge and it is constituted by questions that revolve around the fact that social construction of network is also an expression of knowledge and that knowledge is mobilized in actual 'doings' and 'sayings' and past 'dones' and 'saids'. If a network is not the expression of a set of interorganizational accords – i.e. a form of organization itself – companies, just like individuals, simultaneously belong to numerous networks. It is therefore necessary to bear the complexity of relations among networks in mind.

There are some basic assumptions made in the current literature that are open to challenge. The first is the idea that knowledge is transferred, and in the process of being transferred remains identical; the second is the idea that networks are kept together by collaborative relationships; and the third is that embeddedness is a given that should not need explanation. I start with the last point, noting that when we say 'network as knowledge' we imply not only the firm's know-how in establishing cooperative relationships, but also that knowing how to do so in a competent way means that knowledge is embedded in social relations. The idea that knowledge and knowing are distributed in a network (and kept within it) invites closer consideration of distributed knowledge and of the processes that circulate and translate knowledge. This point will be elaborated by reference to empirical research which analysed how safety knowledge is shaped and circulated in an institutional and territorial network. First, however, I shall briefly review the contribution that the concept of 'distributed knowledge' is able to make to the literature on network learning.

Paradoxically, those who study networks rarely cite the work of those who study 'distributed knowledge', and vice versa, although both bodies of literature take an ecological rather than strictly cognitive approach to their subject matter. Their orientation towards an ecology of learning derives from two lines of inquiry (de Fornel and Quéré, 1999): the ecological psychology of Gibson (1982) and the ecology of thought from a psychological point of view (Hutchins, 1995) or a sociological one (Cicourel, 1994).

Gibson is noted for his notion of 'affordance', which he uses to refer to the fact that individuals directly perceive the functional value of objects, situations or events, and therefore their practical meaning. The use value of 'objects' which afford opportunities for action, which elicit gestures, which signal the possibility or convenience of doing something, which constitute a risk or a threat or an obstacle, are perceived directly. Situated behaviour is directed by a search for these affordances in the environment, and organisms are 'attuned' to the affordances in their environment.[2] Besides research in psychology, Gibson has influenced investigation of objects in their everyday contexts: for instance, the study by Norman (1993), who inquires whether artefacts contain the script of their use, so that humans relate to them by following the instructions and knowledge incorporated in them. Objects, therefore, are not passive and 'ignorant'; rather, they are active containers of expert knowledge and instructions for their use. Likewise, research on technology-in-use (Suchman et al., 1999) suggests that study should be made not of technology itself but of the interactions between technology and the social contexts of its being-in-use. Networks, too, comprise forms of affordance which are more complex than the structural characteristics of relations and which simultaneously facilitate or obstruct the distribution of knowledge. If we transfer the concept of affordance to a network, we can interpret it with its twofold meaning as a network enabling relationships and constraining them. Suffice it to consider how ICTs as mediums of communication influence the contents of relations between humans and non-humans.

Another highly influential author is Hutchins (1995), who has studied work groups such as pilots in an aeroplane cockpit or a ship's crew during docking manoeuvres. He argues that these sets of socio-technical relations should be treated as 'cognitive systems' with their own structures and inner representations of their relationships with the environment and intelligent artefacts. In these systems, cognition is not the expression of an individual mind but the product of a functional system able to convey representational states and to process information. Hutchins stresses the situated character of this distributed cognition: it is situated because it takes place in an environment containing numerous resources, and it acquires form within a system of multiple interactions among components of diverse nature. It unfolds in ordinary activity, that is, within an ecology of thought, by which is meant that thought does not develop within a 'natural' environment but instead in one which is largely artificial and where artefacts and instruments form an ecology.

The sociological version of the ecology of knowledge originated with Cicourel (1994), who pointed out an aspect which I consider to be extremely important: the unequal character of the distribution of knowledge. Cicourel emphasizes that individuals who work together may have very different 'knowledges'. Consequently, although the conception of socially distributed cognition is similar to that of distributed intelligence, it differs from it in important respects. The unequal distribution of knowledge opens the way for investigation into forms of power and whatever else may undermine the excessively harmonious conception of the complementary distribution of knowledge aimed solely at the performance of a task within a structured and hierarchized group.

What does an ecological definition of network learning entail? It requires, for example, reformulation of the question 'How do knowledge and information flow through a network?', which in fact presupposes the existence of knowledge as a discrete object and of a predefined network through which it flows. However, if one assumes a relational view in which what is called 'knowledge' is formed within a set of relations among 'knowing' subjects and a portion of the world defined as knowledge; if one assumes that this set of relations forms a network by means of a relational dynamic, that the interactions are situated in time and space and comprise the materiality of the world and of the artefacts in it, that these artefacts are actively involved in the action taking place around them, then the above question can be reformulated. One may ask how systems of distributed and fragmented knowledge constitute themselves, stabilize themselves and reproduce themselves, and by means of what dynamics knowledge is tied to knowing, practice to practising, network to networking, organization to organizing. One asks, therefore, how knowledge is translated both into relations and by means of them.

The idea of translating knowledge concerns the continuous process by which knowledge practices emerge, are sustained, become enduring and eventually disappear. The process of translation thus creates the network and the actors just as much as it creates the object: actors, relational networks and translation processes are constructed through interactions (Latour, 1992).

If these insights are imported into the literature on network learning and knowing, they enable us to define a network as distributed and fragmented knowledge and they prompt us to investigate the processes by which distributed, dispersed and fragmented items of knowledge are coordinated and connected. Finally, while the literature on the creation of new knowledge is very interesting, the field of social regulation which institutionalizes and supervises the social interpretation of the knowledge thus validated is a less 'heroic' and much more quotidian area of inquiry. Yet it is this that I intend to analyse by examining the ways in which a plurality of organizations interact to establish a normative conception of safety which emerges from a field of situated practices.

7.1   Networks as distributed and fragmented knowledge

Knowledge about safety circulates in a network of organizations consisting of individual building firms, the institutions responsible for prevention, supervision and certification, and the agencies and institutions that provide training, Thus constituted is a dense web of relationships among organizations which, within a territory delimited by the state's administrative apparatus, are all directly or indirectly acquainted with each other. These relationships are by their nature highly diverse: they may consist of collaboration, competition, administrative regulation, or certification. All together they form a network of knowledge exchanges; a network which is the context for the learning and circulation of knowledge and which establishes a local safety culture. The interorganizational relations rest on a set of consolidated practices, which extend from the individual to the institutions and vice versa.

I shall start my analysis with the dissonant voices described in Chapter 5, and with the various discourses on safety that interweave to form the texture which interconnects persons, communities, organizations and institutions within a local safety culture. These voices express diverse logics, notwithstanding the presence of the same situation and a context of interdependent action. I earlier interpreted this state of affairs as action intended to construct identity and difference and to position individuals and their community of belonging within specific discourses on safety. I shall not start with the actors because we have already seen that the voices on safety cut across the phenomenon: in a certain sense they are embodied in artefacts and give rise to institutional forms as agents, or to normative ones as much expressions of a 'voice' as the means by which it is heard at numerous nodes of the network.

In fact we should bear in mind that the term 'discourse' is used to denote a set of texts able to anchor and give a relatively stable form to an object or set of objects, together with the structures and practices involved in their production and circulation. Foucault (1972: 49) defines discourses as 'practices which systematically form the object of which they speak'. Discourses are forms of strategic arranging which are intentional but do not necessarily have a subject (Law, 1994: 21; Foucault, 1977: 95). To every discourse there corresponds an entrenched texture of alliances, which facilitates the translation and mobilization of knowledge and modes of knowing.

We shall see that a safety network within a territorially circumscribed context can be described by the following three 'voices' which locally express three discourses on safety. These three voices respectively express discourses on:

- safety as supervision and punishment;
- safety as safe technologies and artefacts;
- safety as instruction and knowledge.

These three frames of meaning and discursive practices took material form in three groups of actors manifesting a social division of labour and a social and institutional system.

The interorganizational network surrounding the building industry organizations studied[3] comprised three main groups of institutions:

1. those responsible for the legal and normative aspects of safety: local accident prevention agencies and others which supervise compliance with safety standards (e.g. UOPI[4]), the judiciary and other judicial bodies;
2. those concerned with the technical aspects of safety (e.g. the labour inspectorate and the local safety agencies), and in particular with the certification of equipment;

3. those delivering education and training: the building school and the Cassa Edile (Construction Workers' Fund), the provincial administration and safety consultants.

It should be borne in mind that the network does not have boundaries and may be plotted on the basis of numerous other relations and actors: as well as the building firms, therefore, also the trade unions and the employers' associations, INAIL,[5] and others besides, with relations ramifying and linking with numerous other networks.

I shall examine each of these 'voices' in terms of the material-discursive practices by which – through 'doing' and 'saying' and through the mobilization of intermediaries – they translate safety knowledge and anchor it in local practices. In order to analyse how safety knowledge is transferred, and in being transferred is changed, I shall introduce the two concepts of 'intermediary' and 'anchoring'.

The notion of 'intermediary' comprises a wide variety of elements of social interaction, and it relates to aspects rarely considered by other theories of knowledge. Actor network theory stresses this feature by asserting the fundamental 'heterogeneity' of the networks which define the creation and circulation of knowledge.

According to Callon (1992) there are four very general types of intermediary:

*   *human beings*, with the skills and knowledge that they generate and reproduce;
*   *artefacts*, which include all the non-human entities that facilitate performance of a task;
*   *texts and 'inscriptions'*, which include everything that is written or recorded, as well as the channels through which they circulate;
*   *money* in its manifold forms.

A sociology of translation is a sociology of mediation since the intermediaries represent delegations and inscriptions of actions already initiated elsewhere; they do not repeat actions but transform these in surprising and unexpected ways. A model of translation/inscription implies a model of interpretation/reading. Here the concept of anchoring (Goffman, 1974) may help.

The concept of 'anchoring' can be illustrated by referring to the frame of a picture, which performs two functions. On the one hand it frames the picture and in doing so emphasizes its separation from the background; on the other, it serves to attach – to anchor – the picture to the wall, that is, to give it a temporarily stable positioning.

We may therefore imagine that the translation/transformation of the knowledge circulating within a network of interorganizational relations is driven – if it is not discarded – by a series of intermediaries which establish connections-in-action and function as both propellants and anchoring points. I shall now depict the network of interorganizational relations by referring to the principal discourses which engage in dissonant conversation with each other (and which we have already met), on the assumption that discourses are effects of the organizational and institutional actors that sustain them.

7.2 Safety as surveillance and punishment

The discourse on safety as surveillance and repression is institutionally sustained by supervision and prevention agencies, as well as by the judiciary. These agencies share a common interpretative frame because they work closely together, have well-established channels of communication and engage in common and complementary practices. They have two main tasks: to ensure compliance with accident prevention regulations and to assist the judicial police with inquests and inquiries.

These agencies embrace a conception of safety centred on the idea that safety results from the correct application of rules and compliance with safety regulations. They consider safety to depend on control and on information about the regulations. We shall now see by which practices and intermediaries their discourse was translated to, and anchored in, the network's practices.

Inspection is one of the practical principles on which the 'safety as compliance with the rules' discourse is based. Inspection is both the main manner in which the regulatory agency participates in the social construction of safety and one of the principal mechanisms with which it constructs its identity.

Inspections are conducted autonomously by the agency and are performed by one or more inspectors who conduct spot checks on building sites. Because there are more building sites than officials – who spend more than half of their time dealing with paperwork in the office – available to inspect them, blanket inspections are not possible and checks must be performed at random. The criterion for selecting sites for inspection is therefore an attention rule which anchors the inspector's competence to the practices of his/her community and which is part of his/her tacit knowledge.

The criterion used to select building sites for inspection is inscribed in the professional vision:

> if [from outside] the site seems in order, then we don't bother. If instead, something strikes us as irregular, then we stop and inspect the site. From the outside it is possible to see if there are electricity lines and scaffolding, and what this scaffolding is like.

The encounter between an inspector and a building site is thus based on a 'knowing how to see'. But the logic of the encounter is well known to the building site as well, if I may thus anthropomorphize it. In this case, too, a 'mirror game' takes place. In fact one canonical practice in the building site is 'presenting the site well' so that it does not attract an inspector's attention. This is a competence tied directly to inspection activity, as evinced by the fact the most 'visible' sites — those located close to the town centre where the inspectors live and work — are 'neater' than those on the outskirts. It sometimes happens, indeed, that safety barriers are only erected on the side of the building facing the street, so that the inspection practice anchors the work practice in respect to safety issues.

If the inspector decides to stop, he enters the building site and checks its compliance with the safety regulations. He checks whether anti-fall barriers are in place, whether the electrical wiring has been correctly installed, whether equipment and machinery comply with safety standards, and whether they are used in accordance with the instructions. In the inspector's words:

> So in short we check whether the site complies with all the safety regulations. (Chief Inspector)

One notes that the inspector's practice follows a logic similar to that of the engineers, the logic which I have called the 'check-list mentality'. But unlike that of the engineers, the inspector's knowledge is of a procedural type in that it starts from the rules and then verifies compliance with them.

The inspection is the means with which the regulatory agency translates and imposes its decision-making premises, seeking to anchor them in building-site safety. What happens during an inspection is more similar to a negotiation than the simple imposition of orders. In this case, the attention rules are manifest in what the inspector decides to see or to ignore, and in what he decides to report or to let go:

> If the earthing hasn't been done properly, or if anti-fall barriers haven't been installed, then we report it . . .but it's obvious that if I find a plank with a nail sticking out of it on a site which is generally in order, then I let the matter drop.

During a spot check, the site foreman accompanies the inspector, seeking to negotiate the meaning of what the latter sees:

> **Inspector**: This parapet is out of order.
> **Site foreman**: You must be joking, it's standard workmanship.
> **Inspector**: No, no, it's too low.
> **Site foreman**: Aw, come on, it's five centimetres.
> **Inspector**: No, I must be strict about this.

As the site foreman tries to negotiate the meaning of the rule, he is also learning the logic of the inspector's practice so that he can make use of it when the next inspection is made. For his part, the inspector constructs both the situated meaning of a rule and the practice of its implementation, since it is probable that on the next occasion the site foreman will point out that the parapet is of regulation height.

On the site, the competence deriving from this type of interaction with the control authority is described as 'learning to get ready for an inspection'. This involves the ability of the site foreman to identify the aspects on which the inspector will focus and which should therefore comply with the regulations. Interestingly, 'getting ready for the inspection' includes a deliberate decision to neglect certain details so that the inspector can write a 'minimum' report.

All inspections, in fact, must conclude with a fine. Consequently, the organizational actors help the inspector in his work, directing his attention to some minor irregularity so that he is distracted from looking for other, more serious breaches of the regulations. Once this competence has been acquired by the foreman, it is transmitted to the occupational community together with implicit fragments of 'practical wisdom' on how to cosmeticize a building site so that it looks safe. But at the same time the inspector and his community are aware of the mirror game.

When the inspector has completed all the checks, he compiles a report. This is the intermediary which materializes and testifies to the encounter between the two organizations, and it constitutes the text which gives concrete form to memory of the event. The report always imposes a fine and prescribes corrective measures to be undertaken on the site within a certain period of time. On the date specified, the inspector returns to the building site, and if the corrective measures have been taken, the fine can be paid and the offence extinguished. Otherwise – in the event of non-compliance or failure to pay the fine – judicial proceedings begin. Hence the text associates the inspection agency with a building site and then associates it with money. If the association does not come about, the text-as-intermediary is empowered to associate higher level institutions with itself.

The 'voice' of this group of actors (the inspection agency and the judicial authorities) takes material form in the activation of the local meanings of the rules; meanings which are exemplified and negotiated in the practices of the inspection and in the content of the report. 'Seeing', 'doing', 'saying' and 'writing' become precise directions on what constitutes 'good safety practice' in the area under the agency's jurisdiction.

Moreover, the inspection as practice involves reflexive construction of the identity of the control agency as the 'custodian' of the rules, and it reinforces the notion of safety as compliance with the regulations (what may be called 'the bureaucratic vision of safety'). The inspector never explicitly asks whether the building site is safe, but always whether it complies with the rules – accepting and confirming the equation between the two terms. The fact that every inspection concludes with a report and a fine sanctions the idea of safety as an unachievable bureaucratic ideal and confirms the principle that accidents are due to failure to apply the law, which gives further legitimacy to the agency.

Although formally independent, the magistracy and the supervisory agencies are tied to each other by mutually reinforcing complementary practices.

From the magistracy's point of view, safety is a matter of individual responsibility and a potential source of liability and punishment:

I may be stating the obvious, but behind an accident there is always some breach of the safety regulations, or of the law. (magistrate)

The investigation is one of the main practices with which the magistracy constructs and perpetuates its discourse of safety as hinging on liability and punishment. An investigation always ensues from notification of a breach of the regulations or an accident. The law prescribes, in fact, that all information constituting 'notizia di reato' (notice of offence) must be forwarded to the local magistrate's office. In this way the magistracy receives information and data from both the regulatory agencies in regard to non-compliance with safety regulations, and from other agencies involved in the post-accident phase, for example healthcare personnel and the INAIL (which will pay the compensation).

The focus of investigations by the judicial police is the description of the event and determination of liability. The investigative activity therefore consists in collecting evidence and writing a report whose principal purpose is to interpret the event in terms of punishability:

> When at first sight the accident seems quite simple (a worker who's tripped, a brick that's fallen on someone's foot), we get the *Carabinieri* to carry out the inquiries. When instead it seems complex, the investigation is allocated to the accident prevention office. In this case the office holds an inquiry, gathers evidence and writes a report. The inspector first interviews the accident victim, then the witnesses, and gets an idea of the dynamics of the accident, and finally determines whether the accident prevention regulations have been infringed, whether an offence has been committed and consequently whether criminal liability is involved. The inspector's report states which article of law has been breached, then I make a first assessment of the case and send the prosecutor a detailed report which itemizes everything. Finally, the prosecutor takes what he thinks is the right decision: either to dismiss the case or start proceedings. The magistrate's main concern is to establish the causal nexus; that is, determine whether the accident has been due to negligence or breach of the regulations on accident prevention. If the accident has been caused by behaviour not punishable by law, it is evidently a fortuitous or accidental event. So, in order to bring charges, a detailed description is necessary. Normally, an accident occurs by chance (for example a hammer blow on a finger, or someone who slips on the stairs), but one also often finds an illegality. (judicial police expert)

This extract highlights the difference in the accountability system between a layperson and an expert. Because the intention is to identify a miscreant on whom to inflict punishment, not an explanation of the event, the investigation consolidates existing practices and knowledge, and it reinforces a culture of safety predicated on individual 'transgressions' that often obstructs the learning of 'lessons' from the event in question.

However, in the course of investigations, 'enlightened' magistrates, or ones with different 'visions' of safety, may produce new knowledge on safety when they reject current explanatory schemes and construct new ones by mobilizing segments of the institutional network. The investigation thus becomes an opportunity to influence the attention rules of the regulatory agencies, which usually undertake the investigative work, and through those rules influence the local context.

An interesting example of how this happens is provided by an event which led to modification of the technical safety specifications for a porphyry rock cutting machine. Following a large number of accidents, all of the same kind, the magistrate rejected the findings of the investigators, who blamed the accidents on negligence, and asked other technicians to furnish an alternative explanation which would cast doubt, if not on the machine's conformity with technical standards, at least on interpretation of the latter. A seizure order was issued, with the provision that the machine would be released when it had been 'regularized'. Thus, at least at the local level, the magistrate engendered and disseminated a change to practical safety knowledge.

While on the one hand the discourse on safety as compliance with the regulations gives primacy to the institutions of supervision and control, on the other it is reflected in the importance assumed by the safety intermediaries generated by those institutions. Once again, these intermediaries are texts in the form of laws, circulars on application of the regulations, and the like, which constitute the main means and the vocabulary through which instructions on particular aspects of safety competence are transmitted. The circulation of these intermediaries within the network, and the importance of new regulations and circulars issued externally to it, are constant features of every aspect of the construction of safety.

We have therefore seen that one of the most authoritative voices in the network pertains to the institution performing functions of control and repression. The main practices by which this voice makes itself heard and acts upon the 'significant others' are inspection and investigation. The intermediaries that implement these practices and create relationships and linkages consist of both practice-performing humans and non-humans in the form of texts and money. The intermediaries convey – in the sense that they mobilize and negotiate – the local meanings of safety rules, while they anchor their interpretation in the materiality of texts and in the reciprocal expectations of repeated interaction (the mirror game).

7.3   Safety as safe technologies and artefacts

Control over the 'technological' aspects of safety are distributed among a number of agencies following a series of ambiguous changes made to the remits of the various offices concerned with workplace safety. The main activities of these agencies are inspection, conformity checks and certification that machinery complies with safety standards established by law. Their principal task is therefore very similar to that of the other regulatory agencies apart from the fact that it consists mainly in the issue of certificates and authorizations following technical inspections. For example, every crane used on a building site has a log book provided by the crane constructor which certifies compliance with the safety regulations and is used to log the periodic service trials and checks undergone by all complex machinery.

Although these offices undertake activities similar to that of the regulatory agencies, they embrace a rather different notion of safety, one based on the idea that:

> it's possible to incorporate safety in equipment, tools and machinery (safety engineer)

It is widely assumed by engineering culture that knowledge can be transferred by incorporating it in material artefacts and technologies. A significant example of how competence on safety can be conveyed through material artefacts for professional use is provided by the following episode (Gherardi and Nicolini, 2000). One of our informants pointed out an apparently 'irrelevant' difference between a relatively antiquated cement mixer and a technologically 'more advanced' one. Both consisted of the familiar rotating drum, the motor and the 'handle' – that is, the steering wheel which moves the drum into the loading or mixing position (with the 'mouth' upwards) or into the pouring position (the cylinder is tipped downwards so that the cement can be poured out of it).

Whereas the antiquated cement mixer was fitted with a spoked wheel, the modern one had a solid disk instead of the spokes (Figure 7.1).

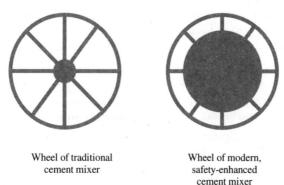

Wheel of traditional
cement mixer

Wheel of modern,
safety-enhanced
cement mixer

Figure 7.1 Technology as intermediary

The function of the disk is to prevent the operator's arm from getting trapped in the spokes during pouring operations, because once the drum starts tipping, its weight builds a momentum which may easily break the operator's arm.

The disk is a simple piece of metal, and it certainly cannot be considered an example of 'high technology'. And yet it conveys a concentrate of knowledge on the building site whereby the new design incorporates the experience gained from a number of accidents and injuries, the search for a solution and its inscription in an artefact.

The spoked wheel is an intermediary in the translation process, and like every technology it enables practical activity but at the same time conditions it. It attempts to introduce into the situation the designer's notion of how a safer practice can be performed. For the translation to be successful from the point of view of the designer, the script implicitly comprised in the artefact must be followed by the user. However, the attempt to exert distant control on the action of the user via the artefact may well be counteracted by the tendency of that user to persevere with established practice, for example by reinterpreting the artefact in terms of normal routine, so that some users may decide to remove the disk and continue to rotate the mixer 'as usual'.

Thus evidenced is how objects – the spoked wheel for example – 'act' upon subjects, asking them to follow a script, embedding in themselves human expertise and also incorporating a prescription in the form of an implicit 'don't do it!'. In this case, embedded in the object is a material-semantic code that blocks human action and shapes human/non-human interaction.

The aim of the regulatory agencies can be summed up as an endeavour to enforce the use of artefacts, which in their turn exert 'control' over situated practices. Possibilities to reinvent or modify the use of artefacts are not limitless, however, for they are restricted by physical and social constraints. On the one hand, this explains the constant interest shown by various 'controllers' in building-site technologies and equipment. These are cases, in fact, where negotiation on compliance with technical standards often consists of no more than verification of the engineering integrity of technologies and equipment. On the other hand, the existence of margins for the modification of artefacts requires the presence of 'institutional' controllers able to discourage the practical 'interpretation' of technology by humans.

Within this discourse on safety, the work of inspectors and certifiers takes the form of an endeavour by the institution concerned to deploy all its coercive and repressive power to compel the use of some artefacts rather than others, and to discourage the 'decomposition' of an artefact and its reinterpretation in consolidated practices. Every item of equipment must comply with safety standards, and it must be used without changes to the technical structure that guarantees its capacity to control the practice of the final user. The institution acts from a distance on the users by forming alliances with artefacts which, by virtue of their presence in the context of use, exert control over the situated action, and in doing so give material form to the values embraced by the institution. The result is the introduction into the network of material intermediaries which tacitly embody knowledge and require users to be competent in their day-to-day use.

However, paradoxically, the capacity of artefacts and technologies to convey knowledge is at times partly a function of their *inflexibility*: the less modifiable and disposable the artefact, the more it is able to exert effects on the user's practice. Authors call this the 'interpretative flexibility of technology' (Giddens, 1979; Barley, 1986; Orlikowski, 1992); an expression which emphasizes the fact that every artefact and technology can be modified when it is first adopted and as it is used, although this reinvention or modification is not infinitely possible because it is restricted by physical and institutional constraints. This, for that matter, is a problem of which the designers and manufacturers of safety devices are well aware, and they endeavour to design devices that are 'human-proof'.

As an expert in safety artefacts put it:

> It's practically impossible to erect normal scaffolding safely [. . .] H-shaped scaffolding, though, has an in-built rigidity which prevents you from erecting and using it incorrectly [. . .] the only way for scaffolding to give this guarantee is if it's made so that even if you want to, it's difficult to erect it incorrectly.

In sum, if one conceives the introduction of innovations, either material, behavioural or conceptual, as a deliberate attempt to exert control from a distance, the success of such translation efforts depends on the effectiveness of the tactics used by the intermediaries to discourage alternative interpretations.

A further example is provided by the above-described changes to the technical specifications of the rock-cutting machine prompted by pressure from the magistrate. The regulations therefore provide an institutional mechanism whereby notification of a malfunction detected during an inspection or inquiries can be transmitted to the central level, where verification is made of whether a structural problem is involved (that is, one relative to the 'safety content' conveyed by the artefact) and requires change to the artefact by its manufacturer.

The ways in which the regulatory agencies seek to impose their discourse of safety – by encouraging or mandating the use of particular artefacts which generate 'safe' practice – also condition the ways in which the actors thus controlled seek to evade the imposition. A first method is obviously the non–use of standard-compliant apparatuses and systems. This may happen intentionally – for example, because new 'compliant' technologies are costly – or semi-intentionally out of plain ignorance. The regulatory agencies respond to this resistance in two ways: by maintaining vigilance and punishing breaches of the regulations, and by circulating additional information on safety standards. In other words, they circulate their textual intermediaries in the form of information and training material which always comprises an 'update' section on the general regulations (concerning compliance and behaviour) and another on devices and equipment (what the regulations prescribe and how it must be used). The technological intermediaries anchor knowledge in artefacts, and by associating their presence with fines and inspections, they anchor further knowledge in textual intermediaries. A network of social, organizational and institutional relations is thus woven and held together by the practices that the intermediaries perform.

7.4   Safety as training and consultancy

Like the regulatory agencies, the local-level education and training organizations are nodes in a broader network comprising both other agencies and national-level institutions: the Ministry of Labour, FORMEDIL, trade associations,[6] research institutes both public (universities and polytechnics) and private.

The education and training agencies have two distinct modes of conceiving and enacting workplace safety. On the one hand they view safety as information about the regulations; on the other, they adopt a somewhat different view of safety as professional competence. I shall now examine the intermediaries by which these agencies participate in creation of the texture of safety. It should be borne in mind that building workers receive various forms of safety instruction and training in the course of their work careers. Safety is a subject on the curriculum during their initial vocational training, in which phase it is mainly the concern of training agencies (the building school or other vocational training institutes). Subsequently, when safety is taught on refresher courses, the initiative passes to other agencies, among which of particular importance is the *Comitato Paritetico* (Joint Committee).[7]

The idea of safety as knowledge of the regulations configures the training agencies as nodes in a network engaged in affirming the bureaucratic discourse on safety. This discourse is based on knowledge of the regulations, therefore, and the training institutions impart it by teaching the jargon required by insiders to produce that discourse competently while performing control practices:

> We do a section on the legislation, where the various laws are explained, the supervisory bodies, and then all the general laws, building regulations and EU norms are explained. And then according to the sector . . . if they're porphyry workers we explain the procedures to follow with the machines. At this point we've totalled around eight to ten hours. Then, in the case of twelve-hour courses, there are two hours of video. There are videos on how to use the elevators, the cranes, the hoists, and on protection measures. We use the regulations to teach. Because the sector is a difficult one, and if you get something wrong you're likely to be prosecuted, it's always better to explain the rules and not their interpretations, explain technical matters but according to what the law says, so you don't make things up, give the wrong information. It's like at university: for good or evil. Technical courses are based on the regulations. (trainer describing the contents of a refresher course)

This example evinces how the normative discourse is conveyed through socialization to vocabulary and is materialized in human intermediaries performing the role of teachers, and in textual intermediaries in the form of books, cassettes, etc. In this case, unlike on the building site, learning takes the more traditional form, which configures it as a specific activity with its own times and places. The separation of learning from working is even more marked because it takes place during the winter months when building work is suspended, or for young job-seekers at the beginning of their working lives.

However, the separation between workplace and training place is only physical, because continuity between the two domains is established by a sort of 'clearing house'. How this operates I shall now describe.

The most popular part of the training course is the question and answer session when 'insiders' have a chance to clarify and negotiate – in a neutral setting – aspects of the regulations that enable them to act within the scope of the regulation without having to conduct negotiations on the building site. In fact, when a regulation's meaning is negotiated on-site with an inspector, it is invariably accompanied by a sanction. Training therefore provides an opportunity for institutional actors to influence each other, and it is an arena for defining the meanings of the rules on safety. Consequently, the training course itself is an intermediary which establishes a connection between control agencies and building firms through specific intermediation practices which co-produce and stabilize a safety culture in a particular territorial area and in a network of interdependent actors.

While on the one hand the training agencies broker information on how to interpret the regulations, on the other they propound an alternative view of safety which conceives it as professionalism. In fact, the importance of the training agencies depends closely on the extent to which safety in firms ceases to be defined mainly in terms of accountability to a corpus of regulations and is instead viewed as accountability to a set of criteria concerning professionalism.

Building firms construct their identity around this 'vision' in contrast to the dominant bureaucratic and repressive discourse:

> . . . the regulation is only a stimulus for training . . . the approach should be changed . . . not being repressive but expanding your mind-set . . . we do courses, we get extremely good participation and response. (building workers' fund official)

Thus, information on the legislation is not withheld; rather, it is subsumed under a professional discourse (the regulations are of service in so far as they enable one to work professionally) which reverses the bureaucratic perspective (working professionally is to abide by the regulations).

The effort to 'expand the mind-set' – that is, develop workers' professionalism or condition their action – takes two forms: the circulation of textual intermediaries able to transmit expertise and direct contact in the form of 'consultancy' by human intermediaries. The term 'consultancy' covers a variety of activities intended to change and condition building-site safety practices. In order to operate more effectively, the *Comitato Paritetico* has 'consultants' who provide training while simultaneously conducting inspections and seek to exploit the persuasive (and coercive) effects of both. The consultants are self-employed professionals who work on behalf of the *Comitato Paritetico* and make spot checks on building sites in a similar manner to the inspectors. They are important intermediaries in that they circulate new practices and transfer them to building firms.

Innovations of external origin and acquired from various sources – personal contacts, articles in professional journals or texts, attendance at conferences or meetings – are suggested to firms:

> When you assemble scaffolding, remember to put footplates under the uprights (question from the site foreman: 'Even when they're on cement?') . . . always, you should always lay the footplates . . . and the scaffolding should always be attached to the building, but not with steel wire: always use bracing tubes in the window openings, or use pressure screws (*Comitato Paritetico* consultant)

Because the consultants combine proposals with prescriptions, they are able to activate a process of institutionalization by which 'putting footplates under scaffolding' or 'using pressure screws' – two new techniques which interpret the general regulation that 'structures must be appropriately anchored to the building' – are disseminated in the community of practice through formal channels (reports, courses) or informal ones (conversations or stories).

It is of interest to analyse what a consultant says and does when inspecting a building site, because it illustrates the practices that circulate knowledge and anchor it (Goffman, 1974). To describe these anchoring practices, I shall use the notion of 'event casting', this being that bracketing operation to isolate a piece of the world which Goffman proposed as a mode of anchoring when he analysed forms of language.

I start with a consultant's description of how he conducts an inspection visit on a building site:

> Generally, when I enter I introduce myself, say I'm from the *Comitato Paritetico* and explain what we do. Except that it's been some years now, and we know each other and introductions aren't necessary. We always explain that we're there to prevent them hurting themselves and set them to rights with the safety regulations.

Note how the consultant first positions himself within his institutional membership, and how he begins with 'I' and then rapidly shifts to a generic 'we' which comprises also his professional and institutional identity as the representative of an agency. By means of this first bracketing operation the consultant anchors his presence, and what he is about to do, in a frame which configures him as someone there to help, not to punish. He continues:

One thing I always look at is the equipment (machines, tools, drills), then I look at the electric cables. Once I've done that, I go into the building and check whether accident prevention work has been done, like parapets on the stairs, whether holes have been filled in. If that's been done, I look at the external scaffolding, how it's been mounted, whether it's complete, if pieces are missing, etcetera. Then, depending on the building site, I look to see what's missing and what isn't. It's not that I follow a specific scheme.

The consultant says that he does not follow a specific scheme or schedule. But at the same time he reveals that he has internalized – and reproduces for the benefit of those accompanying him as he tours the site – the same ceremonial as performed by the inspector, and by reproducing it, he shapes the expectations of those on the site. He does so not with words but with actions. His actions say: an inspector would first look at the machinery, then at the electrical connections, then he would go into the building and inspect the safety devices, and finally (still following the check-list procedure), he would determine what was absent and what was present. With this second bracketing practice, the consultant transmits the temporal sequence and logic of a scenario which comprises the rules that are important and omits those of lesser significance. In fact, after the first sentences he introduced a pause into his description before continuing:

Then I look at the health side of things: if they've got toilets, if they've had anti-tetanus injections, if there's an accident record, if there's a first-aid box.

This second parenthesis encloses the 'health' theme, and the professional gaze shifts from artefacts to texts, from material presence to written testimony of it – as in the case of the anti-tetanus injections, which can only be made present to the consultant in a textual representation which 'stands for' them; that is, acts as their intermediary. Finally, the consultant concerns himself directly with textual representations of operations that are impossible for him to see:

Then in the final phase I look at the documents: the crane log book (if they've got a crane), the scaffolding log book (if they've got scaffolding), the declaration that the wiring is compliant, the earthing diagram . . . and all the documents necessary, hydrogeological reports . . . if they're doing demolition work I look to see whether they've compiled the demolition schedule . . . all the documents they need.

If we imagine ourselves watching the inspection, we observe the consultant and the small group around him walking from the external area of the site into the building and into the office space. This itinerary, as an organizational practice, is similar to that followed by hospital doctors doing the round of their ward. Doing a ward round and touring a building site are working practices which mark out the boundaries of a workplace and physically transmit and anchor a professional mode of looking and seeing. Bracketing renders the constant flow of events discrete — framed — and not only 'evident' but also anchored to an interpretative framework which supports memory work.

The consultant's ability to construct a possible scenario through representation of an inspection is further evidenced by his expedient of compiling a mock report:

> Finally, I mean as I'm touring the site, I compile a report (which is not really a report because only the UOPI can issue one, ours is a check list with defaults pre-printed on it) with the advice given . . . advice in fact, which consists of instructions because on my second visit (if the shortcomings are minor I don't come back: for example if a document is missing I don't return a second time) if they haven't been put right, the committee decides whether a third visit should be made or whether the report should be sent the UOPI.

The situation is ambiguous, therefore. It is only with his final bracketing that the consultant lets it be known that his report is not a 'real' report; that his advice must necessarily be followed; that he will return to check that it has been obeyed; and that if it has not, a 'real' report will follow because an inspector will descend on the building site. Is not this a paradoxical situation? I shall seek to explain it from within the logic of the practice of the building-site community, observing how the ambiguity of the consultants' role is converted into a resource for translation.

The influence exerted by the consultants differs from that of the 'representatives of the law'. The consultants put themselves forward as 'circulating safety experts'. In this guise, they act as temporary participants by using social interaction in practice to transmit knowledge, and by exploiting ongoing processes in the workplace as the basis for their knowledge transfer strategy. In order to emphasize their distinctive approach, and to distinguish themselves from those other consultants who merely provide 'instruction', they call themselves 'preventers':

> I call safety a 'trade': the trade of the preventer. (safety consultant)

A feature shared by the preventers is that they have all acquired relatively long experience of work in the construction industry. According
to the preventers, it is this experience that 'attunes' them to the social
processes that unfold within building-site practices and underpins their
capacity for action:

> I don't consider myself a professional, I consider myself a tradesman . . .
> in the sense that here first of all, how can I put it, you must have worked
> on a building site and then, because you know the trade of site foreman
> through and through, then you can also do the job of preventer . . . only
> if you thoroughly know what the working methods are, and therefore
> the people, and therefore the machinery, plant, equipment . . . according
> to me it should be your last job before you retire. A young lad could do
> it, but he must first have breathed the dust of a building site and heard
> the shouts of the workmen. (safety consultant)

The consultant/preventer's final words remind the researcher that
experience is the main source of knowledge, and they emphasize the
aesthetic dimension of experience. A building site is known through
its practices (experience), and it is known because it is breathed and is
heard, so that a 'feel' for building sites is based on sensible knowledge.
A 'feel' for building sites denotes membership of a community of practitioners. It enables mutual recognition, grants legitimate access to new
building sites and celebrates a collective identity.

All this is not said in words – certainly not with the words that I have
just quoted – but with gestures and indexical references, and by letting
'exemplary' situations say what words fail to convey.

The preventers use their familiarity with practices to attune themselves rapidly to the persons-in-situation:

> the best communication method is to take two or three workmen, go
> into the workplace and discuss the best solution to adopt right in front
> of the machine. (safety consultant)

By creating 'exemplary' situations, the consultants draw on a stock of
language which they have acquired directly on building sites. They use
this resource to assist their audience to reconstruct the situation and
produce different and safer versions of the same practice. We now follow
a consultant on his tour of inspection. The 'preventer' climbs the steps
and looks around. The technique is the same as the one used by a surveyor when he tours a site. As he walks, he looks around and observes
with competence. He makes some comments. He climbs to the first

floor, and as he moves through a thicket of ceiling braces to an area where the ceiling seems to be buckling, he sees an old circular saw. He turns to the site foreman:

> **Preventer**: . . . that circular saw leaves a lot to be desired . . .
> The **site foreman** mumbles an excuse, but does not pay too much attention to the matter. As the preventer moves closer to the unsafe area, he comes across a roll of electric cable. He stops and comments:
> **Preventer**: this electric wire is non-standard . . . this is a kitchen socket . . . you want those blue sockets . . . you've got to remember to use the right wiring.
> He now lists all the different types of wiring and their respective uses. He then returns to the circular saw and announces:
> **Preventer**: this saw is totally out of order.
> The **site foreman** makes an excuse: yes . . . yes, it needs a hand guard . . .
> The preventer looks more carefully at the saw. He asks a worker to switch it on. He unplugs the saw and then plugs it in again. The saw starts up. With a smile denoting that everyone knows exactly what is happening, he tells them that the saw should be fitted with a trip coil:
> **Preventer**: so if the electricity goes off, when it comes back on the saw won't start up again, and nobody will get hurt.
> He then explains and summarises other requirements for the saw to be standards-compliant.

To be noted is both the paucity of the consultant's spoken discourse and the fact that, by bracketing first the cables and then the saw, he creates examples that are self-evident to his audience and require no further comment. In a similar manner to knowledge pointers which direct attention to what is to be seen or heard, the consultant's examples constitute another discursive practice – what I have called 'event casting' – which uses bracketing to isolate portions of the world in the flux of experience so that they can be treated as objects of knowledge. The preventer uses his capacity to comment on practice as it unfolds (event casting) to encourage local reflection and to indicate an alternative course of action. He is thus able to share his practical knowledge without having to furnish an abstract representation of it.

A salient feature of even a brief transaction like the one just described is the unequal power relation presumed and reproduced by the transmission of practical knowledge.

In the above example, the preventer enacts a form of interaction which the workmen present know very well, because it is the way in which they acquired practical knowledge at the beginning of their working careers. During the novitiate phase, in fact, operational and/or physical knowledge is transmitted through the observation/action/talk-in-practice 'circuit' based on direct interaction and the joint performance of tasks in the workplace. As the 'experts', or simply the more expert, produce segments of action accompanied by appropriate comments, they enable their less able audience to appropriate knowledge. The process defines relative positions in the community and distinguishes between experts and apprentices – a distinction which is also a source of power and influence.

By positing himself as an 'expert', the preventer requests those present once again to assume, albeit very briefly, the role of apprentice/inferior. This may cause resistance and barriers against the transmission of knowledge, so that it explains the decision by the *Comitato Paritetico* to attribute repressive powers to the consultant deriving from his ability to activate institutional checks and inspections. In a certain sense, the consultant places himself in a position where he compels learning but runs the risk of evoking 'cosmetic' responses like those described in relation to the regulatory agencies:

> It frequently happens that when they see me coming they all put on hard hats and safety gloves, and I'm sure that ten minutes after I've gone the situation returns to what it was before. I tell them not to try to fool me, because in fact it's themselves that they're fooling. (safety consultant)

The activity of the consultants, and their intermediate position between the training agencies and the regulatory agencies, are important linkages which foster the emergence of consolidated local-level safety practices. The consultants are important intermediaries for the close-knit circulation of new practices and their transfer into businesses.

7.5   To sum up: the woofs and warps of a seamless web

The interorganizational texture of safety is woven into material-semiotic practices which connect people, objects and knowledge in contexts of situated learning and knowledge. This chapter, which concludes the description of my empirical research, has sought to describe the connective tissue which holds together the individuals who work in the building industry, its enterprises and all the institutions which in various capacities and in different ways establish relations with those individuals to co-produce a safety culture within spatio-temporal coordinates constituted by reciprocal relations. The network thus created is a network of knowledge-in-action, knowledge created and deployed by actors who learn and accumulate it in institutions and artefacts which constrain or facilitate connections.

I have proposed a holistic conception of the set of relations-in-action in order to show the fallacy inherent in categorizing the social by dividing it into levels (individual, group, organizational, interorganizational and institutional) and then seeking to explain the relations among them. Just as in a hologram the whole is reproduced in each of its parts, so society and its institutions can be observed in a single interaction. However, I have still not answered the fundamental questions of how connections are established and of how, when established, they acquire form and stability and endure through time and across space.

It should be borne in mind that it is the activity of establishing connections, which constructs the network. Consequently, rather than considering the voluntary and planned nature of a network, we may conceive it as arising from a field of practices which, as they connect persons, objects, knowledge, organizations and institutions together, stabilize and institutionalize collaborative and competitive modes of organizing the social. By choosing to study a territorial network which institutionalizes and regulates safety I have been able to contribute to the literature on network learning by showing that a network of relations is (i) the expression of a social division of labour which has distributed competences on safety among a large number of agencies, and (ii) that an emergent organizational texture aligns both collaborative and conflictual relations within a framework of 'conflictual cooperation' concerning what is meant by safety on construction sites located in the territorial area over which those agencies have jurisdiction. The safety culture thus produced (and which we may legitimately regard as 'social capital' conserved within the network) does not consist solely of non-material values and principles; it is also materialized in cultural practices which mark out a space of interorganizational and intraorganizational relations.

Safety practices are interconnected, and they are merged into each other by a chain of situated relations and interactions. The practices that hold the safety texture together spring from multiple logics of action which in their turn express multiple discourses on safety:

- The discourse on safety as surveillance and punishment expresses a logic of action that considers safety to be a social value which takes concrete form in institutions of control, surveillance and punishment. This discourse is also materialized in laws and regulations which reflect an intentionality (they forbid; they organize a chain of events; they prescribe) implemented – translated into practice – by establishing a field of relations among those institutions, companies, individuals and other institutions involved in the imposition of safety by means of legislative and executive power. Created, conserved, reproduced and developed in this discourse is the normative knowledge that underpins safety practices. The inspection, with its main textual intermediary, the report, exemplifies one of the ways in which the texture is formed, while at the same time it stabilizes the network by prescribing a set of relations, establishing power relationships and creating a system of affordances in the social and material setting for use in situated interactions to 'perform practice'.

- The discourse of safety as safe technologies and artefacts expresses the subjectivity of a set of institutional actors, bodies of specialist knowledge, professionals, their professional associations, and so on. It articulates the belief that safety can be incorporated into artefacts, and that humans can be protected against their foolhardy actions through the control that artefacts exert on contexts of use. Safe artefacts are intermediaries that reflect the intention to prevent improper acts and uses by incorporating a script in technology and inhibiting flexible interpretation of it. They organize the choreography of contexts of use and they control practices by inscribing the affordances offered by the context.

- The discourse on safety as training and institutionalized consultancy oversees the social and institutional production and circulation of expert knowledge on safety in the building industry. It expresses a belief in the power of pedagogy to transmit safety knowledge and techniques through courses, texts, consultancy and so on. More than the others, this discourse views knowledge as residing in relations, and it labels the transmission of knowledge among organizations and people as 'learning'. The practices that express this discourse and 'make it present' – like in consultants' inspections – can be regarded as knowledge-brokering practices because they transmit knowledge from one place to another and institutionalize the figure of the consultant as a socializer to the logics of action present in the interorganizational texture. Within this discourse, the main intermediary for the creation and stabilization of connections is a human being with expert knowledge and relational ability.

I have used these three converging/conflicting discourses to describe three logics of action which are institutionalized – and therefore legitimate subjectivity – and which deploy resources for the social organization of the field of practices examined. This is not the first time that we have met these three discourses; indeed, their pervasiveness has been noted since the beginning of my description of the building site, and I am aware that they traverse all the organizations and institutions and individuals present in the field. However, I would point out the presence of at least two other logics of action to which I may not have given due emphasis. The first is economic logic, to which I paid little attention during the research but which should be mentioned because it conditions the action of building contractors, given their preoccupation with profit, and determines the availability of resources (if institutions do not have sufficient human and material resources, they are less efficient). Economic logic highlights the conflict among the multiple goals pursued by the various interorganizational practices described: there are never enough inspectors to conduct all possible/desirable inspections; safe artefacts may be more costly or less efficient; the exigencies of profit or delivery times conflict with the regulations on accident prevention; the labour market is skewed between the labour supply and demand; and so on. Not only is a complex undertaking of resources optimization necessary; also required is the management of numerous dissonant voices which cannot be harmonized into a canon. This is, that is to say, maintenance of the separation which safeguards individuality and also ensures that there is co-presence, for it is through co-presence that new knowledge is created and translated from one context to another.

In this regard I shall briefly resume discussion of the logic of action analysed in Chapter 3 when I illustrated the discursive practices used by the site foremen with engineers and the main contractor. The logic of the situation expressed by the site foreman can be usefully compared against the three logics outlined above.

The site foreman considered accidents to be 'normal' occurrences, and he contextualized them within the complexity of the co-presence in a limited space of numerous persons with interdependent professions, of objects which did not always 'stay where they should' and of fortuitous events. These various factors presented the site foreman with the logical and logistical problem of both keeping together and separating persons and activities whose modalities of co-presence varied considerably and not always predictably. Hazardous situations exist when those people not directly under the control (and the proper training) of any of the organizations concerned with a building site are in a position to activate the hazard by behaving improperly. They may be members of the general public and in a sense 'strangers' to the site. A building site is the concrete aggregate of whatever abstract systems have been imposed upon it, and its planners or users become involved in that site in a multiplicity of systems, some designed, some unpredictable. The site foreman's logic of action is the one that most completely expresses the logic of situated — that is, context-dependent — action and the manner in which events combine in a context according to temporality and interactions.

The dissonance of voices accompanies their legitimate co-presence, and their co-presence is made possible by the translation of specific logics of action into languages and into changed knowledge. I have expressed this concept on several occasions by saying that knowledge is never transferred without being changed, and several incidents in the field have illustrated how knowledge passes from one community to another in the course of situated interactions and negotiations. I now wish to emphasize the role of intermediaries in the translation process, and in doing so argue that knowledge is translated on a continuum of relations between humans and non-humans.

The intermediaries of knowledge translation — artefacts, texts, money, people — are the means by which the warp and woof are woven together, and they simultaneously constitute the means by which the relation is anchored. We have seen human intermediaries in the form of consultants translate institutionalizing knowledge into instructions; we have seen artefacts like the spoked wheel of the cement mixer incorporating the knowledge produced by analysis of arm-trapping accidents; we have seen reports 'standing for' the authority that punishes forbidden behaviour, and fines extinguishing liability. In all these cases, the intermediaries enable knowledge to circulate while anchoring it in material as well as semiotic forms. In previous chapters I have devoted much space to discursive practices. I would stress now that the materiality which sustains them exerts considerable power over actors and situated practices. I shall therefore briefly dwell on the associative power with which objects hold a network of relations and knowledges together.

If we adopt the principle of symmetry put forward by the actor network theory, we may hypothesize that control over situated activity is exerted by both actors and the practices in which they are engaged. However, while the agency of humans is so taken for granted that relations with the material world escape our notice, attributing agency to non-humans provokes a great deal of resistance. Without going into details of the theoretical debate, I propose that the customary point of view should be reversed and that we should look at how material objects represent constraints and opportunities for humans. In other words, we should look at how control over situated action is also inscribed in artefacts, with the consequence that they too should be attributed the power to establish connections-in-action.

The field of working practices has been made subservient to human activity; it is a space of action that has been tamed by means of two principal instruments: knowledge and rules. The purpose has been to extend the human ability to cope with circumstances which arise as variations of a particular practice, and to consolidate this mastery with rules that pre-structure the practical activity. This activity is accompanied by stabilization of the physical environment in which the knowledge develops in order to reduce its variability. We have seen that management of the physical space of the building site was important to delimit the zones and times of the work activities of diverse groups. The more an environment has been made subservient to a task, the more rapidly the latter can be accomplished. Banally, we can consider how the space of an apartment has been made subservient to the social practices of sleeping, eating, washing and receiving visitors, and how the various rooms have affordances which make it easier to sleep in the bedroom than in the bathroom. Artefacts have therefore incorporated a 'knowing how' which controls a range of possible actions, in that they stabilize a process (sleeping or washing) and reduce margins of freedom in the use of objects. Workplaces provide the most obvious examples of constraints and facilitations delegated to the materiality of the physical world in order to pre-structure working practices. The arrangement of work instruments, the mnemonic function assigned to objects to remind us to do something, the organization of space so that we are able to see the task at hand more clearly: these are all examples of how objects have been made subservient to informational and material tasks, and of how, as they have been delegated to do, to remind, to prevent, to facilitate, they have incorporated control over the practices in which they have been inscribed. We may therefore conclude that objects have the power to associate actors and actions, to anchor meanings and actions, to facilitate choices, to simplify the perception of space organized for a set of practices, to accelerate calculations and whatever else enters into meaningful relations within a material-semiotic network. Objects simultaneously represent the mobility of the intermediary moving in space to connect separate environments and the fixity of the materialization of relations.

NOTES

1. The three perspectives reach the same conclusions as far as the consequences of networks on organizational performance are concerned: increased innovation, greater value creation or product development and better financial performance.

2. David Kirsch (1995) provides illuminating examples of the relation between affordances and repertoires of action. An empty container affords filling, a television switched on affords watching, a hammer affords the act of hammering. But a situation offers affordances for a particular actor: a television does not attract the attention of a blind person just as a hammer does not suggest hammering to a person with no hands.

3. A previous version of this chapter has appeared as Gherardi and Nicolini (2000). Parts of this chapter have also been published in Italian in Nicolini (2001) 'IL Tessuto interorganizzativo della sicurezza: una visione prossimale', *Studi Organizzativi*, No. 2/3, pp. 93–116. This chapter is based on fieldwork carried out by Davide Nicolini, who also wrote the research report 'Il Tessuto interorganizzativo della sicurezza'. Responsibility for the interpretations offered here, however, is mine alone.

4. UOPI (Unità Operativa Prevenzione Infortuni) ensures compliance with accident prevention norms as well as assisting with judicial inquiries.

5. INAIL is the national institute for workplace accident insurance.

6. For example, ANCE, Associazione Nazionale Costruttori Edili.

7. The *Comitato Paritetico* was set up on the basis of an agreement between employers and workers, its purpose being to improve health and safety on building sites by means of training, information and consultancy. The committee has two distinct activities: it runs refresher courses on safety aspects and it advises construction companies on safety by sending professionals for consultation directly on-site.

CHAPTER EIGHT

The Mutual Constitution of Practice and Practising

> *To enter into a practice is to enter into a*
> *relationship not only with its contemporary*
> *practitioners, but also with those who have*
> *preceded us in the practice.*
> **(MacIntyre, 1985: 194)**

We have now concluded our detailed knowledge journey which began with the novice site manager as he learned to produce safety and has brought us to understanding of how safety is managed in a region. We may now ask whether there is a single process that traverses this field of practices and holds it together. However, if we are to determine the linkages among the various connections in action along the spiral from the individual to the institution that I have described, we must abandon the idea that the social order is aggregated or negotiated by a plurality of dissonant voices which eventually blend together to resemble a musical canon. On the contrary, it is antagonism, conflicting ideas, the institutionalization of bodies of knowledge in distinct disciplines and the non–resolution of conflicts that enable multiple discourses on safety to co–exist 'harmoniously'. More importantly, these are the conditions under which safety knowledge is produced though maintenance and mediation of the diverse perspectives of the co–participants in construction of the field of practices that I have described. Co–presence in the joint production of a practice entails the expression of diversity, the sedimentation of a discourse and the affirmation of an identity, as well as respect for the positioning of the other so that the practice in question can proceed in appropriate manner. It is in this light that one should construe practices as mediated by differences among perspectives which in their turn are shaped within more specific contexts of practice. I shall now review the bases for this contention.

My case study has identified five main discourses on safety. Inscribed in them are five logics of action springing from the same number of expert bodies of knowledge grounded on as many occupational or professional identities. The previous chapters have analysed various interactions situated in the field of safety production, and they have distinguished five 'voices', regardless of whether they pertain to a real individual speaking in situation, whether his/her voice is represented by others, or whether there is a system of textually expressed or simply disembodied meanings. These voices are the following:

- A voice which articulates the discourse that the simultaneous occurrence of events in the same place may give rise to breakdowns in the texture of safety. This is the discourse that depicts accidents as 'normal' events due to the complexity of 'being on site'. It expresses the logic of action that attributes value to collectively exercised mastery in the workplace and to vigilance over all the workplace's normalcy conditions. This discourse was articulated mainly by the site foremen, to whom the firm and society gave responsibility for day-to-day management, but it was present in other communities as well, albeit in less distinctive manner.

- A second voice articulates the discourse on safety as embodied in technologies and artefacts. This is the discourse that delegates control over practice-driven actions to the world of objects. It expresses the logic of action that sets value on control exerted over the physical environment through artefacts and technologies and which depicts accidents as errors, as things that should not happen. This discourse was put forward mainly by the engineers and the institutions that ensure that technologies and their producers comply with safety standards.

- A third voice articulates the need for normative control over safety practices. It is the voice that institutionally expresses the fact that safety is a value in our society and that practices which may jeopardize it are morally deplorable and legally punishable. This logic of action is enshrined in laws which prescribe good practices, legitimate forms of social control external to the firm, and punish deviant behaviour. This discourse is affirmed mainly by the institutions that issue laws and enforce compliance with them. Safety as obedience to the law brings with it a conception of accidents as due to 'non-compliance', and it may give rise to a bureaucratic view of safety, both within the firm and in the local safety culture.

- A fourth voice affirms the value of training in transmitting what is deemed to be socially valid knowledge on safety, establishing an ethos in the formation of occupational identities, and controlling individuals through their socialization into a culture. It is this discourse that forms the identity of educational institutions, of the professionals who work for them, and the consultants that act as intermediaries in the circulation of expert knowledge. It expresses the logic of the pedagogical action that seeks to exert control over human beings by teaching and shaping the premises for their actions. From this point of view accidents are due mainly to ignorance.
- The fifth voice is that of the market. This asserts that safety entails costs of prevention besides the organizational and social costs of accidents. Safety, and more generally an organization's reliability, thus become benchmarks for organizational action which flank and/or conflict with the more traditional ones of effectiveness and efficiency. Grounded on this discourse are the identities of both accident insurance institutes and the management responsible for a firm's overall performance.

Table 8.1 summarizes the five discourses on safety that constitute the texture of the safety practices field and mediate the expression of five logics of action by maintaining differences of perspective. Note that these logics found the social division of labour of a society and give rise to institutions that assume specific values and goals and consolidate distinct bodies of knowledge about safety. How are these dissonant voices harmonized?

Though not neglecting the importance of situated negotiation, I have concentrated on the antagonism among the various logics of action that express dissonant discourses on safety. This antagonism provides the democratic guarantee that no single voice will prevail in the 'conversation' among those discourses. In fact, control exercised singularly on issues and ideas turns into reciprocal control. The various discourses on safety are formed and institutionalized independently, and the institutions that implement them organizationally express at once antagonism and complementarity. Together, they constitute the dynamic of the social and institutional division of labour. The negotiation situated in everyday interactions among actors belonging to different organizations and institutions generates 'conflictual coordination' of the various logics of action. In other words, as discourses unfold in practice, logics of action are recast according to their ability to mobilize resources and to assert

Table 8.1 Discourses on safety and their logic of action

Discourses on safety	Logics of action	Conceptions of accident	Occupational identities
CONTEXTUAL	Maintain vigilance on the simultaneity of events	Normal occurrence	Site foreman
TECHNOLOGICAL	Delegate control to objects	Error	Engineer, technology supervision institutions, producers of technology
NORMATIVE	Support good practices normatively. Enforce compliance with the rules	Breach of the rules	Legislative and judicial institutions
PEDAGOGICAL	Exercise control over behaviour through teaching and its inscription in the premises of action	Lack of appropriate knowledge	Educational and vocational training institutions
ECONOMIC	Maintain equilibrium among the parameters of effectiveness, efficiency and reliability	Safety, like an accident, is a cost	Workplace accident insurance institutes, management

their power. But antagonism is part of the same dynamic and reproduces; this becomes particularly evident when we examine discourses *about* practice. As each voice mobilizes and deploys its discourse on practice, it constructs the subject of that discourse as the prime result of 'its' practices. The voice thus not only legitimates the values which it embraces but also celebrates its identity, and does so in the presence of others, socializing this audience into the logic of action embodied in the practices expressive of that discourse. This is the dynamic manifest in the mirror games among diverse communities. Antagonistic discourses are mobilized by discordant voices which do not intend to negotiate; instead, they reflect each other back and forth, thereby reaching mutual understanding and respect for identities founded on different bodies of expert knowledge.

We may therefore conclude that a field of practices is held together by discursive practices which mobilize antagonistic discourses in support of situated identities performed by means of mirror games. However, the answer to the question of how knowledge is created and circulated in a field of practices is not yet complete. Still required is explanation of how practices are 'material-discursive'.

8.1   Material-discursive practices

I shall now develop my point concerning discursive practices as connections in action which hold a field of practices together. The previous section recapitulated the process which connects together, on the one hand, discourses as bodies of knowledge distinct from the subjects that deploy them, and on the other, the situated interactions in which those discourses acquire the historicity of an ongoing conversation and anchor professional and occupational identities. I shall now explain why I have qualified the expression 'discursive practices' with the adjective 'material'.

It might be objected that this explanation is superfluous in that, as Foucault (1973) reminds us, discourses are material anyway because they have a physical basis: be this a voice, a text, or some other concrete medium of communication. However, my emphasis of the material nature of discursive practices has a twofold purpose. First it serves to stress that they are mediated by objects, and secondly it serves to stress that seeing, saying and doing are connected in practice.

To affirm that knowing in practice is mediated by material objects (artefacts, instruments, texts, techniques), and also by the physical space

in which people and objects meet, is to attribute the status of intermediary to materiality. An intermediary is not just something (or someone)
that occurs between two things; it is also something (or someone) that
does intermediating work, that is, connects and translates two things. In
other words, as an intermediary translates, it induces changes of place
and meaning and thus propagates practices. Objects, texts, people and
money are intermediaries, and to ascribe intermediating work to them
is to construct them as 'active' subjects, not as simple instruments used
by humans for their practical activities.

Attributing agency to the material world has provoked considerable
perplexity and controversy, which I have decided not to address. Rather,
I have shown how the material world interrogates humans and gives
persistence to practices, and therefore how knowledge is inscribed in the
material world and thereby acquires tangible form. I have based this
argument on analysis of various situations: the building-site tour of
inspection as a practice of vigilance over a physical space put to
productive use; physical intermediaries which – like the inspector's
report – 'stand for' an ongoing interaction; objects expressing an inter-
diction, like the solid wheel of a cement mixer; or innovative materials
which convey knowledge produced in other places and change the
practices of the building site into which they are imported. Intermediaries also perform an active role in propagating practices and
innovating them.

Hence, by saying that practices are mediated by (and through) the
material world I am also saying that, instead of the ontological antithesis between subject and object, I prefer the relationality in which not
only do subject and object define each other in situation but each subject
is nothing but an 'arrangement', to use John Law's expression:

> Each one of us is an *arrangement*. That arrangement is more or less fragile.
> There are ordering processes which keep (or fail to keep) that arrange-
> ment on the road. And some of those processes, though precious few, are
> partially under our control some of the time.
>
> **(Law, 1994: 33, original emphasis)**

The second significance of the term 'material-discursive' is that it
entails the important methodological consideration that there is a difference *and* a connection between interaction and description of interaction. Producing interaction is different from describing it (Garfinkel
and Sachs, 1970: 350), because the procedures with which we produce
an interaction are not the same as those which we use to describe it: if

they were, everything that we could say about a situation would depend on what people are able to tell us (Fele, 2002: 57). Doing and saying pertain to two distinct practices. Stressing this difference entails that we do not assume the veracity or otherwise of descriptions. Nor does it interest us: we are instead concerned with the way in which descriptions are tied to the actions that they describe from the point of view of their organization in practice. To use Merleau-Ponty's expression (1964: 147, quoted in Fele, 2002), the relation between them is a 'chiasmus', and it is a relation as 'close as that between the sea and the beach'. This emphasizes that practices are observable and analysable as situated practices, and that interaction is also produced through the accountability of practices. This second sense of 'material-discursive' practices is the methodological reason why I have decided to analyse practices as relations between saying and doing in situated settings where objects and context are interwoven and mutually constitutive.[1]

A final aspect clarified by the notion of the materiality of discursive practices is the fact that the material environment contains conditions that both favour action and impede it. That is to say, material practices incorporate and anchor control over action and knowledge. Consider the five discourses on safety, and the five dissonant voices expressing and legitimating five patterns of action intended to achieve: (i) control over the simultaneous occurrence of events in the same place; (ii) control over objects in relation among themselves and with humans; (iii) control over human actions in relation to a system of norms; (iv) control over the knowledge embodied in humans; (v) control over costs. The environment in which interactions take place is prestructured and organized by a system of practices which is not invented *ex novo* whenever a new practice begins, and indeed does not exist unless it is practised. But every practice is practised 'for another first time' (Garfinkel, 1967: 9). As amply shown by the empirical analysis, this means on the one hand that practices are indeterminate, and on the other that it is when they are practised that their indexicality – that is, the relation between discourse and action – is locally and contextually filled with practical meanings that become an integral part of the context.

It is therefore the relation between practice/practising and between knowledge/knowing as a relation of mutual constitution that best describes the everyday reproduction of practices – and in that reproduction the change and dissemination of practices – and the activity of knowing in relation to the enactment of knowledge.

An organization can be conceived as a field of practices, which are constantly practised. As they are reproduced, they are institutionalized as

valid knowledge grounded on a moral and aesthetic order. This view of
the organization implies a model of the organizational actor as different
from the rational decision-maker that follows the logic of consequen-
tiality, and also different from the computational mind of artificial intelligence. It is a social actor enveloped in a network of connections in
action which follows a logic of appropriateness (March and Olsen, 1989).
That is, it creates the objects of knowledge while positioning itself as a
knowing subject.

8.2 Knowing in practice

The litmus test for the successful transmission to a novice of the knowledge inscribed in practices is whether or not s/he has learned to move,
speak, use instruments and establish the social relations appropriate for
the competent reproduction of those practices: that is, whether or not
s/he is able to deploy the knowledge necessary to re-establish the necessary connections. This is the moment of learning in the strict sense,
the situation of ideal-typical learning in which someone who does not
know is socialized into the knowledge enshrined in social relations and
embedded in the contexts where practices take place. This obviously
does not mean that learning does not continue throughout the period
of time in which an individual belongs to a field of practices as a member
of it. It only means that the researcher has easier access to the indexicality of practices when observing a particular situation such as the one
described.

   If we assume the point of view of someone reproducing a practice
under the watchful eye of a master – and through him the entire community of practitioners – we can see the processes by which the novice
learns the 'right' way to say and do things, while we simultaneously see
how the requisite knowledge is available in the context and can be activated at the appropriate moment. I shall not reiterate the individual
processes described in Chapter 3. Instead, having provided an overview
of the field of practices that the novice has entered, I shall specify the
mediations that operate in it.

• Knowledge is mediated by corporeality in the twofold sense that the
  body is a source of aesthetic knowledge, and that knowing how to
  know through the body (and therefore knowing how to develop a
  body disciplined in accordance with the requirements implicit in
  practices) is part of the professional culture.

- Knowledge is mediated by social relations, again in the twofold sense that it is through social relations that access to knowledge is regulated, and that the power asymmetry in social relations mediates the modalities of the transmission and appropriation of knowledge.
- Knowledge is mediated by the material world that incorporates the script for its use and which I have amply discussed.
- Knowledge is mediated by past experiences and by what is already known. When a novice activates situational knowledge or learns something completely new, s/he utilizes knowledge already possessed. For instance, an important source of competence is primary socialization – the novice is already a competent member of society – by which mastery is gained of the tacit knowledge necessary to reproduce this society. And a second source of previous knowledge is represented by formal education.

When we change point of view and ask how practices have incorporated, and made available to the novice, the knowledge appropriate for their reproduction, we can see three processes in operation:

- Categorization, or the various forms of coding that produce a technical vocabulary, a set of appropriate and codified gestures, a situated curriculum, the typification of recurrent situations and the routines of common situations.
- Highlighting, or signalling the salient or exceptional nature of a situation by means of the mobilization by both human and non-human intermediaries of appropriate knowledge pointers.
- The production of texts which can be easily circulated and which 'stand for' a past or more complex experience, or one that is simply non-present.

When a novice – or any practitioner in a situation – competently reproduces one of the common practices of his or her occupation, s/he is mobilizing a knowing-how which associates his/her body, social relations in action, artefacts, his/her knowing how to use abstract knowledge, the codes of his/her community, and his/her capacity to see, hear and react to others, and to the situation, as part of a 'seeing', 'doing' and 'saying' deemed appropriate by the co-participants in the situation. It is in this sense that I have defined knowing in practice as an accomplishment realized by establishing connections in action. Deriving from this notion is my methodological principle of studying practical knowledge as a situated activity.

We are also able to see and describe how knowing in practice rests on an interactional infrastructure which, if it holds together, is invisible, taken for granted and unproblematic. It enables the reproduction of practices as they were previously, or with minor adjustments which do not significantly alter the pattern of activity. Vice versa, when a breakdown occurs – as I have illustrated in the case of accidents – the texture that holds the practices together must be repaired and normality restored by means of repair practices.

At this point we have completed the spiral that links practical knowledge activities from the institutional to the individual level within a single field of practices. Figure 8.1 summarizes in graphical form the processes of knowing in practice that I have illustrated with my case study.

All the elements of the theoretical-interpretative framework have thus been assembled, and I can now answer the question with which I began: how is the knowledge that forms a field of practices woven together?

8.3   A theoretical and methodological framework

My research strategy was not designed to verify theoretical propositions, but rather to generate them. For this reason I shall conclude this book by enumerating the elements which combine to form a theoretical framework and by indicating their methodological implications. My purpose is to propose an interpretative model which, if its use has been convincing in the case study set out in previous chapters, can be used in further research and thereby contribute to establishing a methodology for the practice-based study of organizations. I shall consequently now list a series of theoretical principles, indicating with an arrow those that can be translated into equivalent methodological principles.

1. Knowledge (which is neither mental substance nor an object) is what humans define as such and 'do' together in a physical and material setting ⇒ study knowing in practice as a practical accomplishment, as a set of situated knowings and doings.
2. Embodied in working practices is the knowledge necessary to reproduce them, but practices are indeterminate, open-ended and interrelated ⇒ study practice/practising and knowledge/knowing as processes of mutual constitution.
3. Practice – as practising – arises from a situational logic resulting from the connections in practice among practitioners, artefacts, the

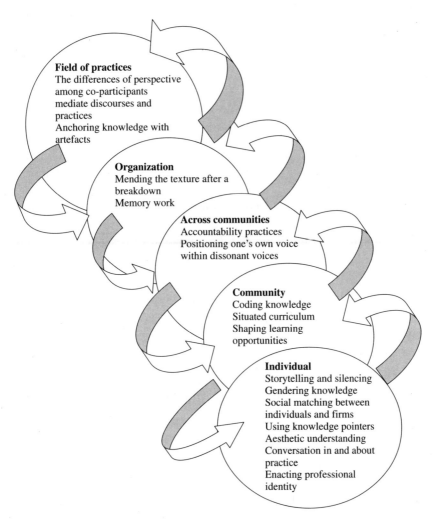

Figure 8.1   How a texture of practices is enacted

context and the normative and aesthetic codes which sustain the performance of practice ⇒ study connections in action, examine the texture of the field of practices.

4. The physical environment and the artefacts in it (including texts and rules) anchor the knowledge required to reproduce practices; as they do so, they retain a portion of control over those practices ⇒ analyse objects as intermediaries in order to study the materiality of the social world.

5. Becoming a practitioner, or being one, is to have mastered the material-discursive practices that perform the occupational identity and sustain a discourse on practice ⇒ study how a professional vision arises and is reproduced.

6. A plurality of dissonant voices and discourses converge and conflict on a field of practices. Whether or not a course of action is possible depends on conversations *in* practice (which produce the negotiated order) and on conversations *about* practice (which produce identity and difference) ⇒ study interactions on the boundaries between communities of practitioners, and study the mirror games between them.

7. The diversity of perspectives among co-participants in a field of practices ensures the circulation of institutionalized knowledge in dominant discourses and the dissemination of practices ⇒ study a field of practices as the locus of institutional learning – that is, within a network of organizations and institutions.

8. The connective texture of practices may be subject to breakdowns or interruptions in the production of normality ⇒ study breakdowns in order to understand the unproblematic reproduction of the practice, and study the repair practices by which normality is restored.

9. Knowing in practice is an interpretative framework where the twofold sense of 'in practice' indicates the production of knowledge in its being in use and the process which, as it reproduces the texture of practices, acquires the second meaning of 'gaining proficiency' ⇒ study organizational learning as knowledge in use and as the development of competence.

This interpretative model contributes to organizational studies in two ways. First, it furnishes precise temporal and spatial coordinates for the analysis of organizing as a dual process of knowing and acting. Second, it shifts the focus to how knowledge is managed by individuals acting in the contexts where that knowledge is produced, and thus eschews the view of management as external control and of knowledge as a mere object for use in the workplace.

8.4 Actionable knowledge

A final point concerns the relation between the descriptive knowledge produced thus far and its translation into practice. In other words, it concerns the relation between understanding and intervening, or what

Argyris (2003: 424) has called 'actionable knowledge', where defined as 'propositions that are actionable are those that actors can use to implement effectively their intentions'. Actionable knowledge also empowers its users, and as the notion is employed by Argyris, it is therefore connected with action research.

Although my research used different methodologies and did not concern itself with action research, I wish to draw attention to this idea of knowledge that generates the action and empowerment of knowing subjects, because there may be an element of action research in the spiral case-study methodology, and because organizational studies often comprise a portion of reflexive knowledge by disciplinary tradition. Consequently, we should interrogate ourselves on the social use made of the knowledge produced by the researcher.

When we speak of actionable knowledge, we should start from the identification of the subject able to translate knowledge into action, and also to take account of what the other subjects will and will not do. In other words, we consider power, the action-net in which it is manifest, and governance of the action system. I shall therefore organize these concluding remarks on the basis of the subjects responsible for action and who therefore have the power to initiate change or translate knowledge into action.

When I reconstructed the texture of practical knowledge in which safety is interwoven, this knowledge was relevant for the institutional actors empowered to devise safety policies. I believe that if safety is considered to be collectively produced by the organization of a social system, a paradox arises. We have seen, in fact, the 'good reasons' which determine the division of labour among institutional actors and agencies, the laying down of different attention rules and competences among the actors in the system; but what is paradoxical is the fact that the specialization that underpins this social organization may produce both an effect of collective responsibilization and collective de-responsibilization. In fact, a system of fragmented and clearly delineated competences may mean that each institutional actor assumes responsibility for a segment of the process and the parameters for its evaluation. But it may also mean that the system as a whole does not accept collective responsibility for outcomes. It does not have, that is to say, governance over its concrete results. The division of competences for safety is as much functional to the development of increasingly specialized knowledges as reciprocal control among competing institutions is functional to the democracy of the system. In organizational terms, one would say that the principle of specialization must be counterbalanced by that of integration, so that actors willing and able to translate a territorial system into an action-net must investigate the processes by which joint actions are undertaken and act accordingly. For example, the bureaucratic safety culture gives rise to formal observance of the rules socially constructed to manage safety through the law, but it ignores the substantial problem of the coherence between those rules and achievement of the ultimate goal of their effectiveness.

On its own, awareness of this potential perverse effect of a social system whose complexity is reduced so that it becomes manageable, but which instead of producing safety produces de-responsibilization for its final effect, is not enough to engender corrective actions. And it is not ignorance or a lack of 'technical' solutions that prevents it from doing so. In fact, the functional integration of competences distributed among diverse actors may be achieved with a variety of means: *ad hoc* integration bodies, concertation boards, interorganizational schemes to integrate individual competences. However, prior to the devising of developing instruments able to translate knowledge into practice, it must be decided whether there is a desire to implement that knowledge. It cannot be taken for granted, in fact, that knowing entails a change of behaviour and a desire to intervene in the *status quo*. The latter may be perfectly suited to the interests that bind the actors together or to the veto power that some of them are able to exercise.

Those who indicate the policy implications of research often adopt the Enlightenment position of 'know in order to intervene'. But the option 'know in order not to intervene' is equally plausible. This latter option is more visible when one considers actionable knowledge at the level of the single organization. Among the courses of action available to a corporate actor, workplace safety policies compete with other criteria and other priorities. Considerations concerning costs and working times, for example, shape the form and extent of the safety to be incorporated into everyday routine. Moreover, the structure of interests within an organization means that the costs and benefits of safety are distributed asymmetrically. Safety thus becomes contentious, and actionable knowledge induces both consideration of the costs of non-safety and analysis of safety cultures with a view to reconciling the numerous priorities and interests mobilized. This requires us to focus on the occupational communities that develop the local meanings of safety and sustain them in practice.

Communities of practitioners constitute, I believe, the fulcrum of the system of safety knowledge governance. However, on the one hand they are constrained by the decisions of organizations which decide the priority to be given to safety with respect to other parameters of organizational action, while on the other they exert coercive power over their members and furnish cultural leadership concerning the values associated with workplace safety. Awareness that – albeit within the same organization and therefore within a frame of action that is the negotiated product of a plurality of interests – several safety cultures are at work may prompt the design of organizational forms that enable the management of knowledge by those who produce, conserve and transmit it.

Without going into details concerning the organization forms that allow the most transparent and effective management of the knowledge produced by a community, and the greatest bargaining power with the other interdependent communities, we may delineate the main processes able to empower the various communities. For example, awareness that expertise is situated expertise may engender a deliberate process of learning from experience and of sharing and institutionalizing it into actionable knowledge. Collective reflection on accidents within the community provides an example of 'good practice' aimed at the management of situated knowledge and its translation into actionable knowledge. Another example is the awareness that it is the community of practitioners which socializes new members and disciplines their behaviour. Translating this awareness into actionable knowledge means operating on training practices, for example by combining formal training with on-the-job training, assigning responsibility for training to the community, recognizing the role of mentor that it implicitly performs, and overtly negotiating the principles, traditions and cultures of safety that are implicitly known and which may be both functional and dysfunctional to the achievement of safety. Without lapsing into a romantic vision of communities of practice as the sole possessors of 'good knowledge', it should be pointed out that recent European regulations have changed attitudes towards safety in that they have sanctioned the co-responsibility of the individual and the organization in accomplishing safety and in combating behaviour contrary to it. But they have not recognized the role of the community of practitioners in the production and management of knowledge.

Finally, also the individual has or can acquire an interest in translating what s/he learns into actionable knowledge, both by active participation at work and in the organization, and by means of individual choices. Resuming Hirshman's (1970) concepts of exit, voice and loyalty, we may reflect on how the possibilities of individual action are confined to a field with narrow boundaries, but also on how within those boundaries individual choices may take the form of adherence to the values and practices of the dominant organizational culture (loyalty), or negotiate the premises of decisions by expressing dissent (voice), or by deciding to withdraw (exit) if they are non-negotiable. Awareness of a match between organizations and individuals, and between individuals and occupational communities, may extend the range of choices available and empower the individual both as a single actor and as a member of a community.

NOTES

1.   I have satisfactorily applied this methodological principle in other research contexts (Bruni, Gherardi and Poggio, 2004) to study gender and entrepreneurship as social practice. Indeed, there is a growing body of research on gender as a situated practice (Martin, 2003).

References

Alcoff, L. (1988) Cultural feminism versus post-structuralism: the identity crisis in feminist theory, *Signs*, **13**(3): 405–36.

Alvesson, M. (1993) Organizations as rhetoric: knowledge-intensive firms and the struggle with ambiguity, *Journal of Management Studies*, **30**: 997–1016.

— (1994) *Management of Knowledge-Intensive Companies*, Berlin: de Gruyter.

— (1996) Leadership studies: from procedure and abstraction to reflexivity and situation, *Leadership Quarterly*, **7**(4): 455–85.

Ambrosini, V. and Bowman, C. (2001) Tacit knowledge: some suggestions for operationalization, *Journal of Management Studies*, **38**(6): 811–29.

Antaki, C. (1985) Ordinary explanations in conversation: causal structures and their defence, *European Journal of Social Psychology*, **15**: 213–30.

— and Fielding, G. (1981) Research on ordinary explanations in the psychology of ordinary explanations of social behaviour, in C. Antaki (ed.), *European Monographs in Social Psychology*, London: Academic Press.

Antonacopoulou, E. and Gabriel, Y. (2001) Emotion, learning and organizational change: towards an integration of psychoanalytic and other perspectives, *Journal of Organizational Change Management*, **14**(5): 435–51.

Araujo, L. (1998) Knowing and learning as networking, *Management Learning*, **29**(3): 317–36.

— and Easton, G. (1999) A relational resource perspective on social capital, in R.T. Leenders and S.M. Gabbay (eds), *Corporate Social Capital and Liability*, Boston, MA: Kluwer, pp. 68–87.

Argyris, C. (2003) Actionable knowledge, in H. Tsoukas and C. Knudsen (eds), *The Oxford Handbook of Organization Theory: Meta-theoretical Perspectives*, Oxford: Oxford University Press.

— and Schön, D.A. (1978) *Organizational Learning: a Theory of Action Perspective*, Reading, MA: Addison-Wesley.

Astley, G. (1985) Administrative science as socially constructed truth, *Administrative Science Quarterly*, **30**: 497–513.

Barad, K. (2003) Posthumanist performativity: toward an understanding of how matter comes to matter, *Signs: Journal of Women in Culture and Society*, **28**(3): 801–31.

Barley, S. (1986) Technology as an occasion for structuring: evidence from the observation of CT scanners and the social order of radiology departments, *Administrative Science Quarterly*, **31**: 78–108.

— and Kunda, G. (2001) Bringing work back in, *Organization Science*, **12**: 76–95.

Barnes, B. (1982) The science-technology relationship: a model and a query, *Social Studies of Science*, **12**: 166–72.

Barthes, R. (1977) *Fragments d'un Discours Amoureux*, Paris: Editions du Seuil (English translation (1990), *A Lover's Discourse. Fragments*, London: Penguin).

Batenson, G. (1979) *Mind and Nature*, Toronto: Bantam Books.

Bauman, Z. (1995) *Life in Fragments. Essays in Postmodern Morality*, Oxford: Blackwell.

Bechky, B. (1999) Creating shared meaning across occupational communities: an ethnographic study of a production floor, paper presented at the Academy of Management Meeting, Chicago, August 1999.

Becker, H. (1953–4) Becoming a marihuana user, *American Journal of Sociology*, **59**: 235–42.

— (1972) A school is a lousy place to learn anything, *American Behavioural Scientist*, **16**(4): 85–105.

— (1982) *Art Worlds*, Berkeley: University of California Press.

Belenky, M., Clinchy, B., Goldberger, N. and Tarule, J. (1986) *Women's Ways of Knowing*, New York: Basic Books.

Berger, P.L. and Luckmann, T. (1966) *The Social Construction of Reality*, London: Penguin (Trad. it. *La realtà come costruzione sociale*, Bologna: Il Mulino, 1979).

Bernstein, B. (1975) Class and pedagogies: visible and invisible, *Studies in the Learning Science*, Paris: OECD.

Blackler, F. (1993) Knowledge and the theory of organizations: organizations as activity systems and the reframing of management, *Journal of Management Studies*, **30**(6): 864–84.

— (1995) Knowledge, knowledge work and organizations: an overview and interpretation, *Organization Studies*, **16**(6): 1021–46.

— Crump, N. and McDonald, S. (2003) Organizing processes in complex activity networks, in D. Nicolini, S. Gherardi and D. Yanow (eds), *Knowing in Organizations: A Practice-based Approach*. Armonk, NY: M.E. Sharpe.

— and McDonald, S. (2000) Power, mastery and organizational learning, *Journal of Management Studies*, **37**(6): 833–51.

Bobrow, C., Cheslow, R. and Whalen, J. (2002) Community knowledge sharing in practice: the Eureka story, *Reflections, the SOL Journal*, **4**(2): 47–59.

Boisot, M. (1998) *Knowledge Assets: Securing Competitive Advantage in the Information Economy*, Oxford: Oxford University Press.

Boje, D. (1994) Organizational storytelling – the struggles of premodern, modern and postmodern organizational learning discourses, *Management Learning*, **25**: 433–61.

Boland, R. and Tenkasi, R. (1995) Perspective making and perspective taking in communities of knowing, *Organization Science*, **6**: 350–72.

Borzeix, A. (1994) Avant-propos. travail et cognition, *Sociologie du Travail*, **4**: 413–17.

Bourdieu, P. (1980/90) *The Logic of Practice*, Stanford: Stanford University Press (trans. Richard Nice).

— (1972) *Esquisse d'une théorie de la pratique précédé de trois etudes de ethnologie kabyle*, Switzerland: Librairie Droz S.A. (Engl. trans. *Outline of a Theory of Practice*, Cambridge University Press, 1977).

Brogan, W. (1989) Plato's pharmacon: between two repetitions, in H. Silverman (ed.), *Derrida and Decostruction*, London: Routledge, pp. 7–23.

Broms, H. and Gahmberg, H. (1983) Communication to self in organizations and cultures, *Administrative Science Quarterly*, **28**: 482–95.

Brown, J. and Duguid, P. (1991) Organizational learning and communities of practice: toward a unified view of working, learning and bureaucratization, *Organization Science*, **2**: 40–57.

Bruni, A. (2004) *Lo studio etnografico delle organizzazioni*, Roma: Carocci.

—, Gherardi, S. and Poggio, B. (2004) *Gender and Entrepreneurship. An Ethnographic Approach*, London: Routledge.

Brunsson, N. (1982) The irrationality of action and action rationality: decision, ideologies and organizational actions, *Journal of Management Studies*, **19**: 29–43.

— (1989) *The Organization of Hypocrisy*, Chichester: Wiley.

Bryant, C.G.A.and Jary, D. (1991) *Giddens' Theory of Structuration. A Critical Appreciation*, New York: Routledge.

Burt, R.S. (1992) *Structural Holes: the Social Structure of Competition*, Cambridge, MA: Harvard University Press.

Butler, J. (1990) *Gender Trouble: Feminism and the Subversion of Identity*, London: Routledge.

— (1993) *Bodies That Matter*, London: Routledge.

Callinicos, A. (1985) Anthony Giddens: a contemporary critique, *Theory and Society*, **14**(2): 133–66.

Callon, M. (1980) Struggles and negotiations to define what is problematic and what is not: the sociology of translation, in K. Knorr-Cetina, R. Krohn and R. Whitley (eds), *The Social Process of Scientific Investigation*, Boston: Reidel, pp. 197–219.

— (1981) Boites noires et operations de traduction, *Economie et Humanisme*, **262**: 53–9.

— (1986) Some elements of a sociology of translation: domestication of the scallops and the fishermen of St Brieuc bay', in J. Law (ed.), *Power, Action and Belief: A New Sociology of Knowledge?* Sociological Review Monograph 32, London: Routledge & Kegan Paul.

— (1992) The dynamics of techno-economic networks, in R. Combs, P. Saviotti and V. Walsh (eds), *Technological Change and Company Strategies. Economic and Social Perspectives*, London: Academic Press.

— and Latour, B. (1981) Unscrewing the big Leviathan or how do actors macrostructure reality and how do sociologists help them to do so, in K. Knorr-Cetina and A. Cicourel (eds), *Advances in Social Theory and Methodology: Toward an Integration of Micro and Macro Sociologies*, London: Routledge & Kegan Paul, pp. 277–303.

Cantiere Scuola (1995) *The Curriculum of the Course for Construction Site Managers*, Cantiere Scuola 1(VI).

Carroll, J. (1998) Organizational learning activities in high-hazard industries: the logics underlying self-analysis, *Journal of Management Studies*, **35/6**: 699–717.

Castells, M. (1996) *The Rise of the Network Society*, Cambridge, MA: Blackwell.

Cavalli, A. (1997) Gedächtnis und Identität. Wie das Gedächtnis nach katastrophalen Ereignissen rekonstruirert wird, in K.E. Muller and J. Rüsen (eds), *Historishe Sinnbilding. Problemstelellungen, Zeitkonzepte, Wahrnehmugshorizonte, Darstellungsstrategien*, Hamburg: Rowollt, pp. 455–70.

Chaiklin, S. and Lave, J. (1993) *Understanding Practice: Perspectives on Activity and Context*, Cambridge: Cambridge University Press.

Child, J. and Markoczy, L. (1993) Host-country managerial behaviour and learning in Chinese and Hungarian joint ventures, *Journal of Management Studies*, **30**(4): 611–30.

— and Rodrigues, S. (2003) Social identity and organizational learning, in M. Easterby-Smith and M. Lyles (eds), *The Blackwell Handbook of Organizational Learning and Knowledge Management*, Oxford: Blackwell, pp. 535–56.

Cicourel, A. (1994) La connaissance distribuée dans le diagnostic médical, *Sociologie du Travail*, **4**: 427–49.

Clegg, S.R. (1975) *Power, Rule and Domination*, London: Routledge & Kegan Paul.

— (1979) *The Theory of Power and Organization*, London: Routledge & Kegan Paul.

— and Hardy, C. (1996) Organizations, organization and organizing, in S.R. Clegg, C. Hardy and W.R. Nord (eds), *Handbook of Organization Studies*, London: Sage, pp. 1–28.

Cohen, I.J. (1987) Structuration theory and social praxis, in A. Giddens and J. Turner (eds), *Social Theory Today*, Cambridge: Polity Press, pp. 273–308.

Cohen, M. and Bacdayan, F. (1994) Organizational routines as stored and procedural memory: evidence from a laboratory study, *Organization Science*, **5**(49): 554–68.

— and Levinthal, D.A. (1990) Absorptive capacity: a new perspective on learning and innovation, *Administrative Science Quarterly*, **35**(1): 128–52.

Coleman, J.S. (1988) Social capital and the creation of human capital, *American Journal of Sociology*, **94**(supplement): 95–120.

Collinson, D.L. (1988) Engineering humour: masculinity, joking and conflict in shop-floor relations, *Organization Studies*, **9**: 181–99.

— (1992) *Managing the Shopfloor: Subjectivity, Masculinity and Workplace Culture*, Berlin: de Gruyter.

Conein, B. and Jacopin, E. (1994) Action située et cognition: le savoir en place, *Sociologie du Travail*, **94**(4): 475–500.

Constant II, E.W. (1984) Communities and hierarchies: structure in the practice of science and technology, in R. Laudan (ed.), *The Nature of Technological Knowledge. Are Models of Scientific Change Relevant?* Dordrecht: Reidel.

— (1989) The social locus of technological practice: community, system, or organization? in W.E. Bijker, T.P. Hughes and T. Pinch (eds), *The Social Construction of Technological Systems*, Cambridge, MA: The MIT press.

Contu, A. (2000) L'apprendimento situato e la semiotica della pratica: nuovi vocabolari per l'apprendimento organizzativo, *Studi Organizzativi*, **2**: 83–106.

— and Willmott, H. (2000) Comment on Wenger and Yanow. Knowing in practice: a 'delicate flower' in the organizational learning field, *Organization*, **7**(2): 269–76.

— and Willmott, H. (2003) Re-embedding situatedness: the importance of power relations in learning theory, *Organization Science*, **14**(3): 283–96.

Cook, S. and Yanow, D. (1993) Culture and organizational learning, *Journal of Management Inquiry*, **2**(4): 373–90.

Cooper, R. and Fox, S. (1990) The texture of organizing, *Journal of Management Studies*, **27**(6): 575–82.

— and Law, J. (1995) Organisation: distal and proximal views, in S. Bacharach, P. Gagliardi and B. Mundell (eds), *Studies of Organisations in the European Tradition*, Greenwich: JAI Press.

Coopey, J. (1995) The learning organization, power, politics, and ideology, *Management Learning*, **26**: 193–214.

Cyert, R.M. and March, J.G. (1963) *A Behavioral Theory of the Firm*, Englewood Cliffs, NJ: Prentice Hall.

Czarniawska, B. and Jorges, B. (1995) Winds of change, in S. Bacharach, P. Gagliardi and B. Mundell (eds), *Studies of Organisations in the European Tradition*, Greenwich: JAI Press.

Czarniawska, B. and Sevón, G. (eds) (1996) *Translating Organisational Change*, Berlin: de Gruyter.

Czarniawska-Jorges, B. (1991) Culture is the medium of life, in P.J. Frost, L.F. Moore, M.R. Louis, C.C. Lundberg and J. Martin (eds), *Reframing Organizational Culture*, Newbury Park, CA: Sage, pp. 285–97.

— (1996) Learning organization in a changing institutional order: examples from city management in Warsaw, *Management Learning*, **28**: 475–95.

Davenport, L. and Prusak, L. (1998) *Working Knowledge*, Boston: Harvard Business School Press.

Davidson, D. (1986) A nice derangement of epitaphs, in E. Lepore (ed.), *Truth and Interpretation: Perspectives on the Philosophy of Donald Davidson*, Oxford: Blackwell, pp. 433–46.

Davies, B. and Harré, R. (1990) Positioning: the discursive production of selves, *Journal of the Theory of Social Behaviour*, **1**: 43–63.

De Lauretis, T. (1987) *Technologies of Gender. Essays in Theory, Film and Fiction*, Bloomington: Indiana University Press.

Dean, J.W. Jr, Ottensmeyer, E. and Ramirez, R. (1997) An aesthetic perspective on organizations, in C. Cooper and S. Jackson (eds), *Creating Tomorrow's Organizations: A Handbook for Future Research in Organizational Behavior*, Chichester: Wiley.

Deetz, S. (1996) Discursive formations, strategized subordination, and self-surveillance: an empirical case, in A. McKinlay and K. Starkey (eds), *Managing Foucault: A Reader*, London: Sage, pp. 157–71.

Deleuze, G. and Guattari, F. (1983) *Anti-Oedipus. Capitalisme and Schizophrenia*, Minneapolis: University of Minnesota Press.

Depolo, M. (1988) *Entrare nelle Organizzazioni*, Bologna: Il Mulino.

Derrida, J. (1967) *De la Grammatologie*, Paris: de Seuil.

— (1981) *Dissemination*, Chicago: University of Chicago Press (trans. Barbara Johnson).

Dewey, J. (1922) *Human Nature and Conduct*, New York: Holt.

Dierkes, H., Berthoin, A., Child, J. and Nonaka, I. (eds) (2001) *The Handbook of Organizational Learning and Knowledge*, Oxford: Oxford University Press.

Dixon, N. (2000) *Common Knowledge*, Boston: Harvard Business School Press.

Dodgson, M. (1993) Organizational learning: a review of some literature, *Organization Studies*, **14**(3): 375–94.

Douglas, M. (1985) *Risk Acceptability according to the Social Sciences*, New York: Sage.

— (1986) *How Institutions Think*, Syracuse: Syracuse University Press.

Drucker, P. (1939) *Post-Capitalist Society*, New York: Harper Collins.

Easterby-Smith, M. (1997) Disciplines of organizational learning: contributions and critiques. *Human Relations*, **50**: 1085–114.

— and Lyles, M. (eds), *The Blackwell Handbook of Organizational Learning and Knowledge Management*, Oxford: Blackwell.

—, Snell, R. and Gherardi, S. (1998) Organizational learning and learning organization: diverging communities of practice?, *Management Learning*, **29**: 259–72.

Eckert, P. (1989) *Jocks and Burnouts: Social Categories and Identity in the High School*, New York: Teachers College Press.

Ehn, P. (1988) *Work-oriented Design of Computer Artifacts*, Stockholm: Arbetlivscentrum.

Eisenhardt, K. (1999) Building theories from case study research, in A. Bryman and R. Burgess (eds), *Qualitative Research*, London: Sage, pp. 135–59.

Elkjaer, B. (2000) The continuity of action and thinking in learning: revisiting John Dewey, outlines, *Critical Social Studies*, **2**: 85–101.

Elster, J. (2000) *Ulysses Unbound*, Cambridge: Cambridge University Press.

Emery, F. and Trist, E.L. (1965) The causal texture of organizational environments, *Human Relations*, **18**: 21–32.

Empson, L. (2001) Introduction: knowledge management in professional service firms, *Human Relations*, **54**/**7**: 811–17.

Engestrom, Y. (1987) *Learning by Expanding: An Activity Theoretical Approach to Developmental Research*, Helsinki: Orienta-Consultit Oy.

— and Middleton, D. (1996) Introduction: studying work as mindful practice, in Y. Engestrom and D. Middleton (eds), *Cognition and Communication at Work*, Cambridge: Cambridge University Press.

—, Puonti, A. and Seppänen, L. (2003) Spatial and temporal expansion of the object as a challenge for reorganizing work, in D. Nicolini, S. Gherardi, D. Yanow (eds), *Knowing in Organizations: a Practice-based Approach*, Armonk, NY: M.E. Sharpe.

Feldman, M.S. (1995) *Strategies for Interpreting Qualitative Data*, Thousand Oaks: Sage.

Fele, G. (2002) *Etnometodologia. Introduzione allo studio delle attività ordinarie*, Roma: Carocci.

Ferguson, E. (1977) The mind's eye: non-verbal thought in technology, *Science*, **197**: 827–36.

Fineman, S. (2003) Emotionalizing organizational learning, in M. Easterby-Smith and M. Lyles (eds), *The Blackwell Handbook of Organizational Learning and Knowledge Management*, Oxford: Blackwell, pp. 557–74.

Fiol, C.M. and Lyles, M.A. (1985) Organizational learning, *Academy of Management Review*, **10/4**: 803–13.

Fitchen, J. (1961) *The Construction of Gothic Cathedrals: A Study of Medieval Vault Construction*, Chicago: Chicago University Press.

Flynn, P. (1991) *The Ethnomethodological Movement*, New York: Mouton de Gruyter.

Fornel, M. de, and Quéré, L. (1999) *Presentation. La Logique des Situations*, Paris: Editions de l'Ecole des Hautes Etudies en Sciences Sociales, pp. 7–32.

Foucault, M. (1972) *The Archeology of Knowledge*, London: Tavistock.

— (1977) *Power/Knowledge*, New York: Basic Books.

— (1984) *L' usage des plaisirs*, Paris: Gallimard.

Fox, S. (1997) Situated learning theory versus traditional cognitive learning theory: why management education should not ignore management learning, *Systems Practice*, **10**: 727–47.

— and Grey, C. (1999) Emergent fields in management: connecting learning and critique, *Management Learning*, **31**: 1.

Frey, K. (1977) *Teorie del Curriculum*, Milan: Feltrinelli.

Fujimura, J. (1995) Ecologies of action: recombining genes, molecularizing cancer, and transforming biology, in S.L. Star (ed.), *Ecologies of Knowledge*, Albany, NY: State University of New York Press, pp. 302–46.

—, Star, S. and Gerson, E. (1987) Metode de recherche en sociologie des sciences: travail, pragmatisme et interactionnisme symbolique, *Cahiers de Recherches Sociologique*, **5**: 65–85.

Gagliardi, P. (1990) Artifacts as pathways and remains of organizational life, in P. Gagliardi (ed.), *Symbols and Artifacts: Views of the Corporate Landscape*, Berlin: de Gruyter, pp. 3–37.

244   REFERENCES

— (1990a) *Symbols and Artifacts*, Berlin: de Gruyter.

— (1996) Exploring the aesthetic side of organizational life, in S.R. Clegg, C. Hardy and W.R. Nord (eds), *Handbook of Organization Studies*, London: Sage.

Garfinkel, H. (1967) *Studies in Ethnomethodology*, Englewood Cliffs, NJ: Prentice Hall.

— (1986) *Ethnomethodological Studies of Work*, London: Routledge & Kegan Paul.

— and Sacks, H. (1970) On formal structures of practical actions, in J. McKinney and E. Tiryakian (eds), *Theoretical Sociology: Perspectives and Development*, New York: Appleton-Century-Crofts.

Garratt, B. (1990) *Creating a Learning Organization. A Guide to Leadership, Learning and Development*, London: Simon and Schuster.

Geertz, C. (1973) *The Interpretation of Cultures*, New York: Basic Books.

Gephart, R., Steier, L. and Lawrence, T. (1990) Cultural rationalities in crisis sensemaking: a study of a public inquiry into a major industrial accident, *Industrial Crisis Quarterly*, **4**: 27–48.

Gergen, K.J. (1991) *The Saturated Self: Dilemmas of Identity in Contemporary Life*, New York: Basic Books.

Gherardi, S. (1995) When will he say: 'Today the plates are soft'?: management of ambiguity and situated decision-making in studies in cultures, *Organizations and Societies*, **1**: 9–27.

— (1995a) *Gender, Symbolism and Organizational Culture*, London: Sage.

— (1995b) Organizational learning, in M. Warner (ed.), *International Encyclopedia of Business and Management*, London: Routledge, pp. 3934–42.

— (1999) Learning as problem-driven or learning in the face of mystery?, *Organization Studies*, **20**: 101–24.

— (2000a) Practice-based theorizing on learning and knowing in organizations: An introduction. *Organization*, **7**(2): 211–23.

— (2000b) Where learning is: metaphors and situated learning in a planning group, *Human Relations*, **53**(8): 1057–80.

— (2001a) From organizational learning to practice-based knowing, *Human Relations*, **54**(1): 131–9.

— (2001b) Learning, organizational, *International Encyclopedia of the Social and Behavioral Sciences*, **5.1**: 31, Elsevier.

— (2003) Feminist theory and organizational theory: a dialogue on new bases, in H. Tsoukas and C. Knudsen (eds), *The Oxford Handbook of Organization Theory: Meta-theoretical Perspectives*, Oxford: Oxford University Press.

— and Nicolini, D. (2000) The organizational learning of safety in communities of practice, *Journal of Management Inquiry*, **9**(1): 7–18.

— and Nicolini, D. (2000a) To transfer is to transform: the circulation of safety knowledge, *Organization*, **7**(2): 329–48.

— and Nicolini, D. (2001) Sociological foundation of organizational learning, in M. Dierkes, A. Berthoin Antal, J. Child and I. Nonaka (eds), *The Handbook of Organizational Learning*, Oxford: Oxford University Press, pp. 35–60.

— and Nicolini, D. (2002a) Learning the trade. A culture of safety in practice, *Organization*, **8**(4): 191–223.

— and Nicolini, D. (2003) Learning in a constellation of interconnected practices: canon or dissonance?, *Journal of Management Studies*, **39**(4): 419–36.

— Nicolini, D. and Odella, F. (1998a) What do you mean by safety? Conflicting perspectives on accident causation and safety management inside a construction firm, *Journal of Contingencies and Crisis Management*, **7**(4): 202–13.

—, Nicolini, D. and Odella, F. (1998b) Toward a social understanding of how people learn in organisations: the notion of situated curriculum, *Management Learning*, **29**(3): 273–98.

—, Nicolini, D. and Odella, F. (1999) How people learn in organizations, in D. Wilson and R. Rosenfeld (eds), *Managing Organizations: Text, Readings, and Cases*, New York: McGraw-Hill, pp. 121–31.

— and Poggio, B. (2003) *Donna per fortuna, uomo per destino*, Milan: Etas.

— and Strati, A. (1988) The temporal dimension in organizational studies, *Organization Studies*, **2**: 149–64.

— and Strati, A. (1990) The 'texture' of organizing in an Italian university department, *Journal of Management Studies*, **27**(6): 605–18.

Gibson, J.J. (1982) Notes on action, in E. Reed and R. Jones (eds), *Reasons for Realism. Selected Essays of J.J. Gibson*, Hillsdale, NJ: Lawrence Erlbaum, pp. 385–92.

Giddens, A. (1976) *New Rules of Sociological Method*, London: Hutchinson.

— (1979) *Central Problems in Social Theory*, London: Macmillan.

— (1984) *The Constitution of Society*, Cambridge: Polity Press.

— (1986) Action, subjectivity and the constitution of meaning, *Social Research*, **53**(3): 529–45.

— (1990) *The Consequences of Modernity*, Cambridge: Polity Press.

Giglioli, P.P. (1990) *Rituale, interazione, vita quotidiana*, Bologna: Il Mulino.

Glaser, B. and Strauss, A. (1967) *The Discovery of Grounded Theory*, Mill Valley, CA: Sociology Press.

Goffman, E. (1959) *The Presentation of Self in Everyday Life*, London: Allen Lane.

— (1971a) *Relations in Public*. New York: Harper & Row.

— (1971b) 'The territories of the self', in E. Goffman (ed.), *Relations in Public: Microstudies of the Public Order*, New York: Harper & Row.

— (1974) *Frame Analysis*, Boston, MA: Northeastern University Press.

Goodall, H.L. (1991) *Living In The Rock 'n Roll Mystery: Reading Context, Self and Others as Clues*, Carbondale, IL: Southern Illinois University Press.

Goode, W. and Hatt, P. (1952) *Method in Social Research*, New York: McGraw-Hill.

Goodwin, C. (1994) Professional vision, *American Anthropologist*, **96**(3): 606–33.

Goodwin, C. and Goodwin, M.H. (1996) Seeing as situated activity: formulating planes, in Y. Engestrom and D. Middleton (eds), *Cognition and Communication at Work*, Cambridge: Cambridge University Press, pp. 61–95.

Gouldner, W.A. (1954) *Patterns of Industrial Bureaucracy. A Study of Modern Factory Administration*, Glencoe, IL: Free Press.

Granovetter, M.S. (1992) Problems of explanation in economic sociology, in N. Nohria and R.G. Eccles (eds), *Networks and Organizations: Structure, Form and Action*, Boston, MA: Harvard Business School Press, pp. 25–56.

Habermas, J. (1971) *Knowledge and Human Interest*, London: Heinemann.

Haraway, D. (1991) *A Manifesto for Cyborgs*, New York: Routledge.

— (1991a) Situated knowledges: the science question in feminism and the privilege of partial perspectives, in D. Haraway (ed.) *Simians, Cyborgs and Women: the Reinvention of Nature*, London: Free Association Books, pp. 183–202.

Harding, S. (1986) *The Science Question in Feminism*, Ithaca: Cornell University.

Hardy, C. and Clegg, S. (1996) Some dare call it power, in S. Clegg, C. Hardy and W. Nord (eds), *Handbook of Organization Studies*, London: Sage, pp. 622–41.

Hassard, J., Holliday, R. and Willmott, H. (eds) (2000) *Body and Organization*, London: Sage.

Hatch, M.J. (1997) *Organization Theory. Modern, Symbolic and Postmodern Perspectives*, Oxford: Oxford University Press.

Haug, F. (1987) *Female Sexualization: A Collective Work of Memory*, London: Verso.

Hawkesworth, M. (1989) Knowers, knowing, known: feminist theory and claims of truth, *Signs*, **14**: 533–57.

Heath, C. and Button, G. (2002) Special issue on workplace studies: editorial introduction, *The British Journal of Sociology*, **53**(2): 157–61.

Heidegger, M. (1969) *Zur Sache des Denkens*, Tubingen: Niemeyer.

— (1971) *On the Way to Language*, San Francisco: Harper & Row (trans. Peter Hertz).

Henke, C. (2000) The mechanics of workplace order: toward a sociology of repair, *Berkeley Journal of Sociology*, **44**: 55–81.

Heritage, J.C. (1987) Ethnomethodology, in A. Giddens and J. Turner (eds), *Social Theory Today*, Cambridge: Polity Press, pp. 224–72.

Hirshman, A.O. (1970) *Exit, Voice and Loyalty*, Cambridge, MA: Cambridge University Press.

hooks, belle (1994) *Teaching to Transgress: Education as the Practice of Freedom*, New York: Routledge.

Horlick-Jones, T. (1996) Is safety a by-product of quality management?, in D. Jones and C. Hood (eds), *Accident And Design*, London: University College London Press.

Huber, G. (1991) Organizational learning: the contributing processes and the literatures, *Organization Science*, **2**(1): 88–117.

Hughes, T.P. (1983) *Networks of Power: Electrification in Western Society*, Baltimore, MA: The John Hopkins University Press.

Hutchins, E. (1991) The technology of team navigation, in J. Galegher and C. Kraut (eds), *Intellectual Team Work*, Hillsdale: Lawrence Erlbaum.

— (1993) Learning to navigate, in S. Chaiklin and J. Lave (eds), *Understanding Practice: Perspectives on Activity and Context*, Cambridge: Cambridge University Press, pp. 35–63.

— (1995) *Cognition in the Wild*, Cambridge, MA: The MIT Press.

Hynes, T. and Prasad, P. (1997) Patterns of 'mock bureaucracy' in mining disasters: an analysis of the Westray coal mine explosion, *Journal of Management Studies*, **34**(4): 601–23.

Huysman, M. (1999) Balancing biases: a critical review of the literature on organizational learning, in M. Easterby-Smith, J. Burgoyne and L. Araujo (eds), *Organizational Learning and the Learning Organization. Development in Theory and Practice*, London: Sage.

ISFOL (1992) *Glossario di Didattica della Formazione*, Milano: Angeli.

Jermier, J., Slocum, J., Fry, L. and Gaines, J. (1991) Organizational subcultures in a soft bureaucracy: resistance behind the myth and façade of an official culture, *Organizational Science*, **2**: 21–30.

Jick, T. (1979) Mixing qualitative and quantitative methods: triangulation in action, *Administrative Science Quarterly*, **24**: 602–11.

Joerges, B. (1999) Do politics have artifacts? *Social Studies of Science*, **29**(3): 411–31.

Kalling, T. and Styhre, A. (2003) *Knowledge Sharing in Organizations*, Copenhagen: Copenhagen Business School Press.

Kay, J. (1993) *Foundations of Corporate Success: How Business Strategies Add Value*, Oxford: Oxford University Press.

Kirsch, D. (1995) The intelligent use of space, *Artificial Intelligence*, **73**: 36–68.

Kieser, A., Beck, N. and Taino, R. (2001) Rules and organizational learning: the behavioral theory approach, in M. Dierkes, A. Berthoin Antal, J. Child and I. Nonaka (eds), *The Handbook of Organizational Learning*, Oxford: Oxford University Press, pp. 598–625.

— (1997) Sociality with objects: social relations in post-social knowledge societies, *Theory, Culture and Society*, **14**(4): 1–30.

— (2001) Objectual practice, in T.R. Schatzki, K. Knorr-Cetina and E. von Savigny (eds), *The Practice Turn in Contemporary Theory*, London: Routledge, pp. 175–88.

Kogut, B. (2000) The network as knowledge: generative rules and the emergence of structure, *Strategic Management Journal*, **21**(Special Issue): 405–25.

—, Shan, W. and Walker, G. (1993) Knowledge in the network and the network as knowledge: the structuring of new industries, in G. Grabher (ed.), *The Embedded Firm: on the Socio-economics of Industrial Networks*, London: Routledge, pp. 67–94.

Lakoff, G. (1987) *Women, Fire and Dangerous Things*, Chicago: The University of Chicago Press.

Latour, B. (1986) The power of association, in J. Law (ed.), *Power, Action and Belief: A New Sociology of Knowledge?* London: Routledge & Kegan Paul.

— (1987) *Science in Action*. Cambridge, MA: Harvard University Press.

— (1992) Where are the missing masses? The sociology of a few mundane artifacts, in W.E. Bijker and J. Law (eds), *Shaping Technology/Building Society: Studies
in Sociotechnical Change*, Cambridge, MA: MIT Press.

— (1999) On recalling ANT, in J. Law and J. Hassard (eds), *Actor Network and
After*, Oxford: Blackwell, pp. 15–25.

Laudan, R. (1984) *The Nature of Technological Knowledge. Are Models of Scientific
Change Relevant?* Dordrecht: D. Reidel.

Lave, J. (1988) *Cognition in Practice*, Cambridge: Cambridge University Press.

— and Wenger, E. (1991) *Situated Learning: Legitimate Peripheral Participation*,
New York: Cambridge University Press.

Law, J. (1987) Technology and heterogeneous engineering: the case of the
Portuguese expansion, in W.E. Bijker, T.P. Hughes and T.J. Pinch (eds), *The
Social Construction of Technical Systems: New Directions in The Sociology and
History of Technology*, Cambridge, MA: MIT Press, pp. 111–34.

— (1992) Notes on the theory of the actor-network: ordering, strategy and
heterogeneity, *System/Practice*, **5**(4): 379–93.

— (1994) *Organizing Modernity*, Oxford: Blackwell.

— (1999) After ANT: complexity, naming and topology, in J. Law and J. Hassard
(eds) (1999) *Actor Network Theory and After*, Oxford: Blackwell, pp. 220–47.

Layton, E. (1974) Technology as knowledge, *Technology and Culture*, **15**: 31–41.

Leplat, J. (1982) Fiabilitè et securitè, *Le Travail Humain*, **45**(1): 101–8.

Levinthal, D.A. and March, J.G. (1993) The myopia of learning, *Strategic
Management Journal*, **14**(winter special issue): 95–112.

Levitt, B. and March, J.G. (1988) Organizational learning, *Annual Review of
Sociology*, **14**: 319–40.

Lincoln, J.R. (1982) Intra- (and inter-) organizational networks, in S.B.
Bacharach (ed.), *Research in the Sociology of Organization*, Greenwich, CT: JAI
Press, vol 1: 1–38.

Linstead, S. (1985) Jokers wild: the importance of humour in the maintenance
of organizational culture, *Sociological Review*, **4**: 741–67.

Lorenzoni, G. and Lipparini, A. (1999) The leveraging of interfirm relationships
as a distinctive organizational capability: a longitudinal study, *Strategic Management Journal*, **20**(4): 317–38.

Luff, P., Hindmarsh, J. and Heath, C. (2000) Introduction, in P. Luff,
J. Hindmarsh and C. Heath (eds), *Workplace Studies*, Cambridge: Cambridge
University Press.

Lyles, M. and Easterby-Smith, M. (2003) Organizational learning and knowl-
edge management: agendas for future research, in M. Easterby-Smith and
M. Lyles (eds), *The Blackwell Handbook of Organizational Learning and
Knowledge Management*, Oxford: Blackwell, pp. 639–52.

Lynch, M. (1995) The idylls of the academy, *Social Studies of Science*, **25**: 582–600.

— (1997) Theorizing practice, *Human Studies*, **20**: 335–44.

— (2000) Against reflexivity as an academic virtue and source of privileged
knowledge, *Theory, Culture and Society*, **17**(3): 26–54.

Lyotard, J. (1977) The unconscious as mise-en-scène, in M. Benamou and C. Caramello (eds), *Performance in Postmodern Culture*, Madison, WI: Coda Press.

— (1984) *The Postmodern Condition*, Manchester: Manchester University Press.

MacIntyre, A. (1985) *After Virtue*, London: Duckworth.

Manning, P.K. (1987) *Semiotics and Fieldwork*, Newbury Park: Sage.

March, J. and Olsen, J. (eds) (1976) *Ambiguity and Choice in Organizations*, Bergen: Universitetforlaget.

— and Olsen J. (1989) *Rediscovering Institutions*, London: Free Press.

— and Simon, H. (1958) *Organizations*, New York: Wiley.

Martin, J., Feldman, M., Hatch, M.J. and Sitkin, S. (1983) The uniqueness paradox in organizational stories, *Administrative Science Quarterly*, **28**: 438–53.

Martin, P.Y. (2003) 'Said & done' vs. 'Saying & doing'. Gendered practices/practicing gender at work, *Gender & Society*, **17**.

McDermott, R. (1999) Why information technology inspired but cannot deliver knowledge management, *California Management Review*, **41**(4): 103–17.

Mead, G.H. (1934) *Mind, Self and Society*, Chicago: University of Chicago Press.

Merleau-Ponty, M. (1964) *Le Visible et L'Invisible*, Paris: Gallimard.

Miner, A. and Mezias, S. (1966) Ugly duckling no more. Pasts and futures of organizational learning research, *Organization Science*, **7**(1):88–99.

Mitchell, J.C. (1999) Case and situation analysis, in A. Bryman and R. Burgess (eds), *Qualitative Research,* London: Sage, pp. 180–200.

Miyazaki, K. (1994) *Building Competences in the Firm: Lessons from Japanese and European Optoelectronics*, London: Macmillan.

Mol, A. (1999) Ontological politics. A word and some questions, in J. Law and J. Hassard (eds), *Actor Network Theory and After*, Oxford: Blackwell.

Morgan, G. (1992) *Images of Organization*, second edition, Thousand Oaks, CA: Sage.

Mouzelis, N. (1989) Restructuring structuration theory, *The Sociological Review*, **37**(4): 613–34.

Nicolini, D. and Meznar, R. (1995) The social construction of organizational learning: concepts and practical issues in the field, *Human Relations*, **48**(7): 727–46.

—, Gherardi, S. and Yanow, D. (eds) (2003) *Knowing in Organizations: A Practice-based Approach*, Armonk, NY: M.E. Sharpe.

Nicotera, F. (1996) *Etnometodologia e azione sociale*, Milano: Prometheus.

Norman, D. (1993) Les artefacts cognitifs, in B. Conein, N. Dodier and L. Thévenot (eds), *Les Objects dans l'Action*, Paris: Edition de l'Ecole des Hautes Etudes en Sciences Sociales, pp. 15–34.

Orr, J. (1996) *Talking about Machines: An Ethnography of a Modern Job*, Ithaca: Cornell University Press.

Orlikowski, W. (1992) The duality of technology: rethinking the concept of technology in organisations, *Organisational Science*, **3**(3): 398–427.

Owen, M. (1983) *Apologies and Remedial Interchanges*, Berlin: Mouton.

Parker Follet, M. (1942) *Dynamic Administration: the Collected Papers of Mary Parker Follett*, H.C. Metcalf and L. Urwick (eds), New York: Harper.

Pedler, M., Boydell, T. and Burgoyne, J. (1991) *The Learning Company: A Strategy for Sustainable Development*, London: McGraw-Hill.

Pepper, S. (1942) *World Hypotheses*, second edition, Berkeley: University of California Press.

Pickering, A. (1992) *Science as Practice and Culture*, Chicago: University of Chicago Press.

Pidgeon, N. (1995) Safety culture and risk management in organizations, *Journal of Cross-Cultural Psychology*, **22**(1): 129–40.

Polanyi, M. (1962) *Personal Knowledge*, London: Routledge and Kegan Paul (original work published in 1958).

— (1966) *The Tacit Dimension*, London: Routledge & Kegan Paul.

Porter, L.W., Lawler, E.E. and Hackman, J.R. (1975) *Behavior in Organizations*, New York: McGraw-Hill.

Prahalad, C.K. and Hamel, G. (1990) The core competence of the corporation, *Harvard Business Review*, May–June: 79–91.

Raeithel, A. (1996) On the ethnography of co-operative work, in Y. Engenstrom and D. Middleton (eds), *Cognition and Communication at Work*, Cambridge: Cambridge University Press.

Resnick, L.B. (1987) Learning in school and out, *Educational Researcher*, **6**(9): 13–20.

Ricolfi, L. (1997) La ricerca empirica nelle scienze sociali: una tassonomia, in L. Ricolfi (ed.), *La Ricerca Qualitativa*, Roma: La Nuova Italia Scientifica, pp. 19–44.

Ryle, G. (1949) *The Concept of Mind*, London: Hutchinson.

Rogoff, B. (1995) Observing sociocultural activity on three planes: participatory appropriation, guided participation, and apprenticeship, in J. Wertsch, P. Del Rio and A. Alvarez (eds), *Sociocultural Studies of Mind*, Cambridge: Cambridge University Press.

Rorty, R. (1989) *Contingency, Irony and Solidarity*, Cambridge: Cambridge University Press.

Rouse, J. (2001) Two concepts of practices, in T.R. Schatzki, K. Knorr-Cetina and E. von Savigny (eds), *The Practice Turn in Contemporary Theory*, London: Routledge, pp. 189–98.

— (2002) *How Scientific Practices Matter*, Chicago: University of Chicago Press.

Sachs, P. (1993) Shadows in the soup: conceptions of work and nature of evidence, *The Quarterly Newsletter of the Laboratory of Human Cognition*, **15**: 125–32.

Scarbrough, H., Swan, J. and Preston, J. (1998) *Knowledge Management and the Learning Organization: the IPD Report*, Institute of Personnel Development.

Schank, R.C. and Abelson, R.P. (1977) *Scripts, Plans, Goals, and Understanding*, Hillsdale: Lawrence Erlbaum.

Schatzki, T.R. (2001a) Introduction. Practice theory, in T.R. Schatzki, K. Knorr-Cetina and E. von Savigny (eds), *The Practice Turn in Contemporary Theory*, London and New York: Routledge, pp. 1–14.

— (2001b) Practice mind-ed orders, in T.R. Schatzki, K. Knorr-Cetina and E. von Savigny (eds), *The Practice Turn in Contemporary Theory*, London: Routledge, pp. 42–55.

—, Knorr-Cetina, K. and von Savigny, E. (eds) (2001) *The Practice Turn in Contemporary Theory*, London: Routledge.

Schegloff, E. (1992) Repair after the next turn: the last structurally provided defense of intersubjectivity in conversation, *American Journal of Sociology*, **97**: 1295–345.

—, Jefferson, G. and Sacks, H. (1977) The preference for self-correction in the organization of repair for conversation, *Language*, **53**: 361–82.

Schein, E. (1996) The three cultures of management: implications for organizational learning, *Sloan Management Review*, **38**: 9–20.

Scheler, M. (1926) *Die Wissensformen und die Gesellschaft*, Liepzig: Neue Geist.

Schön, D. (1983) *The Reflective Practitioner. How Professionals Think in Action*, New York: Basic Books.

Schutz, A. (1962) *Collected Papers I. The Problem of Social Reality*, The Hague: Nijhoff.

— (1964) *Collected Papers II. Studies in Social Theory*, The Hague: Nijhoff.

Senge, P.M. (1990) *The Fifth Discipline: The Art and Practice of the Learning Organization*, Sydney: Random House.

Serres, M. (1974) *La Traduction, Hermes III*, Paris: Les Editions de Minuit.

Shrivastava, P. (1983) A typology of organizational learning systems, *Journal of Management Studies*, **20**(1): 7–28.

Siegel, S. and Castellan, J.N. (1988) *Non-Parametric Statistics for the Behavioural Sciences*, New York: McGraw-Hill.

Silverman, D. (2000) *Doing Qualitative Research. A Practical Guide*, London: Sage.

Simon, H. (1991) Bounded rationality and organizational learning, *Organization Science*, **2**(1): 125–34.

Sims, D., Fineman, S. and Gabriel, Y. (1993) *Organizing and Organizations*, London: Sage.

Snell, R. and Chak, A.M. (1998) The learning organization: learning and empowerment for whom?, *Management Learning*, **29**: 337–64.

Spinosa, C. (2001) Derridian dispersion and Heideggerian articulation: general tendencies in the practices that govern intelligibility, in T.R. Schatzki, K. Knorr-Cetina and E. von Savigny (eds), *The Practice Turn in Contemporary Theory*, London: Routledge, pp. 198–212.

Star, S.L. (1991) Power, technologies and the phenomenology of standards: on being allergic to onions, in J. Law (ed.), *A Sociology of Monsters? Power, Technology and the Modern World, Sociological Review Monograph*, no. 38, London: Routledge.

— (1995) *Ecologies of Knowledge*, Albany, NY: State University of New York Press.

— (1996) Working together: symbolic interactionism, activity theory, and information systems, in Y. Engestrom and D. Middleton (eds), *Cognition and Communication at Work*, Cambridge: Cambridge University Press, pp. 296–318.

StatXact (1992) *Statistical Software for Exact Nonparametric Inference*, Cambridge, MA: Cytel Sotware Corporation.

Stevenson, R.J. (1993) *Language, Thought and Representation*, Chichester: Wiley.

Strathern, M. (1991) *Partial Connections*, Savage: Rowan and Littlefield.

Strati, A. (1992) Aesthetic understanding of organizational life, in *Academy of Management Review* (special issue on New Intellectual Currents in Organization and Management Theory. Theory Development Forum), **17**(3): 568–81.

— (1999) *Organization and Aesthetics*, London: Sage.

— (2000) Estetica, conoscenza tacita e apprendimento organizzativo, *Studi Organizzativi*, **2**.

— (2000a) The aesthetic approach in organization studies' in S. Linstead and H. Hopfl (eds), *The Aesthetic of Organization*, London: Sage.

— (2000b) *Theory and Method in Organization Studies: Paradigms and Choices*, London: Sage.

— (2003) Knowing in practice: aesthetic understanding and tacit knowledge, in D. Nicolini, S. Gherardi and D. Yanow (eds), *Knowing in Organizations*, Armonk, NY: M.E. Sharpe, pp. 53–75.

Strauss, A. (1978) *Negotiations*, San Francisco: Jossey-Bass.

Strauss, A. and Corbin, J. (1990) *Basics of Qualitative Research: Grounded Theory Procedures and Techniques*. Newbury Park, CA: Sage.

Stucky, S. (1995) Technology in support of organizational learning, in C. Zucchermaglio, S. Bagnara and S. Stucky (eds), *Organizational Learning and Technological Change*, New York: Springer Verlag, pp. 4–15.

Suchman, L. (1987) *Plans and Situated Action: the Problem of Human–Machine Communication*, Cambridge: Cambridge University Press.

— (1996) Constituting shared workspaces, in Y. Engestrom and D. Middleton (eds), *Cognition and Communication at Work*, Cambridge: Cambridge University Press.

— (2000) Organizing alignment: a case of bridge-building, *Organization*, **7**(2): 311–28.

—, Blomberg, J., Orr, J.E. and Trigg, R. (1999) Reconstructing technologies as social practice, *American Behavioural Scientist*, **43**(3): 392–408.

Sudnow, D. (1978) *Ways of the Hand: The World of Improvised Conduct*, Cambridge, MA: Harvard University Press.

Sulkunen, P. (1982) Society made visible. On the cultural sociology of Pierre Bourdieu, *Acta Sociologica*, **25**(2): 103–15.

Swan, J., Scarbrough, H. and Robertson, M. (2002) The construction of 'Communities of Practice' in the management of innovation, *Management Learning*, **33**(4): 477–96.

Swidler, A. (2001) What anchors cultural practices, in T.R. Schatzki, K. Knorr-Cetina and E. von Savigny (eds), *The Practice Turn in Contemporary Theory*, London and New York: Routledge, pp. 74–92.

Toft, B. and Reynolds, S. (1994) *Learning from Disasters: A Management Approach*, Oxford: Butterworth-Heinemann.

— and Turner, B.A. (1987) The schematic report analysis diagram: a simple aid to learning from large-scale failures, *International CIS Journal*, **1**(2): 12–23.

Tolman, E. and Brunswick, E. (1935) The organism and the causal texture of the environment, *Psychological Review*, **42**: 43–77.

Tota, A. (1999) Memorie in conflitto: i narratives della commemorazione, *Comunicazioni Sociali*, **3**: 336–50.

— (2001) I nonluoghi della commemorazione: la stazione di Bologna, 1980–2000, in A. Tota (ed.), *La Memoria Contesa*, Milan: Angeli.

Townley, B. (1993) Foucault, power/knowledge, and its relevance for human resource management, *Academy of Management Review*, **18**: 518–45.

Tsang, E. (1997) Organizational learning and the learning organization: a dichotomy between descriptive and prescriptive research, *Human Relations*, **50**(1): 73–90.

Tsoukas, H. (1991) The missing link: a transformational view of metaphors on organizational science, *Academy of Management Review*, **16**(3): 566–85.

— and Knudsen, C. (2003) 'Introduction: the need for meta-theoretical reflection in organization theory', in H. Tsoukas and C. Knudsen (eds), *The Oxford Handbook of Organization Theory. Meta-theoretical Perspectives*, Oxford: Oxford University Press, pp. 1–36.

Turner, B.A. (1978) *Man Made Disasters*, London: Wykeham Press.

— (1988) Connoisseurship in the study of organizational cultures, in A. Bryman (ed.), *Doing Research in Organisations*, London: Routledge, pp. 108–22.

— (1991) Rethinking organizations: organizational learning in the nineties, Paper presented at the EFMD Research Conference, Isida, Palermo.

— (1991a) The development of a safety culture, *Chemistry and Industry*, **1**: 241–3.

— and Pidgeon, N. (1997) *Man-Made Disasters*, 2nd edition, Oxford: Butterworth-Heinemann.

Turner, S. (1994) *The Social Theory of Practices: Tradition, Tacit Knowledge, and Presuppositions*, Chicago: University of Chicago Press.

Tversky, A. and Kahneman, D. (1974) Judgement under uncertainty: heuristics and biases, *Science*, **185**: 59–80.

Van Maanen, J. and Schein, E.H. (1979) Toward a theory of organizational socialization, *Research in Organizational Behavior*, **1**: 209–64.

Van Wijk, R., Van Den Bosch, F. and Volberda, H. (2003) Knowledge and networks, in M. Easterby-Smith and M. Lyles (eds), *The Blackwell Handbook of Organizational Learning and Knowledge Management*, Oxford: Blackwell, pp. 428–53.

Vaux, J. (1999) Social groups and discursive communities: context and audience in the explanatory practices of the artificial intelligence (AI) community, Paper presented at The Transformation of Knowledge conference, University of Surrey, 12–13 January.

Wacquant, L.D.J. (1992) *Toward a Social Praxeology*, in P. Bourdieu and L.D.J. Wacquant (eds), *An Invitation to Reflexive Sociology*, Cambridge: Polity Press, pp. 1–59.

Wallace, A. (1982) *The Social Context of Innovation*, Princeton: Princeton University Press.

Weber, M. (1922) *Wirtschaft und Gesellschaft. Grundriss der verstehenden Soziologie*, Tubingen: Mohr (Eng. transl.: (1978) *Economy and Society*. Berkeley: University of California Press).

Weick, K. (1979) *The Social Psychology of Organizing*, Reading, MA: Addison Wesley.

— (1988) Enacted sensemaking in crisis situations, *Journal of Management Studies*, **25**: 305–17.

— (1989) Theory construction as disciplined imagination, *Academy of Management Review*, **14**(4): 516–31.

— (1991) The non-traditional quality of organizational learning, *Organization Science*, **2**: 16–23.

— (1995) *Sensemaking in Organizations*, Thousand Oaks, CA: Sage.

— and Westley, F. (1996) Organizational learning: affirming an oxymoron, in S.R. Clegg, C. Hardy and W.R. Nord (eds), *Handbook of Organization Studies*, London: Sage, pp. 440–58.

Wenger, E. (1998) *Communities of Practice. Learning, Meaning and Identity*. New York: Cambridge University Press.

— (2000) Comunità di pratica e sistemi sociali di apprendimento, *Studi Organizzativi*, **1**: 11–34.

Whitley, R. (1984) The fragmented state of management studies: reasons and consequences, *Journal of Management Studies*, **21**(3): 331–48.

Winner, L. (1985) Do artifacts have politics?, in D. MacKenzie and J. Wajcman (eds), *The Social Shaping of Technology*, Philadelphia: Open University Press, pp. 26–38.

Winograd, T. and Flores, F. (1986) *Understanding Computers and Cognition: A New Foundation for Design*, Norwood: Ablex.

Wittgenstein, L. (1953) *Philosophical Investigations*, Oxford: Blackwell.

Wood, D., Bruner, J.S. and Ross, G. (1976) The role of tutoring in problem solving, *Journal of Child Psychology and Psychiatry*, **17**: 89–100.

Wright, C. (1994) A fallible safety system: institutionalized irrationality in the offshore and gas industry, *Sociological Review*, **1**: 79–103.

Yin, R. (1981) The case study crisis: some answers, *Administrative Science Quarterly*, **26**: 58–65.

— (1984) *Case Study Research*, Beverly Hills, CA: Sage.

Zimmermann, D.H. and Pollner, M. (1970) The everyday world as a phenomenon, in J.D. Douglas (ed.), *Understanding Everyday Life*, London: Routledge & Kegan Paul, pp. 80–103.

Index